❖

THE LURE OF THE HONEY BIRD

❖

The Storytellers of Ethiopia

First published in Great Britain in 2013 by Polygon, an imprint of Birlinn Ltd.

Birlinn Ltd, West Newington House, 10 Newington Road, Edinburgh EH9 1QS

www.polygonbooks.co.uk

ISBN 978 1 84697 246 1
eBook ISBN 978 0 85790 581 9

British Library Cataloguing-in-Publication Data
A catalogue record for this book is available on request from the British Library.
Printed and bound by ScandBook AB, Sweden

Text design by Teresa Monachino.

For the storytellers of Ethiopia

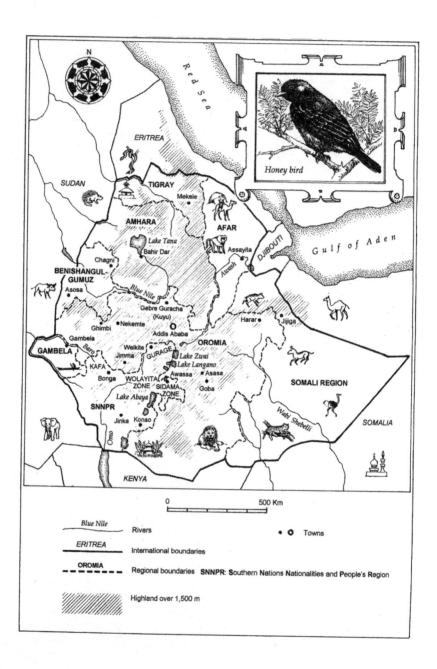

Honey bird

❖

CONTENTS

❖

❖

ACKNOWLEDGEMENTS

❖

This book is a personal account of a project with many collaborators. The British Council and the Ethiopian Ministry of Education were joint partners. They organised and supported the collection of stories and the publication of the readers with generous help from the Foreign and Commonwealth Office. Michael Sargent, Director of the British Council in Ethiopia, was the prime mover, and with his wife Patsy a constant support and inspiration, but I must also thank Dr Simon Ingram-Hill, the late Michael Daniel Ambatchew and Dr Solomon Hailu of the British Council, as well as Dirije and Tekle, the brave and tireless drivers. The three talented and cheerful translators on the project, Michael Daniel Ambatchew, Mikhail Negussie and Mesfin Habte-Mariam, accompanied me on my journeys, put up with many difficulties, patiently resolved dilemmas and often made me laugh. At the Ministry of Education, special thanks are due to all those who showed such interest in the project and gave it essential practical support, under the guidance of the Minister of Education, Woizero Genet Zewdie.

Throughout Ethiopia, the practical arrangements for my visits, the meetings with storytellers and the organisation of translators were handled enthusiastically and with great kindness by officers of the Regional Cultural and Education Bureaux. Their names are listed below, and apologies are due to any who have been omitted.

AFAR: Mohammed Ahmed Algani and Ousman Mohammed Ahmed;
AMHARA: Alemayehu Gebrehiwot and Daniel Legesse;
BENI SHANGUL: Dires Gebremeskel and Belay Makonnen;
GAMBELA: Ogota Agiw;
HARAR: Nejaha Ahmed;
OROMIA: Merga Debelo and Bekar Hadji;
SOUTHERN REGION: Nigatu Wolde, Tiringo Segatu, Yacob Woldemariam Dimeno, Mamo Malla and Mitachew Belay;
SOMALIA: Moge Abdi Omar;
TIGRAY: Mesele Zeleke and Tschaynesh Gebre Yohannes.

The artist Yosef Kebede worked on the reader project from the start, taking great pains with the complexity of cultural references in the different regions. A few of his illustrations have been reproduced in this book. Thanks are also due to Eric Robson for the map of Ethiopia and the illustrations on pages 228 and 254.

This book owes its very existence to Wolde Gossa Tadesse and to the generosity of the Christensen Foundation, who funded the website www.ethiopianfolktales.com in both English and Amharic, on which all the stories can be read and heard, and supported the publication of this book. Michael Sargent was a co-creator of the website, along with Gareth Cromie, who with his team designed and produced it.

My personal thanks are due to Robin and Merril Christopher, who kindly put me up in Addis Ababa, to Fiona Kenshole of Oxford University Press, to Marc Lambert of Scottish Book Trust, to Jane Fior, best of friends and encouragers, to all at Polygon, to my agent Hilary Delamere and, as ever, to my husband, David McDowall, who has supported and encouraged me throughout.

❖ 1 ❖

ADDIS ABABA

Addis Ababa leans against the slope of Mount Entoto like a child lying on the shoulder of its mother. I like to take the steep road up to the top of the mountain's long ridge every time I visit Ethiopia. The land beneath one's feet swoops away to the south, levelling out onto a vast plain where the hot light shimmers in shifting shades of green and blue, before it rises again up the sides of Mount Wuchacha.

From this vantage point, the city below looks like a vast shanty town, intersected by the sweeps of grand avenues. This is an illusion. It is true that most houses are small, that the walls, made of mud and straw, list alarmingly when of a certain age, and that all the roofs are of corrugated iron, on which the downpours of the Big Rains clatter with a roar. But unlike a shanty town, Addis Ababa has an underlying structure, even a certain orderliness. Each district has a controlling administration, called the 'kebele', and although many back streets are little more than lanes, treacherous with mud in the Rains, and negotiable only by donkey hooves and human feet, they are less haphazard than they seem.

They do not, however, yield their secrets easily. There are no A–Z maps of Addis Ababa, no plans or directories. To find the house of a friend you have to follow elaborate directions.

'You know the Bio-Diversity Foundation?'

'No.'

'Yes, you do. There's a sign near it saying A Twist Night Club. Turn up the lane beyond it, then the next one to the right after the Paradise Heaven Pasterie. You'll probably see a priest sitting on the corner under a striped umbrella. Our place is just beyond him.'

Up on Entoto, the thin cool air is spiced with the scent of eucalyptus and the city is a hundred years and a mind's journey away. Forty years ago, when I used to ride Meskel, my nervous grey pony, along the ridge of Entoto, the city was a fraction of the size it is now, the air was polluted only with the smoke of cooking fires and the sky was blue all the way down to the horizon. These days, one looks down on a smudge of pollution, and one is no longer struck by the sound of barking dogs, squealing children, saws, hammers and the clatter of small workshops, but the drone of traffic.

The temperature always catches you out in Ethiopia. The sun beats down with equatorial intensity on your bare skin. But as soon as you step into the shade, it's so cool that you need a sweater. As a result, a fussy person like me is constantly fiddling with hats and over-garments.

I was doing this while strolling along the Entoto ridge one afternoon in 1996, chatting with my companion, a mechanic called Tesfaye, who could perform miracles of rejuvenation on obsolete vehicles.

'So, Liz,' he said, 'I see you are feeling chilled. But in Britain I have heard that it is colder than Ethiopia. How are you managing there to keep warm?'

'Oh, you know, coats and hats and scarves. And in the winter we have heating inside our houses.'

He thought about this.

'Each person has a fire in their house, not only for the cooking? From where do you get the wood?'

'Not a fire exactly. We have a system called central heating. There are pipes that bring hot water into each room, supplying tanks called radiators. A radiator can warm a whole room.'

He nodded.

'That is a very nice idea. What is the fuel used to heat the pipes?'

'In our house we use gas.'

'Gas? In bottles?'

'No, it comes to the house in pipes.'

'Like water?'

'Like water.'

"I see. How do you pay for it?'

'We have meters which measure . . .'

But at this point we both became aware of something moving on the ground beside our feet. We bent down to look.

Across the ground in front of us ran a groove about a centimetre wide and deep. It started from a hole under the tarmac of the roadway to our right, and went in a straight line towards the field on our left. I saw that it was a miniature highway formed by the feet of ants, a column of which was marching in each direction. The ants coming from the field were carrying morsels of food in their mouths – a seed, a grain, or even a small flower. They disappeared down the hole under the tarmac, presumably to their nest, manoeuvring their loads past their colleagues, who were emerging from the hole and setting out along the road towards the field to fetch more supplies. Fascinated, Tesfaye and I squatted down to watch.

After a moment or so, I became aware of a pair of bare feet on the far side of the groove. Their soles were hardened to a thick hide, and their nails were as tough as horns. I struggled to my feet. An elderly man, carrying a farmer's stick over his shoulders, which were draped in a cream-coloured shamma,[1] was looking down at us with concern.

'Have you lost something of value?' he asked Tesfaye in Amharic. 'Are you looking for it?'

Tesfaye explained about the ants. The man smiled, lowered one end of his stick to the ground and leaned on it, making himself comfortable.

'The ant is very good animal,' he said. 'I will tell you a story about him.'

He did so, pausing at the end of each sentence so that Tesfaye could translate for me, and finishing off with a moral which made us smile and nod. Then off he went, back to his village, and down the mountain went Tesfaye and I, never to meet again.

I told the story of the ant to the friends I was staying with. I mulled it over. I compared it in my head to the fables of Aesop and La Fontaine. I relished its perfection, and promised myself to preserve it in my diary. But somehow I never did. And it went clean out of my head. All I can now remember is a fragment about a man pinching his wife on the ankle, and the woman blaming the ants.

That moment in the cool air on Mount Entoto, with the trail of ants on the ground and the old farmer shaking back the folds of his shamma as he embellished his story with gestures, struck me with the force of a revelation. I felt as if I had caught a pearl falling from a treasure chest and that I only had to reach out and prise off the lid to reveal a priceless hoard.

That evening, in one of those reversals of experience that make life so enthrallingly dislocated in Ethiopia, I found myself standing on the lawn of the British Embassy under the windows

[1] The hand-woven shawl worn by both men and women in the highlands of Ethiopia.

of the august Edwardian residence, while the band of the Royal Marines in their shockingly white tropical uniforms and solar topees rapped out a drum tattoo. Beside me stood the director of the British Council in Ethiopia, Michael Sargent.

'I've got an idea,' I said, trying to restrain myself from grasping his sleeve. 'I want to tell you about it.'

'Tomorrow. My office. Eleven o'clock,' he said.

And so it began.

The British Council, like all successful organisations, is an evolving creature, reinventing itself in twists and turns of policy. One of its virtues is autonomy. Separate from the Foreign Office, it can pursue its generally worthwhile goals of development and 'soft diplomacy' at some distance from the machinations of Her Majesty's Government's foreign policy. Another strength is the British Council's ability to attract good people. Within its ranks there are of course the usual careerists, hacks and bureaucrats, but it has had more than its share of romantics and idealists, who plunge into whichever country they find themselves in and look for creative things to do.

It seems to me that there were more such people in the British Council thirty years ago. This was partly because they were out of touch with their controllers in London. It could take a day to book an expensive telephone call from Addis Ababa to Spring Gardens. The diplomatic bag went and returned once a week, and even telexes, when they came in, were cumbersome. Faxes speeded things up alarmingly, but with the advent of email, the game was up for the old style director, who ran his fiefdom with independence.

Michael Sargent was a British Council director in the grand old tradition.

❖

There can't be many cities in the world where you can step into a taxi, say 'British Council' and be taken to its doors, as you can in Addis Ababa. This gave some Addis Ababa residents an inflated idea of the importance of the British Council in British national life. I heard of an Ethiopian visiting London who hailed a taxi, said 'British Council', and was of course met with a blank stare.

I was nostalgic as I walked into Artistic Buildings where the British Council was then housed. Thirty years earlier, when I had been a teacher in Addis Ababa, I had often walked up those chipped marble steps to visit the library, where I had sent my students to register so that they could borrow books. I had hoped that they would develop the habit of reading, an unusual phenomenon in Ethiopia, where until recently there were no public libraries; many schools still possess almost no books, and the rare bookshop has few titles on its shelves. The British Council, after one of its policy reviews, was soon to close the library, but even when it was open the books on offer were often not accessible to inexperienced readers. (I remember leafing through Southey's *Life of Nelson* and shutting it with a snap.) Where were the books that Ethiopian children could read and enjoy? Where could they find reflections of themselves and their own world? It was these thoughts that had given me my big idea.

'Could you possibly,' I said to Michael Sargent, 'provide me with the means to make a journey or two out of Addis Ababa in order to collect some stories? What I'll do is write them in simplified English easy enough for schoolchildren to understand. I'll produce a couple of little books to give to schools so that children can have reading practice in English with familiar Ethiopian subject matter.'

Luckily for me, two developments had made my idea timely. The first was that the Ministry of Education had decided that English should be the medium of instruction from the seventh grade onwards. The rationale for this was partly to sidestep political and social tensions over language in a country with over seventy diverse tongues, all jockeying for formal recognition, and partly to make students competitive in the wider world beyond Ethiopia, where few people understand Amharic, the Ethiopian lingua franca, and even fewer can read its ancient and beautiful script.

The second factor was that, since the change of government in 1991, when the dictator Mengistu Haile Mariam had been swept from power, and the country had risked fracturing along ethnic and linguistic lines, the incoming government had offered some autonomy to Ethiopia's widely different ethnicities and had created fourteen regions. Each of these had its own ministries of education, culture, agriculture and so on, and were joined in a federation under the national government operating out of Addis Ababa.

I was barely aware of all this as I sat in Michael Sargent's office.

'Collect stories?' he said. 'Readers in English? Yes.'

He sat thinking, his blue eyes bright between the thick crown of white hair above them and the neat white beard beneath, while I sat, stupefied, appalled at what I was proposing.

'But,' he continued, 'two readers won't do. You should visit each of the fourteen regions and write two books of stories for each one.'

❖

It's not easy to grasp the intricacies of Ethiopia's cultural, linguistic and religious life. Vastly varying landscapes and climates, criss-crossing camel and mule trade routes, and two millennia of written history have produced not one but many widely differing cultures. Ethiopia's monuments include giant stelae from the fourth and fifth centuries, twelfth-century rock-hewn churches and seventeenth-century castles. In the churches, frescoes surge from the walls, and the priests may well show you manuscripts dating back hundreds of years illustrated with a vibrancy that makes you blink. Musical instruments, forms of dance, a love of wordplay in poetry and stories – all these make for a richness largely unknown to the rest of the world. Given all this, I knew in my bones, without any evidence to back it up, that there must be troves of oral stories waiting for me to discover.

It's galling to Ethiopians that the name of their country evokes in most outsiders images of poverty and famine.

'Going to Ethiopia?' the nurse in my London surgery said as I offered my arm for a typhoid jab. 'Do you take your own food with you?'

I tried to tell her that I was already salivating at the prospect of Ethiopia's delicious cuisine, but I could tell she didn't believe me.

This is ironic, given the hold which Ethiopia has in times past held on the imaginations of the West. The Mountains of Rasselas, Prester John and the Lion of Judah ring down the ages.[2]

The old heartland of Ethiopia is the central highland region, a massive cool plateau that rises in the north to the peaks of the

2 The legend of Prester John, a Christian king said to rule over a lost nation of Christians surviving amid a sea of Muslims, was popular in Europe in the Middle Ages. Samuel Johnson, exploiting the eighteenth-century obsession with the exotic, set his philosophical romance *Rasselas* in the mountains of Abyssinia, while the Lion of Judah, one of the titles of the Emperor Haile Selassie, echoes the Old Testament, so well known in the West, where the term refers to the Israelite tribe of Judah.

Semien Mountains, and is intersected by gorges below whose dizzying cliffs run powerful rivers: the Nile, the Omo and the Takazze. The land shelves down towards the Red Sea in the east in a series of giant lurches to bottom out in the Danakil Depression, an arid, inhospitable region which claims to be the hottest place on earth. In the north-west, an even more spectacular escarpment plunges down thousands of feet to the deserts of Sudan. Hollows in the Rift Valley, which runs from the north to the south, have filled with water to make a string of lakes. In the south-east there are vast plains of semi-arid grassland, and in the south-west steam rises from the hot lowlands where the Baro river snakes its marshy way towards the Nile.

Human beings, as they do everywhere, have created diverse ways to survive in these different and sometimes uncomfortable environments. It's hardly surprising that settled cereal farmers have for millennia cultivated the cool fertile uplands, that nomadic pastoralists populate the semi-arid east, and that small groups of hunter-gatherers have until recently lived in the relatively empty lands of the south-west. Michael Sargent was proposing to send me to visit all of them.

❖

Back in London, I had the shakes about what I'd taken on. I would wake with a jerk in the night and horrid visions would crowd in. I'd get malaria. I'd die of exhaustion. No one in Ethiopia would know any stories and I would embarrass myself and everyone else.

I went over the memory of the old farmer on Entoto again and again. If only I could remember his fable about the ant! If only I could be sure that I'd find enough stories to fill a few little books! I had on my shelf a much-thumbed volume of Ethiopian folk tales,[3] but it had been published half a century earlier, and by now, surely, such tales would no longer be living in people's memories. I delved into the London Library, losing my way as I always did in those dim, dusty stacks, but unearthed only collections of stories from all over Africa, the religious legends of Ethiopian saints and the tale of Solomon and the Queen of Sheba.

I started to think about stories. What was I looking for? What did the word 'story' mean, anyway?

❖

I was a child with aunts. I had five in New Zealand, who seemed as remote and exotic as baroque goddesses on a *trompe l'oeil* ceiling, and six aunts and great aunts, whom I knew well, in Scotland. Their names were Mary, Marie, Mona, May, Martha and Nancy. My understanding of oral literature, if I had any at all, came from them.

Mary, my grandmother's sister, had fallen in love with a missionary to the Inuit in her youth. He had informed her that the Arctic was no place for a woman, so she had concentrated on her career as a nurse, ending up as matron of the Glasgow Royal Infirmary. She would sing snatches of verse and offer the tag ends of tales to small nieces like me. I took from her a love of rhymes and riddles and jingles.

Marie, my grandfather's sister, was among the millions of young female victims of the First World War forced into

---

3 *Fire on the Mountain* by Harold Courlander and Wolf Leslau (Holt, Rinehart and Winston, 1950).

involuntary spinsterhood by the shortage of young men. She looked after her parents into their old age and became a repository of knowledge on the history of our family. She made up genealogical trees, talked of an ancestress arraigned as a witch, and was proud of our Covenanting heroes standing up to the bullying troops of the Stewart kings. From her, I learned that history has meaning when it's the story of one's own family, and (much later) that tales of the ancestors move from history into myth, and don't necessarily agree with the views of real historians.

May was the one I knew least well. She was married to an uncle, and was from a Highland family.

'She sees beyond the every day world,' my mother would say, but May, like all my other aunts, was deeply religious, and her special gift was not something she liked to discuss. She was also the kindest woman alive. I learned from May to respect the un-knowable.

Mona, Martha and Nancy were my father's sisters. Mona was a true storyteller. She was the headmistress of a girls' boarding school and had a weakness for titles and the aristocracy. She was bossy, imaginative and wildly generous. I adored her. She drove my sister and me all the way from London to Scotland in her small car, defiantly negotiating blind corners on the wrong side of the road, while she spun fabulous yarns of the Three Adventurers setting sail on the high seas. (I was the cabin boy.) Mona taught me that stories can be made up, embroidered, added to, changed, laughed over, remembered and forgotten.

Martha joined the Indian army as a nurse in 1939 and was sent to Burma, where she experienced such horrors in her jungle hospital that she could never speak of them afterwards without weeping. I suppose I learned from her the power of real stories, of the dark emotions their telling and concealment suggests.

Nancy was a missionary in Angola. She too was a gifted storyteller. She sent us tales she had written herself. The postman would bring them in envelopes with colourful Angolan stamps, which I would soak off and stick into my album. Her stories were of leopards and monkeys, of brave missionaries and of Africans brought to salvation. For Nancy, stories were a means of spreading the gospel and bringing children to the Lord.

This education in story didn't seem much to go on as I contemplated my task in Ethiopia, but in retrospect I can see that my aunts didn't give me such a bad grounding, after all.

❖

The night before I left London for my first story-collecting expedition, I dreamed that the man checking passports at the airport in Addis Ababa was the king of Saudi Arabia. He gave me an old-fashioned look as I approached the desk because my sleeves were too short. I was anxious, I suppose, at the thought of being a woman alone in Ethiopia. Ethiopia may be ahead of many countries in the world when it comes to the rights of women, but there is still a long way to go. Decades ago, during the 1960s, when I had been a young, single teacher of English in Addis Ababa, I had had to learn the art of side-stepping out of many an ambiguous situation.

Flying to Ethiopia, if you are lucky enough to get a window seat, is a lesson in geography. Once you have skimmed over the Alps, you find yourself peering down the funnel of Vesuvius. Shortly afterwards you are following the winding snake of the Nile, with irrigation channels glinting between the geometrically precise rectangles of Egyptian fields. Some time after Khartoum, the great escarpment of the Ethiopian highlands rises beneath you, and you float across the plateau and land in Addis Ababa as the sun sinks behind the mountains in the west.

❖

It was a soft landing for me on that first expedition because I was to stay with Robin and Merril Christopher, old friends from England. They were entertaining on the night of my arrival, and an hour after the plane had landed I had washed my face and hands, put on a clean blouse, and was sitting at their dinner table, listening to a Russian diplomat discoursing on the life of a young boy from a noble Ethiopian family who had somehow become a page boy at the court of Peter the Great. The Tsar had adopted him, and he had married a Russian princess. His great grandson was Alexander Pushkin.

The talk turned to the White Russians who had fled to Addis Ababa after the revolution, of the restaurants they had opened, their mysterious comings and goings and sudden disappearances. Nazis, too, had sought concealment in Ethiopia after the fall of Germany. One of them, indeed, had presided over the stables of the Imperial Bodyguard, where I had been taught to ride.

'Anybody remember that old Austrian woman?' I chipped in. 'The one who was reputed to have been the mistress of an archduke? I used to go to her restaurant on the Ambo road. She served up *Wiener schnitzel* and *apfeltorte*.'

'And those dynasties of Armenian merchants! And the Greeks! Why didn't anyone collect their stories?' everyone kept saying. 'It's too late now. They've all gone.'

Stories lost and gone. I tried not to feel discouraged.

❖

At over 2,300 metres, Addis Ababa is one of the highest capital cities in the world. High altitude induces in me a sense of irrepressible joy. The downside of this euphoria is an inability to sleep.

I did sleep that night, however, which was just as well, because in the days to come there would be a gruelling round of meetings as the details of the project were hammered out with the Ministry of Education, the British Council and the various officials whose blessing needed to be sought.

It was a piece of luck that the man at the British Council in charge of my project was Ato[4] Mulugeta Hunde. I was catching him just before he retired after his long career. I found myself looking at him carefully as we sat over our first lunch together in Castelli's, a venerable restaurant, which, with its *buffet fredo* and pasta *al funghi* would have graced a side street in old Palermo. Mulugeta was an old man, moving with an extreme slowness which belied the sharpness of his mind.

'Weren't you the librarian at the Council in the sixties?' I asked him at last. 'Wasn't it you who sat by the door with a rack of tickets in a long wooden box, and stamped the books as they went out?'

This memory of his early career enchanted him, and we promised each other that when we were less pressed for time we would meet and swap our life stories, and so we did, weeks later. This is what Mulugeta told me.

He had been working at the British Council for some years before the revolution which had toppled Emperor Haile Selassie,

---

4   Ato equates to Mr in English.

and when the old order changed he concentrated on keeping his head down and pressing on quietly with his work.

'I saw him, you know, His Majesty, when they were taking him away to the barracks on the day they arrested him. I was standing there, by the underpass, and he came past in a small Volkswagen car. A little car like that! For him! Children and young people were running along shouting abuse at him. 'Burn him! Burn him!' I was so shocked. It was very terrible. He was a man we all respected, with a very great charisma. To see him like that! On that day!'

A few months later, the British Council had sent him to Aberystwyth to do a degree in librarianship and he was out of the country for three years.

'When I was going into breakfast one day, some English students said to me, 'You Ethiopians are very cruel people. You have shot all your ministers.' I ran to find a newspaper, and it was true. All the cabinet ministers executed. Men I had looked up to!'

He had nearly decided to stay in Britain but in the end he had returned to Ethiopia and gone on working for the British Council. He had been afraid all the time, and with reason.

'Working for foreigners at that time, you know . . . Every day you go out of your house and you don't know if you will come home. Even our food! We could only buy tef[5] on the black market, because it was considered to be a bourgeois luxury. You had to pretend to eat only maize and if you wanted tef you must buy and eat it secretly. But time is healing, you know. Time is healing us from all those things.'

---

[5] The staple cereal unique to Ethiopia from which injera is made.

❖ 2 ❖

JESTERS AND ZOMBIES
IN AMHARA

One does not prepare lightly for journeys in rural Ethiopia. In 1968, with the self-confidence of youth, I had embarked on a sixty-mile trek across the mountains to Lalibela provisioned only with twenty hard boiled eggs and a pair of semi high-heeled shoes. This time my packing list had covered two columns of typing and took weeks to assemble.

'Have you packed a bath plug?' my husband David said, coming into our bedroom where I had laid everything out on the bed. 'Have you checked your mosquito net for holes?'

'What do you take me for? Why don't you come with me, anyway?'

'You'll do much better on your own. I'd only distract you.'

A veteran of journeys to unlikely places (where he had had too many close shaves with bandits, gunmen and dodgy politicians) David knew what he was talking about.

'A torch and batteries,' he added as he ambled back to work in the study we shared.

❖

A week later, with my kit stowed in a small bag and tucked away in the hold of an Ethiopian Airlines plane, I was arriving in Bahir Dar, the administrative centre of the first of the regions I was to cover, and it was time to put the project to the test.

Bahir Dar, the capital of the Amhara region, is barely sixty years old. It was laid out in the 1960s with industrial development in mind. This led to an ambitious town plan based on wide boulevards, and though these are planted with flowering trees, they are meant for wheeled traffic and are achingly long and hot when one has to plod along them on foot in pursuit of storytellers.

Bahir Dar lies at the northern tip of the old province of Gojjam which, in pre-revolutionary times, was the fiefdom of powerful lords. One of these, Ras Hailu (the title Ras roughly equals duke) was a man of immense power and charisma, closely associated with the imperial family. He travelled widely in Europe, and his memory is alive today. From his headquarters in Debre Marcos, Ras Hailu presided over the fates of hundreds of thousands and commanded many armed men. His court was attended by Major Cheesman, the British consul in north-west Abyssinia in the 1920s. The detail which fascinated me most in Cheesman's account[6] was the fact that Ras Hailu had a jester, who, in the manner of such men in the medieval courts of Europe, could say what he liked to anyone, and whose scurrilous, bawdy wit made everyone clutch their sides with laughter.

Another tradition from those courtly times was the 'azmari', or wandering troubadour – the singing gazelle of Ethiopia. He would travel about the country with his 'masenqo' (a simple single-stringed instrument played with a bow), improvising songs as the occasion arose, lauding guests and heroes and teasing his hosts with satire.

The tradition was still just alive in the 1960s. When I walked the pilgrim route to Lalibela in 1968, I stayed overnight in a

[6] *Lake Tana and the Blue Nile*, Major R.E. Cheesman (Macmillan and Co, 1936).

village. A man who had been sitting against the wall of the little round house stood up while the mistress of the house was preparing coffee, took his masenqo off its nail and began to play and sing. A few familiar words stood out from his song: England, queen, Elsabet, Lalibela, Haile Selassie King of Kings. Our hosts' faces reaction showed the shifts in the verses' mood as they shook their heads and drew in their breath with emotion or fell on each others' shoulders, laughing.

The glory of Bahir Dar is the lake on whose banks it lies. Lake Tana is big, about fifty miles from north to south, and forty from east to west. Fed by many streams, it pours out at its southernmost tip into a great river, the Blue Nile (known as the Abay in Ethiopia), which is impressive even so near the place of its birth, and will become more so as it cuts its way through colossal canyons and spills down stupendous rapids, carrying the fertile silt of Ethiopia to the Sudan, where it will mingle with the waters of the White Nile flowing north from Uganda to create one broad stream giving life and wealth, as it always has done, to Egypt.

For millennia, the Abay has been revered by the people who lived at its source, and has fascinated those to the east and north, in Egypt and in Europe beyond. The Book of Genesis states: 'And a river went out of Eden to water the garden; and from there it was parted and became four heads . . . And the name of the second river is Gihon, the same it is that encompasseth the whole land of Ethiopia.'

Ethiopians took this reference to mean the Abay, and the name Gihon, or Ghion, is a favourite one for hotels and businesses all over Ethiopia.

The Nile has cast its enchantment over Europeans, too. Alexander the Great sent an expedition to find its source. Julius

Caesar claimed that he longed to know of it, more than anything else in the world. And Nero despatched two luckless centurions to explore it. Ethiopians have always known how valuable the river is as a diplomatic bargaining chip, and over the centuries have used a threat to divert it in their dealings with Egypt. It is only in modern times that they have had the ability to do so, a fact which strains their relationship with the countries downstream.

The Portuguese, in the early seventeenth century, were the first Europeans to reach Lake Tana and discover the actual source of the Nile, the spring which feeds the Little Abay, which is the principle stream flowing into Lake Tana, although their claims were dismissed by James Bruce of Kinnaird, the colourful Scot who found it for himself in 1770.

Right up until 1968, the course of the river to the Sudan had never been explored, owing to the dangerous territory through which it flows: the ravines, the leopard-haunted forests and death-defying rapids, not to mention lurking crocodiles and hippos. The river was finally conquered during an expedition in 1968 organised by the British army. At the time, I was immersed in the round of my teaching routine, busy with lesson preparation, marking and staff meetings. I was invited to a party to meet these Boy's Own heroes, and their leader John Blashford-Snell, on their triumphant return to Addis Ababa. They were all so dashing, so muscular, so sun-tanned and joyful that I had heart-flutters for at least a week after they had gone home.

Like most other regions of Ethiopia, Gojjam is populated by a patchwork of communities and religions, each with its own customs and rituals. These groups have lived alongside each other for centuries in a complex hierarchy of status and occupation. The Amharas, who moved into the highlands of Ethiopia from the east thousands of years ago, and who formed the ruling élite of Ethiopia, were at the top of the pecking order. They were the feudal lords, government officials, soldiers and farmers. No self-respecting Amhara would engage in crafts, such as pottery or weaving, or work as smiths. Those pursuing such occupations still come from minority groups, live separately and are often thought to possess the evil eye. This belief is by no means unique to Ethiopia. Skilled artisans are thought to have sinister powers in many parts of the world. In the Highlands of Scotland metal work was in the past done only by 'tinkers' (the name means menders of metal objects) who were thought to be linked with the fairies – a tradition probably going back to the Iron Age.

Among the minorities in Gojjam were the Beta Israel (or Falasha, as they were commonly called – a term considered derogatory today). These legendary Jews of Ethiopia had practised their religion for millennia, out of touch with mainstream Judaism. When I had visited Gojjam during the 1960s, there were still numerous members of the Beta Israel living in the area, making and selling their distinctive black glazed pottery. Like every other ferenji,[7] my house filled up with swan-necked coffee pots, shallow bowls and branched candlesticks which I had bought at the roadside near Beta Israel villages. By the time I had returned to collect stories, thirty years later, almost every member of the Beta Israel population had been swept up in airlifts to Israel. I was sorry that none of their stories would be in the collection.

Lake Tana is shallow and studded with islands which are of immense historical and symbolic importance to Ethiopia's ancient Orthodox Christian church. There are churches and monasteries on many of these islands, some dating back to the thirteenth

---

[7] A term commonly used throughout Ethiopia and the Middle East to describe Europeans. It derives from the word 'Franks' and dates from the Middle Ages.

century. Vellum manuscripts illuminated with glowing paintings, in the uniquely Ethiopian style descended from Byzantium, have long been in the possession of the clergy here, and the walls of many churches are adorned with brilliantly coloured frescoes. Given the religious importance of Lake Tana, and the many legends which, I knew, floated about in the rich atmosphere, I might have expected, while sitting on the lake shore, to hear stories of saints, raisings from the dead, rescues from devils, and the visit by the Virgin Mary during the Flight into Egypt. None of these were offered to me. Later, I realised that for Ethiopians (as for Christians, Jews and Muslims everywhere) there is a clear distinction between 'scripture' and 'story'. The same is true in Europe, where folk tales are not confused with Bible stories or hagiographies. You will not find the story of Daniel and his lions or Noah and his ark in collections of secular animal stories for children in Europe.

The flight to Bahir Dar from Addis Ababa was bumpy. To my relief, Ato Alemayehu Gebrehiwot, head of the Culture, Tourism and Information Bureau of the Amhara National Regional State (to give him his full title) was there to pick me up. He was the first such officer I was to meet, and like many of the others, living and working in vastly different circumstances in other regions of Ethiopia, he was impressive. He told me about his passion for drama and his hope to encourage theatrical productions in the Amhara region. He had, he explained, put me in the hands of Daniel Legesse, his assistant, who would ferret out stories for me and translate them into English. In the meantime, I would be staying in the grand old hotel of Bahir Dar (naturally named the 'Ghion'), which was set on the shore of Lake Tana under a canopy of majestic trees.

That afternoon, I went to sit on the tumbled basalt rocks at the water's edge to watch the day fade into night. It was the wedding season, and several honeymoon couples were scattered along the shore, intent only on each other. I felt lonely, and was annoyed with myself. Earlier in the day, I'd gone for a walk into town from the hotel and, as so often happens round tourist honey pots, I had been besieged by beggars and harassed by clamorous children. I'd always resolved, before a visit to Ethiopia, to be easy-going on these occasions, but the old school-marmy stand-offishness had kicked in and I'd scuttled back to the sanctuary of the hotel. Now, sitting on my rock, I was falling into another typically European cast of mind: the controller, the exploiter, the organiser. Before the sun had set, I had put a fish farm on the lake, established a fleet of boats for the hotel guests, swapped the plastic chairs in the garden for wooden seats, retiled the bathrooms and changed the 20-watt light bulbs for ones you could actually read by. In doing so, I would have imposed cruel strains on Bahir Dar's energy resources, contributed to global warming and wrecked the laid-back charm of the place. As I walked slowly back to the restaurant for my supper, I reflected on how Ethiopia is forever at the mercy of bright ideas from foreign 'improvers', and I hoped that my story-collecting project would not end up in the over-stocked graveyard of ill-conceived do-gooding schemes.

The next morning, filled with enthusiasm, Daniel and I found ourselves standing outside the closed door of a neatly kept house in a quiet corner of Bahir Dar. The window shutters at one side were open – an encouraging sign – and a couple of chairs were set out under the covered area in the front of the house.

Daniel knocked on the door, coughing to signal his presence. Nothing happened. He knocked a bit louder, knocked again, coughed again, then gave the door a thump. It opened a crack. A young woman stared at us with suspicion in her one visible eye.

Daniel smiled, bending forward from the hips. This ferenji woman, I understood him to say, would like to see Ato Shimeles, and ask him to tell her stories.

Not surprisingly, the girl's face remained blank. Daniel spoke some more. At last, she reluctantly opened the door and stepped aside. Daniel bounced ahead of me into a small dark room lined with chairs. It was the classic sitting room of an Ethiopian house. The floor, of polished concrete, was swept clear of dust. On the walls hung a few faded pictures cut from magazines and several studio photographs of serious men and women in formal clothes. A curtain was suspended across a door at the back of the room.

We waited. I was consumed with embarrassment. What a cheek to march into someone's house in the middle of the morning, and demand that they tell me stories! Come to think of it, what effrontery this whole project showed, for a person as ignorant and unprepared as I was.

A tall man, who seemed to be a servant, appeared through the curtained doorway. He was unsmiling. What was the purpose of our visit? What did we want Ato Shimeles to do for us?

He came and went several more times, and then at last another door at the side of the room opened and we were beckoned through.

'Ato Shimeles was a diplomat in the time of His Majesty,' Daniel hissed in my ear. 'He suffered very much under the Derg.'

Then I understood the blank stare which the maid had given me when she had opened the door, the toings and froings of the manservant, and the long wait before Ato Shimeles was ready to see us. He belonged to the generation who had suffered unspeakably at the hands of Mengistu Haile Mariam and his government (always referred to as the 'Derg'), which in 1973 had toppled the emperor, Haile Selassie, and his ancient Solomonic dynasty and replaced it with a revolutionary Stalinist tyranny, only to be ousted in his turn in 1991. Tens of thousands of students, teachers and intellectuals had died in the Red Terror unleashed by Mengistu. A sudden knock on the door and the appearance of strangers must have been unnerving to the household of Ato Shimeles.

He was standing behind his desk in what was clearly his study. He had the fair skin of a high-born Amhara, and a neat white beard gave him a resemblance to the old emperor, who is now so rehabilitated in the people's esteem that nearly everyone refers to him as 'His Majesty'.

The room was lined with books in Amharic and English. A collection of antique Ethiopian jewellery hung from a frame near the window. Behind the large desk, on which stood ivory ornaments, was a bed covered in handsome woven cloth. It was the room of a scholar.

Ato Shimeles greeted us in perfect English. He had lived in London, he said, in the 1950s. He probed me gently about myself. I'd known one of his former colleagues. My stock rose. I explained my mission. Could he tell us any stories? He wasn't sure. He needed time to think. We should meet him in a couple of hours' time at his office, some way from his home.

Ato Shimeles's office was a small mud-plastered single-room hut, roofed with tin. He was a practising lawyer and several clients were waiting to see him. It was dark inside the little office, the open door providing the sole source of light, which fell in a rectangle onto the floor and showed a scattering of freshly cut leaves and grass.

'You can see by the floor that we are honouring you,' he said, as I crunched across the greenery to perch on a plastic chair. And I did feel honoured. Strewing leaves is a festive thing, a mark of respect for a guest.

I took out my tape recorder and pencil, excited at the thought that stories would now start to flow. But Ato Shimeles was fiddling with his pen.

'There are some books you should consult,' he said. 'I have the titles for you.'

Daniel, fidgeting on his chair, urged him to tell a story himself.

'Just one,' he coaxed.

At last, Ato Shimeles cleared his throat. I switched on my tape recorder.

'It must be in Amharic,' he warned.

'No problem,' said Daniel. 'I will translate later for Mrs Elizabeth.'

And so the first storytelling session began. As Ato Shimeles's voice rose and fell, his clients began to cluster round the open door, sucking their breath in through their teeth to show their appreciation. But I was dying to ask this man for another kind of story, about his own life, and the painful road he must have travelled, from his academic education through the gilded embassies of Europe, perhaps through the torture chambers of the Derg, to end here in this hut, listening to the grievances of the clients.

We hurried back to the Ghion Hotel and settled down in the garden under the shade of giant fig trees. Black-headed herons flapped and clattered in the branches. Every now and then a fruit would splatter down, making us flinch for fear that it was something worse.

I couldn't wait to hear the translations of Ato Shimeles's stories, but when Daniel, doing his best, had stumbled through them, I sat back, chewing the end of my pen, discouraged. I had in my notebook only a few fragments of wit and snatches of anecdote. There was a tale of young lovers found dead on one of the islands in the lake, which sounded like a real incident, and some sayings, riddles and short poems.

'Here is one,' Daniel said, his ear to the tape recorder. He wrinkled his brow with the effort of teasing out the convoluted meaning in English. 'Her chest looks like the orange of Shenno. And he said, "She is mad, let me also be mad." There is a double meaning. Mad. It is associated with sex. This is wax and gold, you see. Wax and gold!'

He beamed at me. My confidence, already dented, fizzled to a new low. Wax and gold is the term used to describe the most prized form of Ethiopian prose and poetry, in which the surface meaning, the wax, must be melted in the crucible of thought to reveal the hidden core, the gold, underneath. This art form, perfected in Amhara culture, relies on densely impacted sentences and double meanings. It's almost impossible to translate. Would I be offered only wax and gold on my journeys? Had the farmer on Entoto misled me? Perhaps the robust folk tales I was after didn't exist at all.

But Daniel was still listening to the cassette player, holding it to his ear, his plump cheeks quivering with amusement.

'There is one more, but it is not really a story like you want. It is like a joke. From the Derg time. Not very interesting for you.'

'Let me hear it anyway.'

He translated it, between gusts of laughter.

At the time of the Derg there was a self-important official called Kumche Ambau. Wanting to show that he was decisive and forward-looking, he decided to create a football field in his town. To work on this project, he took men away from more important tasks until at last the field was finished.

Kumche Ambau decided to make a splash of the opening football game and invited bigwigs down from Addis Ababa, but as the players ran out onto the field, he saw that something was terribly wrong.

'Oh sirs,' he cried, 'we are only a poor district. We have done our best, but due to economic circumstances we have only been able to buy one ball. But let me tell you this, when we have made more revolutionary progress, you will come back again, and then, I promise you, every player shall have his own ball!'

Later, I was to hear more of the exploits of Kumche Ambau, and I realised that he was evolving into a classic character of oral fiction – the fool, the jester, the simpleton, who sometimes stumbles upon a truth. I didn't understand at that moment by the lapping water of Lake Tana, that Kumche Ambau and his football field were living proof that the oral storytelling tradition was alive and well in Ethiopia, changing with the times to meet, mock and make sense of the modern world. And it was only later, too, that I realised that a highly educated, cultured man like Ato Shimeles was not likely to be a fount of oral stories from a folk tradition. We would have had more luck, perhaps, in going through to the back of his house and talking to the old woman who was sweeping out the yard.

The Kumche Ambau story had inspired Daniel.

'Now I will tell you a story that I know myself.' He clicked his fingers, and a waiter, who had been hovering on the hotel's veranda, his sharp ears tuned to the sound, hurried over to us. 'Two Mirandas.'

'Not for me,' I put in hastily. I couldn't face another bottle of the chemical orange fizz to which Daniel was addicted. 'Tea. With no sugar.'

'No sugar?' The waiter's brows rose in disbelief.

'No sugar.'

'This story is about a wise and witty man called Aleka Gebrehana,' began Daniel.

And so I had my first introduction to the joker of Gojjam. Later, I would hear from others how he deceived rapacious policemen; how he wangled his way from purgatory into heaven to meet the Empress Menen, and was only persuaded to leave when he couldn't resist scrabbling after a handful of coins which St Peter threw out of the pearly gates; how he shat himself when a medicine man applied a hot poker to a sore on his behind. 'What did you expect?' he cried indignantly, on being reproved. 'When the house is burning, the goods must be removed.'

I began to build up a picture of Aleka Gebrehana. His character seemed to be based on one of the court jesters whom Cheesman had described. A man with a reputation for searing wit, he seemed to be allowed an astonishing degree of latitude in his digs at those in power. With the passage of time many fantastical stories have been added to the repertoire of Aleka Gebrehana's exploits and he has acquired legendary status, becoming cousin to the trickster Abu Nawas whom I would later meet in Harar, and Nasruddin, whose wily irreverence is celebrated in countless stories across the Middle East. But there was an earthiness and directness to Aleka Gebrehana that provoked a belly laugh rather than a titter.

There was much running about that afternoon from offices to

schools in pursuit of possible narrators. Ethiopian government offices usually conform to one pattern. A long, one-storey building is entered at the end. Rooms give off to left and right down the central corridor. The head man's sanctum, at the far end, is accessible only through the office of his secretary, who fiercely guards the portal. Inside the holy of holies, the chief's desk forms the short arm of a T-shaped arrangement, with a table running down the length of the room away from it. This is where guests, committee members and supplicants are seated. I had seen an identical office arrangement in China and Kazakhstan, and assumed that it was a Communist import. In the more rural areas of Ethiopia, where in the late 1990s photocopiers and computers were rarities, I was sometimes brought up short by the smell of Gestetner skins, evoking long forgotten memories of the hours I had once spent typing students' exam papers, and the blobs of pink fluid that had covered up my frequent mistakes.

At last we ran to earth two elderly teachers. They would meet us tomorrow, they said, when they would have had time to prepare some stories.

Daniel, watching me ease my sandal straps around my blisters, was struck by an idea.

'You will return to your hotel on a bicycle!' he beamed. 'And later you will ride it to my house for dinner!'

I have never had a good relationship with a bicycle. A childhood spell in bed with rheumatic fever had left me with weak knees.

'Promise me, *promise me*, Elizabeth,' a teacher at my school had once pleaded, stopping her car alongside as I had wobbled down a busy road in an effort to cycle to school, 'that you will *never* ride a bicycle on a main road again.'

But Daniel was insistent, and I began to be afraid that I was looking feeble. In any case, I quailed at the thought of another long walk.

Daniel was smiling encouragingly, like a parent with a child.

'I will come with you, Mrs Elizabeth. You will find it very easy.'

As it turned out, he was right. The road was long and straight. No children rushed at me as I feared they would, and although an ox cart pulled out suddenly from a side turning, and the bike proved to have no brakes, I reached the Ghion in one piece.

'I'll come to your house tonight in a taxi,' I told Daniel firmly, then I lay down in my room and slept.

❖

Daniel's wife, Sari, had laid on a delicious meal. Good, home-cooked food is, in my view, one of the pleasures of travel in Ethiopia. Hot, rich curries (called 'wat') and strips of crisply fried meat ('tibs') are served on large, flat sourdough pancakes ('injera'). On the frequent fasting days in Christian households no animal products, including eggs, butter and honey, are eaten, but the vegan alternatives are tasty vegetable and lentil stews. Before the meal began, Daniel bowed his head to say grace, and I was startled by the well-worn phrases, so familiar from my Evangelical childhood, which fell from his lips.

'Oh Lord, we bring before you . . . your many goodnesses and the richness of your blessings . . . this hour of fellowship with our sister . . .'

The missionaries had been busy indeed.

I enjoyed my dinner, but I was tired and the evening was a strain. I was concerned about Sari, who was very thin. She had been severely ill with malaria, Daniel explained. I wasn't surprised. The whine of mosquitoes buzzing about the hot little house was a constant backdrop to our conversation, and I was worried in case there was a gap between my trousers and my socks which the jungle juice I had plastered on myself might not have reached. Malaria, of the most deadly and virulent kind, is a frightening killer in parts of Ethiopia, especially around Lake Tana, and I watched with foreboding as the toddler, Prophet, pushed his toy car along the surface of the table, his eyes on the black and white fuzz emanating from the television in the corner of the room, which gave more light than the dim bulb hanging from ceiling.

❖

Government offices are not good places for storytelling, and I was to learn that creating an atmosphere was a necessary prerequisite to a successful session. But the following day, a group of four young employees of the Cultural Bureau, sitting in embarrassed silence behind their desks, began at last to egg each other on.

'I know one.'

'Mine's better. Once there was a lion and an ape . . .'

'The one with the bull's placenta in it? Not that one.'

'Here, listen to this. It's called "The Marriage Chain",' said one of them at last. His name was Yirga Ejigu.

The hero of Yirga's story is a poor man whose rich neighbour covets his wife. The rich man offers the woman luxurious clothes and jewels if she will divorce her husband and marry him. She starts to badger her husband to buy her all that the rich man has promised. He does his best, and falls into debt.

'But what are clothes and jewels?' the rich man says to her. 'If your husband really loved you, he would perform miracles for you. Divorce him and marry me, and see what I can do.'

The poor man's wife, her head turned, complains to her husband that he never performs miracles. In despair, he prays for help. A wizard appears, and gives the poor man two sticks. 'The first,' he says, 'will change a human being into a donkey. The second will change him back into a man.'

Jubilant, the poor man runs home.

'I'll show you a miracle,' he says, and changes his wife into a donkey. Then he returns her to herself. 'And now,' he tells her, 'I'm going to punish our enemy, the man who has tried to come between us. You know who I mean.'

The wife confesses that her head had been turned by the rich man's promises, and is sorry. Her husband changes the rich man into a donkey, then hides the magic sticks in the roof of his house. He makes his donkey work hard for many years, until with its help he has become rich. Only when the donkey is lame and beaten down with toil does he relent and turn him back into a man – old, worn out and poor, and tells him to go home, with a final admonition to stay away from other men's wives.

There are versions of this story around the world with similar features: the theme of justice and retribution, the motif of the good poor man versus the wicked rich man, and of tolerance and gentleness between a husband and wife, while the magic sticks are first cousins of wands in European witch lore. I enjoyed the echo of Nebuchadnezzar in the Bible, who in punishment is turned from a tyrant into a comic character: 'He was driven from men, and did eat grass as oxen . . . till his hairs were grown like eagle feathers, and his nails like birds' claws.'[8] It was the

---

[8] Daniel, chapter 4.

first time I had encountered shape-shifting in an Ethiopian story, a concept common in some parts of the country, where fear of were-hyena women still seems to be active. The magical significance of sticks taken from or kept in the roof of the house would occur again and again.

It was also my first story featuring a donkey in the typical role of fall-guy, a stock character of literature in Europe from Aesop to A.A. Milne. The donkey's role is to be eaten by a lion or hyena. He is to be ridiculed, like Bottom or Eeyore. But in his humility, he is blessed with wisdom. A donkey's colt takes Christ into Jerusalem.

G.K. Chesterton caught this ambiguity in his poem, 'The Donkey'.

> *With monstrous head and sickening cry*
> *And ears like errant wings,*
> *The devil's walking parody*
> *On all four-footed things . . .*
> *Fools! For I also had my hour;*
> *One far fierce hour and sweet:*
> *There was a shout about my ears,*
> *And palms beneath my feet.*

The donkey in Ethiopian folk stories runs true to form and is the brother of his counterparts everywhere, as this story demonstrates:

The hyena's son has died and the donkeys realise that, in spite of their misgivings, they must attend the funeral or risk causing grave offence. The hyenas, seeing them coming, accuse them of mocking their grief.

The frightened donkeys sing:

Great hyenas, you hunt all night,
And we hear you sing in the cold moonlight.
Your teeth are long, your eyes are bright,
Though your food is black, your dung is white.
But now your son lies on his bed,
Your son is dead! Our lord is dead!

They pretend to weep. But the dead hyena's uncle asks what they have brought for the mourners to eat. The donkeys have brought nothing and start to back away, but the hyenas demand that they cut off their lips for them to eat. The donkeys have no choice but to comply, but once they have lost their lips, the hyenas accuse them of grinning.

'You're laughing at us!' they howl, then fall on the donkeys and eat them. Before the oldest donkey dies, he looks up at the hyenas and says,

Wicked hyenas, we came with song
To comfort you but we were wrong.
Next time you're hungry, don't pretend
That you need a reason to eat your friend.

I was to encounter short verses of this kind within stories many times, although it took a conscientious translator to point them out. They made me think of the role of verse and jingle in European stories: 'Fee-Fi-Fo-Fum'; 'Little pig, little pig, let me come in'; 'Mirror, mirror on the wall', and countless other instances. Such verses have a ritualising effect in the story, at once distancing, familiar, and often with an underlying menace.

There is a vast store of animal fables in oral literatures around the world, from Aesop to the ancient Sanskrit tales of Kalilah and

Dimnah, from Anansi in West Africa to Brer Rabbit in the USA
and La Fontaine in Europe. Their purpose is often to impart
wisdom and point morals, and they are usually more overtly
instructive than other types of story. Almost identical fables,
with specific local trimmings, crop up in widely separate cultural
and geographical contexts, and one can speculate forever on
their origins and kinship.

Iona and Peter Opie, authors of *The Lore and Language of
Schoolchildren*, pointed out the astonishing speed with which
playground games, clapping rhymes and skipping chants spread
around the world, traversing continents and oceans with ease.
The same is no doubt true of stories. Ethiopia is crisscrossed
with ancient trade routes, along which salt cut from the Danakil
desert was transported up into the highlands and beyond, to
other parts of North and Central Africa.

I sat once for a whole day on a hillside watching the comings
and goings at the marketplace in Bati, a town set on an outcrop
of the escarpment that falls from the highlands of Ethiopia
westwards towards the Red Sea. The peoples of the Danakil
depression were arriving with strings of camels laden with bars
of salt which they had hacked out of the cruelly hot salt flats
below. Their camels could go no higher up the rocky mountain
tracks. The peoples of the highlands were tripping down from
the cool hills above, their donkeys and mules weighed down
under sacks of grain and gourds of butter and honey. Their
animals could go no lower into the heat. The grain, butter and
honey were necessities of life for the desert people. The salt was
a form of currency for the highlanders. Some of it would cross
donkey and mule trains right over the Ethiopian highlands and
descend to the Sudan, where, transferred once more onto the
backs of camels, it would embark on another journey ending in

trading centres such as Timbuktu. News must always have been traded as well as goods, and why not stories also?

I dragged my mind back to the present. The men in the office were embarking on other stories. There were more doings of Aleka Gebrehana, including a series of misunderstandings between deaf people (politically incorrect to our ears). The quietest young man, who hadn't taken part in the banter, offered the title of a tale which provoked nervous laughs from the other three.

'Yes, go on. Mrs Elizabeth wants all the stories,' urged Daniel, and turning to me, with an unusually serious expression, he said, 'This is a story but it is also true.'

We filled a couple of tapes that afternoon, and it wasn't until the evening, when I sat with Daniel once more in the garden of the Ghion, that I heard the quiet young man's story. Daniel told it seriously, urging its truth upon me.

Two girls lived near to each other. The mother of one of them died, and the child was now alone with her father. After some time, the neighbour's daughter told the motherless girl that she has seen her mother alive, inside her own house. She took the child home with her, pulled a stick from the roof and touched a pot with it. The pot changed into the body of the dead woman, lying lifeless on the ground.

The neighbour's daughter told the child not to let the secret out, but the girl couldn't resist telling her father. He didn't believe her, until she described the pot to him, saying that it had a chip on its rim.

'Your mother had a chipped tooth,' he said, and was at last convinced.

He waited until the first anniversary of his wife's death, when he prepared a ceremony of remembrance. In order to provide food and drink, he asked his neighbour to lend him his pots. The neighbour reluctantly handed them all over.

The dead woman's husband touched the chipped pot with his stick but nothing happened. The child remembered that the stick that had brought her mother to life came from the roof of the neighbour's house. Her father waited until the neighbour had arrived for the ceremony and his house was empty, then he sent his daughter to fetch the stick. When she returned with it, he touched the pot and it was transformed into the body of his dead wife. Quickly, he turned it back into a pot. He told his relatives to fetch their weapons. When they returned, he touched the pot once more in front of all his guests.

'That man has the evil eye!' he shouted, pointing at his neighbour. 'He transformed my wife into a zombie to be his slave!'

The neighbour tried to escape but was caught.

'Give back my wife's soul,' said the woman's husband, 'or we will kill you.'

The neighbour did so. The woman was fully restored to life. The neighbour and his daughter slipped away and were never seen again.

'Are you seriously telling me that this is a true story?' I asked Daniel.

'Yes, yes,' he insisted. 'Tomorrow we will go back. We will ask Worku Alemu, who told it to us. He will corroborate. The evil eye is very dangerous. It kills many people.'

Worku Alemu was in the office when we returned the next day.

'Tell me where you heard this story,' I asked him.

'My mother told it to me.'

'Where?' I wanted him to paint a picture for me. He did so, with some prompting.

'At night, when we sat by the fire. She would make sure that the door was shut, because of the hyenas, and pull her shamma over us because we were frightened, and tell us this story to make us beware of people with the evil eye.'

I didn't like to ask him if he still believed in zombies.

'What happens to people if they are thought to have this magic power?' I asked.

'It is very terrible for them. They will be left on their own.'

He stood up and came round from behind his desk. I saw that one of his legs was shorter than the other.

'What happened to him?' I asked Daniel afterwards. 'Why is he lame?' I feared some tale of a curse. The curse in question, however, had been a childhood attack of polio.

The zombie woman was only the first of several frightening female characters I was to meet in Ethiopia. There would be cannibalistic ogresses, usually with innocent daughters; a sorceress who murders her hapless suitors; a malevolent mistress of porcupines with the power to change men into animals, and several were-hyena women. These characters point to a fear of women, of their power and sexuality, and these stories still send shivers down the spines of their Ethiopian hearers. Fairy tales of all kinds have become fare only for children in Europe, where friendly witches, schoolboy wizards and big friendly giants abound in children's fiction, little girls dress in pink fairy costumes carrying toy wands in their hands, and little boys run about in Superman costumes (a fairy-tale character if ever there was one).

As Daniel and I discussed the zombie story, we were sitting in an airy thatched tea house waiting for two retired teachers to join us. Such rustic shelters are common in public buildings, providing rest areas for staff and entertainment spaces for guests.

The two old teachers came. One was tall and stocky. The other barely topped his shoulder, and his head was crowned with fluffy white hair.

'Let's go somewhere nice, by the lake,' they said, and led us out of the school compound to a café on the far side of the road. Sitting in the dappled shade of an old tree, I relished the heat-softening breeze that rises each afternoon off the waters of the lake. The two old friends' heads stood out like chiselled copper bas-reliefs against the blue-green water, framed by the pink flowers on the oleander bushes nearby.

I explained my project to them. They had heard about it already, but people in Ethiopia like to mull things over and look at something from every angle. Slowly, they got round to telling stories.

Even with my rudimentary Amharic I couldn't help noticing that every story started with the same phrase:

'*Teret, teret, ye lam beret.*'

After saying this, the storyteller would pause as if to collect his thoughts.

I asked for a translation.

'It's like "Once upon a time," said Daniel.

'But what does it mean?' I persisted.

He worked at it for a while. The translation came out as something like this: 'The evening has come, the cows are shut in the byre, and it's time for stories.'

If you're thinking that this is rather a long sentence with which to explain five short words, you are of course right. Literally, the phrase means 'Story, story, cow in byre', and it illustrates the sparse economy of Ethiopian sayings which were to give my various translators so many headaches.

I relished every moment of that afternoon by the lakeside.

I couldn't understand much of what the old friends had said until Daniel and I worked on the translations later, but I could watch them enjoying the occasion, and I laughed with them whenever they laughed, which was frequently. The following reconstruction may not be accurate, but it gives the flavour of the occasion.

'This one's about Ras Hailu of Gojjam,' one would begin. 'He was in Geneva with Haile Selassie, getting Ethiopia enrolled in the League of Nations. On the way he stopped in Rome and tried to buy an expensive razor. "You can't afford this," the shopkeeper said. "They're all beggars in your country." "Just tell me the price," Ras Hailu said. He bought the razor, and when he came home he set up a man to run a first-class barber's shop in Addis Ababa. Anyway, when he was walking down the road in Italy, a woman called out, "You blacks look like baboons!" "Very true, Madam," said Ras Hailu. "My face looks like a baboon's face, but yours looks like her bottom."'

There followed snippets of history about the wisdom of the Emperor Theodore, the guns of Queen Victoria, the triumphs of the nineteenth-century Emperor Yohannes in his wars against the Mahdi of Sudan, some victory poems and a little joke which still makes me laugh years afterwards.

A shepherd boy starts going to school but finds his lessons very difficult, especially Maths.

'Take three from five,' says the teacher. 'What's the answer?'

The boy shakes his head.

'Four minus two? It's easy.'

But the boy can't do it.

'Well,' says the teacher. 'Here's an example you ought to understand. Say you have five sheep in your fold and one of them runs out through a hole. How many will be left?'

'None, of course,' answers the shepherd boy.

'How can you be so stupid?'

'I'm not stupid! I don't know much about maths, but I know all about sheep. If one goes out through a hole in the fence, all the others will follow.'

Before I had to say goodbye, I asked the two teachers about themselves. They had been friends all their lives, they told me, since their schooldays long ago. One had outstripped the other, moving up from teaching into administrative posts in the civil service, while his friend had remained in the classroom. But when the Derg fell, and the new government led by Tigrayans had swept to power, they had been arrested at the same time and shared a cell for three months.

'They had nothing to punish us for, so they let us go,' one said.

They denied having suffered during the Derg years, from which I concluded that they had been loyal servants of the revolutionary government. I wanted to ask them how they felt about the present situation, but they discouraged me with grimaces.

'We can't talk here,' one said as we got up to leave, moving away from other tea drinkers at nearby tables. 'Who knows who will hear us?'

Ethiopian politics is not my subject, and indeed I find politics in general hard to grasp. But it's impossible to understand Ethiopia, and indeed the meaning of some of the stories I was to encounter, without a little background knowledge.

The Amhara people were in power in the Ethiopian highlands for many centuries. Over the last thousand years or so, the Amhara emperors had gradually gained dominance over many other ethnic groups in the surrounding lands, some alliances being made by marriage, and some as the result of conquest, and when national boundaries from colonial times were set permanently in the map-oriented minds of the modern era, the boundaries of their empire were fixed. There is an astonishing diversity of lands and peoples within Ethiopia, with about seventy-five languages in common use.

Although efforts were made both by Haile Selassie and Mengistu Haile Mariam to downplay distinctions between different groups, and to encourage a sense of Ethiopian-ness, Amhara dominance never lost its grip. Amharic was the national language and the medium of instruction in schools. The army, the civil service and the class of feudal landlords were dominated by Amharas. But as the population increased, education spread and weapons infiltrated the country, pressure built up from the peoples who had long felt hard done by, and Mengistu faced challenges to the very existence of Ethiopia from the many restive groups who resented continued Amhara domination. The Oromo in the south, the Tigrayans and Eritreans in the north and the Somalis in the east all raised their banners against him, embarking on a series of bloody wars which led in their turn to famines and the deaths of tens of thousands.

In 1991, after a long and bitter struggle, Mengistu Haile Mariam was toppled by a disciplined force of young fighters from Tigray in the north. They swept into Addis Ababa in their tanks, scarcely able to believe that at last the prize was theirs. The challenges they faced were formidable, and one of their solutions was to create a federated country composed of different 'nations' which would offer some autonomy to the regions while they attempted to hold the centre firm. 'Divide and rule,' some people muttered, as they tried to explain this to me.

Only Eritrea broke away completely. The new Ethiopian government recognised the Eritreans' right to hold a referendum.

They voted almost unanimously for independence, and this was achieved in 1993.

I had much to think of as I set out for the airport on the next leg of my journey. In different ways, the storytellers I had met had told me a great deal about how it felt to be an Amhara in modern Ethiopia. Their sense of loss was palpable. Ato Shimeles, who had been bred into the 'effortless superiority' of the old feudal days, had fallen victim to the Derg. The retired teachers, who had flourished under the revolution, had lost out in their turn to the triumphant young northerners. The young men at the Cultural Bureau were the new faces of Ethiopia, whose job it was to promote Amhara culture, which for the first time was no longer thought to be the culture of Ethiopia itself, but only of one group within it.

Ato Alemayehu from the Cultural Bureau kindly drove me to the airport. The evening before, at the Ghion Hotel, we had talked for a while about the stories I'd heard, and I'd expressed my gratitude for his and Daniel's efforts.

'There's one story,' I had told him, 'which I can't get out of my mind. It's about a zombie woman.'

He had nodded.

'This superstition is a big thing around here. It's very common to believe it.'

He went on to tell me that when he was a child, all the Beta Israel people were said to have the evil eye. Sometimes he would go with his mother to the market and she would pull him to her side and cover his face with her shamma if she saw a person from that community in the distance.

'Even they themselves learned to take care. When they came to a person's house they would shout from far away, 'Hide your children! I am Falasha! I am coming!' They did so because if their glance had fallen on a child, and the child had died, they would be accused. It was a very terrible thing, and I feel bad about it now.'

I told him that I didn't know what to do with this story. Was it suitable for a school reader? Would the subject be too sensitive?

As we walked around the veranda of the hotel, we had a lucky encounter. Bikala Seyoum, an old boy of the school where I had taught in Addis Ababa so long ago, was sitting with some friends. He had now become the head of the Amhara Education Bureau. We reminisced for a while, then I told him of my dilemma.

'You should put this story in your book,' he said, 'but place it in a context where you can show what harm it has done to people, and how false it is. This will be doing everyone here a service.'

I was thinking of this as I left Alemayehu and walked into the airport. I could hear my missionary Aunt Nancy's voice in my head.

'Using stories to counteract superstition, dear. Quite right too.'

I wasn't sure why the idea made me feel so uneasy.

❖ *3* ❖

FORTY DOGS IN TIGRAY

I had to brace myself for the flight to Mekele, which as usual I dreaded. I had no fear of accidents. The safety record of Ethiopian Airlines is admirable, but I am easily airsick, and the little planes used on internal flights are buffeted about in the violent air currents rising from the mountains and gorges below, resulting in nauseating swoops and dives.

Being prone to airsickness hasn't always been a disadvantage. I was flying from Bombay to Bhopal in 1973 when the plane hit turbulence above the Deccan plateau. I reached for the sick bag, but the man in the seat next to mine got there first. He looked after me. That was how I first met David. We were married a year later, and he has been looking after me ever since.

In spite of queasiness, I was excited to be returning to Tigray, a part of Ethiopia which had gripped my imagination on every previous visit.

Tigray is the northernmost region of Ethiopia. Mankind has been destroying and creating in this place since history began. In ancient times, a great empire (recorded by Josephus, the first-century AD Romano-Jewish historian) was centred on Axum. Its people sculpted towering stelae, precision-carved needles of stone which still make visitors gasp, and built palaces for their kings, who converted to Christianity in the fourth century, thus making Ethiopia the first officially Christian country in the world. But at the same time, the environment on which the wealth of Axum depended has slowly been depleted. With the loss of trees, the erosion of soil and the vagaries of climate change, the once rich farmlands of Tigray have become arid and hard to cultivate, and the Tigrayans, enterprising and resourceful as they are, have had to leave their traditional heartlands in their thousands to settle elsewhere.

The region boasts wonders unique in Africa. Parts of Tigray are as spectacular as Arizona. Ridges of red-coloured rock, weathered into columns of Grand Canyon-like magnificence, rise in tiers from the valley floors. Caves burrow into the sides of these cliffs, some natural, some chiselled out centuries ago by the hand of man to form exquisite churches. You can plunge through a hole in a rock face and find yourself in a basilica, with aisles and columns carved with mathematical precision. Saints, prophets, angels and devils surge out at you from the brilliantly coloured frescoes, some many centuries old.

Wood is a scarce resource in Tigray. Elsewhere in Ethiopia, the classic country dwelling is a round structure with a tall central pole. The roof is thatched, and the walls are made of laths plastered with 'chikka' – a mixture of mud and cow dung. In Tigray, farmsteads are built of squared-off blocks of honey-coloured stone. They dot the landscape in their walled compounds, and if their roofs were not flat but pitched, they would remind you of cottages in the Cotswolds.

Mekele is the regional capital of Tigray. The small town – hot, and plagued with gritty winds – is dominated by two impressive grey stone castles. One was built as a palace by the nineteenth-century Emperor Yohannes. The other, erected by a competitive nobleman, has for a long time been a hotel, called the Castle Abraha.

I had stayed at the Castle Abraha in the 1960s. The great man of Tigray at that time was Ras Mengesha, an energetic, idealistic and public-spirited aristocrat, who was married to Princess Aida, one of Haile Selassie's British-educated granddaughters. Ras Mengesha had invited a small but dauntless New Zealander, Ivy Pearce, to lead a team from the University of Addis Ababa to explore and survey the rock churches of Tigray and I had been lucky enough to tag along.

The ras had provided his own richly embroidered Egyptian tents, Land Rovers, trucks, drivers, cooks, servants and even a waiter. Camp was pitched each night in a different place, and the country people would approach with gifts of eggs, chickens and mead. Every day we walked, climbed, photographed and sketched, knowing that we were under the special protection of a man who, enlightened though he was, had the power of a great medieval prince.

Since that time (which many Ethiopians sentimentalise, without wishing to return to the evils of the feudal system), the Four Horsemen of the Apocalypse have ravaged the country. Pestilence, war, famine and death have left scarcely a family untouched by tragedy. During the 1980s, in a drastic attempt to crush the rebellious Tigrayan nationalists (while ostensibly easing the endemic problems of overpopulation and environmental degradation), Mengistu Haile Mariam forcibly resettled over 800,000 Tigrayans in the relatively empty and more fertile lands of the south-west. People were rounded up in market places, packed into trucks and driven away. Families were separated. There was little or no provision for them in the resettlement sites, where hunger and malaria took their toll. Tens of thousands of people died.

The Tigrayan rebels took to the mountains and caves, and waged a guerrilla war of breathtaking ingenuity. Men and women fought as equals alongside each other. Pharmacists produced antibiotics in cave laboratories. Meanwhile, the tectonic plates of world politics had shifted. The once solid walls of communism were crumbling. Out-manoeuvred, increasingly brutal and out of touch with the suffering of his people, Mengistu fell at last in 1991.

Tigrayans are a small minority within the population of Ethiopia. The Oromos, an ancient people with a rich culture of their own, have for centuries been vying with the Amharas for control over the highlands of Ethiopia from their heartlands in the south and west. They are the largest minority group in Ethiopia, followed by the Amharas. But in 1991 the Tigrayans became the rulers of Ethiopia. They found themselves on the bridge of power, steering the ship of state with a small team of trusted comrades while the lower decks seethed with resentful passengers, many of whom were inclined to plot mutiny in the name of their own national struggles.

The Tigrayans, with some self-indulgence, have spent money on their old capital of Mekele. A bombastic war memorial has been erected. Larger-than-life figures representing the lean fighters of the Tigrayan People's Liberation Front march upwards on a sloping stone plinth, their guns in their hands. On a second plinth, emaciated victims of the famines struggle forward, women and children falling and dying.

On my first return visit to Mekele, I was with an Amhara friend. He could scarcely control his irritation as we walked around town. He would kick out at the finely cut kerbstones and pavements which lined the city streets, the smartest I had seen in Ethiopia.

'How much do you think all this has cost?' he would growl, afraid of being overheard. 'And they just let Addis rot. Look at that pharmacy! All those medicines! You can't get any of this stuff in Addis.'

❖

This time, I arrived in Mekele by air. The runway was no more than a dirt strip across open ground, and the airport building was a single room with a bar attached. There was no one to meet me and no visible transport to town, but in the typical Ethiopian way my predicament was noticed and I was given the choice of two lifts. I was dropped off at the smart stone office of the Regional Cultural Bureau in which a pretty secretary, with nothing in her in-tray, was playing solitaire on her computer – an up-to-date model rare in most parts of Ethiopia.

It took a while to establish who I was and what I was doing. Messages from Addis Ababa have a way of being lost in the ether in Ethiopia, and in spite of reassurances from the British Council staff in Addis that hotels had been booked and the local cultural bureaux had signed up to the project, I often had to start from scratch to explain what I was doing.

The young government official tapped his pen on his desk as I spoke and seemed puzzled about what to do with me. Then I saw, behind his desk, a poster of one of the rock churches I had visited so long ago.

'I was part of the expedition that Ras Mengesha set up with the university in 1968,' I remarked, 'led by Ivy Pearce.'

He dropped his pen and leaned forward.

'You were on Pearce's Pilgrimage? But that is famous. I have documents about it here. You know, I am the wrong person to help you. I think it is Ato Mesele you need.'

He made a phone call and turned back, beaming.

'They were expecting you yesterday! They came to the airport but you did not arrive.'

'Well, I'm here now.'

A large, four-wheel drive car was summoned and I was driven through the dust-blown streets of Mekele to the district cultural office beside Ras Mengesha's old palace at the bottom of the hill. This was no long, prefabricated shed smelling of Gestetner skins, but a two-storey building which looked as if it dated from the Fascist era of Italian occupation in the 1930s. A gateway led into a walled compound, in the centre of which a magenta bougainvillea almost hurt the eyes with the intensity of its colour, while behind it a jacaranda tree rose in a cloud of blue flowers. The turquoise window shutters on the upper floor of the building were flung open.

Ato Mesele, head of the Tigray Education Bureau, was waiting for me in his upstairs office.

'You were not here yesterday, Mrs Elizabeth! We came to meet you!'

The misunderstanding was ironed out. The project was explained.

'You will work with my assistant.' Ato Mesele indicated the woman at another desk in the room. 'She is an expert in stories. She has been collecting them from schoolchildren. I can assure you that she will assist you.'

The woman didn't seem so certain. Small and thin, she stared at me with eyes that were disconcertingly close together. Her hennaed hair was tied back in an untidy bunch. She stood up, and I saw the words 'I love Jesus and Jesus loves you' emblazoned in large red letters on her yellow T-shirt. It read like a threat.

It was only four o'clock, ten o'clock in Ethiopian terms.[9]

'You have time,' Ato Mesele said encouragingly. 'Why not start the good work at once?'

The woman was tense and I couldn't understand her hostility. With reluctance, she pulled a sheaf of pages from a drawer and began to look through them. I could see that they were all written in different hands in Amharic script. These were the stories supplied by the schoolchildren.

She chose one at last, and translated it with difficulty. It was a classic fable, which I had encountered already in the ancient Sanskrit collection of Kalilah wa Dimnah, which was translated into Arabic in the eighth century and became popular throughout the Middle East from that time. I would have liked to ask the child who submitted this story where he or she had heard it. Whatever its source, this celebration of a tyrant's downfall must have a real punch for Ethiopians, who have had centuries of experience of one kind of tyranny or another.

The story's main character is a bird whose chicks are trampled to death in their nest by a careless elephant. She calls her relatives, and together they peck out the unrepentant elephant's eyes. Not content with this revenge, she persuades a group of frogs to sing at the edge of a cliff. The now blinded elephant, wanting to bathe his sore eyes, stumbles towards the sound of the frogs, thinking he will find water, and falls over the edge of the cliff to his death. The weak have finally triumphed over the strong.

I felt that the translator relished the downfall of the elephant in a rather pointed way. She paused to unscrew the cap from a

---

[9] The Ethiopian clock works on the ancient biblical system, with the hours counted from the break of day until nightfall. Thus, the first hour of the day is six in the morning and the first hour of the night is six in the evening. You have to add six hours to the time on your watch to know where you are.

bottle of water, shutting her eyes and muttering a grace before she took a sip, then began to leaf through her papers again.

'This one is not interesting. You will not like that one either.'

We had been working for only half an hour when she said that she was too tired to carry on, and needed to go home.

'Try one more story,' Ato Mesele coaxed her, with what I thought was remarkable restraint.

She stumbled through a muddled summary of a second story, looking sharply at me at the end, and saying, 'No, you should have written down at the beginning how the monkey finds the stick. And there is something else about the lion.'

I had given up trying to make sense of it and had stopped writing. I leaned back in my chair. Ato Mesele had left the room. The woman slapped down her papers and said, 'I want to know. What is the basis of agreement for your work?'

I explained my project again. She found my explanation inadequate.

'What are they paying you for these stories?'

'What do you mean? I . . .'

'Before we continue, I must have it in writing. The agreement.'

I was beginning to understand. The bundle of stories represented a large body of work, both of her own in collecting them and of the children, who had written them down. She could see them being snatched away from her, the credit going to elephantine foreigners, who could barge in and take what they wanted, and who would probably profit financially from the whole scam.

I assured her that when the readers were published, she would be credited as the translator and her work as the collector would be acknowledged. The whole point of the project was to make the stories useful to schools. She was unconvinced.

'I feel you are worried in case I'm taking your work from you,' I said at last, seeing that I was making no headway.

'No. I am not worried. I love the Lord Jesus so I can let you take what you like.'

I didn't know what to say. She put her hand on my arm.

'Have you accepted the Lord Jesus Christ as your own personal saviour? Are you born again?'

She could have had no idea how often that question had been hurled at me in my childhood and adolescence, how it had filled me with guilt and a knowledge of my own inadequacy, how often I had tried to be 'born again', and how at last I had been able to free myself from the manipulations of enthusiastic evangelicals to find refuge in a gentler, more tolerant and inclusive Christianity. It was partly the need to escape the suffocation of the evangelical world in which I had grown up that had caused me to take a job in Ethiopia as soon as I had qualified as a teacher, so long ago.

I tried to shake her off.

'Are you my sister in Christ?' she insisted, her face inches from mine.

'Yes of course,' I said cravenly, then dodged past her and beetled off out of the room on the pretext of finding a toilet.

'Come again in the morning,' Ato Mesele said, meeting me on the stairs. 'We will make good progress tomorrow.'

I had hoped to stay in the old Castle Abraha Hotel, remembering with affectionate anticipation the high-ceilinged, airy bedrooms, the old-fashioned easy chairs round which waiters had hovered with trays of gin, and the charming Indian managers who had welcomed their guest as graciously as hosts at a weekend house party. The hotel was full. No, they had no record of a booking. I had been 'bumped'.

I settled discontentedly into a noisy room over a restaurant in a small hotel down town. The communal toilet leaked. The only window opened onto a stairwell. The restaurant belted out tinny music. I was out of love already with my project and afraid that I would quickly finish the book I had brought with me and have nothing to read. I decided to go for a walk.

It was pleasant to stroll through Mekele. The town had been set out by Ras Mengesha on a grid pattern, and it was impossible to get lost. No children shouted 'You! You! Money! Mister! Pen! One dollar!' at me, as they do so persistently elsewhere in Ethiopia. Not one young man sidled up to me in the hope that I could supply him with a scholarship to a British university or a visa for the USA. I returned to my hotel in a better frame of mind.

The next morning, my irritation with Ato Mesele's assistant had had time to cool, and I was able to think about her reaction as I walked down to the office. She had a fair point. In every sphere of life, European entrepreneurs have been busy ferreting out the knowledge and skills of people in traditional societies and patenting them, often excluding their original owners in the process. Pharmaceutical companies have been plundering the expertise of herbal healers and making profits with their discoveries, with never a cent returning to the communities from which the knowledge came.[10]

A seed of anxiety had been planted in my mind. I had every intention of producing a children's book for the UK market if I managed to collect enough suitable stories. Was I a story pirate? Could there be such a thing? Or was I at least a profiteer from

---

[10] In 1997, the American company RiceTec controversially patented basmati rice, the glory of India's centuries-long expertise in the development of rice strains. (RiceTec only lost their right to call their own product 'basmati rice' after an outraged Indian government persuaded the United States Patent Office to review their decision.)

the work of other people, such as Ato Mesele's assistant? I didn't think so, but other people might. Later, eyebrows would be raised when I inserted a copyright notice in my little reader books. I learned that it was important to clarify that © mark, and I added a paragraph pointing out that the stories were the copyright of the Ethiopian people and could be retold in anyone's words, but my exact words could not be copied without my permission, or claimed to be the work of anyone else. However, the question of copyright would come up again from time to time and cause anxiety and suspicion.

The next day was spent in Ato Mesele's office with the door locked 'to prevent from interruptions'. He had, to my relief, decided to take over the work of translation himself, and as his English was good, and his pleasure in the stories unabashed, the work went with a swing. He sat behind his desk, chuckling over his assistant's thick file of stories, while I perched, scribbling, on a plastic chair, and his assistant glowered at us from her desk in the corner of the room.

The advantage of this method of story gathering was that it was possible to hear many stories from different sources in one session, but that was the only one. The students, writing down the tales they had gleaned from their parents or grandparents, had had to turn them into written prose, leaving out the storytellers' flourishes. There were no colourful voice changes for the different characters, no dramatic pauses, no sing-song rhymes. I realised how fragile oral storytelling is, and how easily it can be crushed by the very act of preserving it.

Mesele (a charming man, with sweeping eyelashes and distinguished touches of grey in the hair above his ears) was enjoying himself, finding storytelling more fun than his daily round of administrative tasks.

The first he chose to translate featured a crane, a fox and a vulture. The fox persuades the crane to throw her chicks down to him one by one, threatening to cut down the tree in which she has built her nest if she refuses. A passing vulture, hearing her cries of grief, tells her that the fox is fooling her. He can't cut down her tree because he has no axe. When the fox returns to demand the last chick, the crane calls his bluff. The fox realises that the clever vulture has put her up to this, and vows to be revenged. He finds the placenta from a new-born calf, drapes it over his head, and waits. The vulture swoops down to eat it and the fox catches her. She pretends to shake with fright.

'Please, Fox,' she croaks. 'You can beat me and bite me and cut off my tail but don't throw me into the grain store!'

Of course, the fox does just that, and the vulture happily feasts on the grain. The fox sees that he has been tricked and catches the vulture again.

'I beg of you, Fox!' she screeches. 'Kill me and cook me and cut off my head, but don't throw me over the cliff!'

The fox is fooled again, throws the vulture over the cliff and she flies away, laughing at him.

This story evoked such a sharp memory of my mother that I could almost smell the hot ironed rayon of her blouse and feel the sharpness of her elbow as I tried to nestle into her side. And I could see the black and red pictures on the page of the open book from which she was (rather impatiently) reading the story of Brer Fox and the Tar Baby retold by 'Uncle Remus'. For those unfamiliar with this tale, Brer Fox makes a Tar Baby. Brer Rabbit attacks it and gets stuck in the tar. Brer Fox catches Brer Rabbit who escapes by pleading not to be thrown into the briar patch.

Through how many mouths did the stories which gave birth to Brer Rabbit pass in their journey from Africa to the plantations of Louisiana where they were apparently first written down? Underneath the faint aroma of my mother's fawn-coloured blouse, there were other, darker smells, the stench of the slave ships and the hot dry earth of the cotton fields.

I had no time to convey all this to Ato Mesele, who was already frowning over the next story.

'This student writes that the story happened to someone in his village,' he said. 'Perhaps it is true, perhaps not.'

'It sounds like an urban myth,' I told him. 'The sort of story that everyone claims happened to someone they know. Let's hear it, anyway.'

The heroine of this strange tale is called Almaz. She takes her father's cattle to water them at the spring, but the water has been muddied and they refuse to drink. Her father comes to see what the problem is. The demon of the spring leaps out and demands Almaz in exchange for clean water. The man agrees, and pretending that he has lost a shoe, sends Almaz back to the spring to find it. The demon leaps out at her and says,

> *Beautiful girl with long fine hair,*
> *Beautiful girl with swelling breasts,*
> *I will take you, take you, take you!*

The terrified girl runs home only to find to find that her mother has barred the door against her. She runs to her aunt's house.

'The demon of the spring has tried to catch me! He says,

> *Beautiful girl with long fine hair,*
> *Beautiful girl with swelling breasts,*
> *I will take you, take you, take you!*

Her aunt refuses to take her in, so Almaz runs to her friend. She gives Almaz a flower and sends her on to her grandmother.

'Pick the petals of this flower as you go,' she says. 'Eat one and throw one away, eat one and throw one away, until they've all gone. The demon will try to pick them up and he'll be too distracted to catch you.'

Almaz stays with her grandmother and becomes the owner of dogs. She breeds them until she has a pack of forty. Her parents at last come and visit her. Almaz calls out:

> *My father gave me to a demon.*
> *My mother barred the door.*
> *Bark, my forty dogs!*

The dogs rush out and eat her parents. The same fate befalls her aunt, but when her friend comes, Almaz runs out to greet her.

> *My friend has come, my friend!*
> *The saviour of my life!*
> *Don't bark, my forty dogs.*

'Go on,' I said, gripped by this tale.

'That's all there is,' said Ato Mesele, except for a little rhyme.'

'What rhyme?'

'It's just the small saying that comes at the end of the story.'

'Can you translate it?'

He tried, and when we'd worked it out, we agreed that it meant something like this,

> *If this story you do forget, may*
> *death also you forget.*

There was so much in this saga (the unlikeliest urban myth that I'd ever come across) that I hardly knew where to begin. Several themes in it would turn out to be perennials. It was, however, the only time that I came across the plucking of flower petals, so similar to our childhood trick with daisies: 'He loves me, he loves me not.'

The demon of the spring, or river, (in one case a talking snake) would rise, dripping, to meet me in many parts of Ethiopia. He was usually intent on catching girls. In some of the more remote parts of the country storytellers would assume that I shared their belief that it was dangerous for women to visit rivers or springs in the middle of the day, when no sensible girl would dream of approaching water.

The collection of water is one of the main tasks of women and girls in Ethiopia. The water is carried in heavy pots strapped to women's backs, and little girls are initiated early, graduating to larger and larger pots as their strength increases. This back-breaking chore sometimes involves a walk of several hours, twice a day, and is always accomplished first thing in the morning and late in the afternoon. There is perhaps an assumption that visits to a water source at other times of the day might involve romantic assignations. Were stories of water demons instilled into young girls to keep them away from trouble? It was at the well, after all, that the Patriarch Jacob met and fell in love with Rachel as she watered her father's camels.

Perhaps the Ethiopian water demon is the cousin of the Scottish water kelpie which made even the dauntless Alan Breck shiver with fright in R.L. Stevenson's *Kidnapped*, or indeed of the troll who pesters the Billy Goats Gruff as they try to cross his bridge. The naiads of Greek myth are friendlier creatures on the whole. On the spectrum of river spirits around the world, from full-blown gods to pretty nymphs, the Ethiopian water demons inhabit the nastier end. They remind me of crocodiles.

Dogs in Ethiopian stories are more commonly associated with men than with women, and especially with hunters. Every farmstead in the Ethiopian countryside has its own dogs. They are yellow-coloured, sturdy little animals, which bark enthusiastically to warn off strangers and will rush to the attack. In a country where there is little surplus human food, dogs have to scavenge to survive, and a large part of their diet is the excrement of their owners. People are fond of their dogs and children often have a favourite puppy.

But it is Almaz herself who carries this story so thrillingly. Strong and independent, she defies the world with her forty dogs. There is no saccharine ending here. The cruel parents and timorous aunt are gobbled up in a fitting act of revenge. I wished most particularly with this story that I had met the student who recorded it. I imagined a young girl anxious about the forthcoming separation from her family at the time of her marriage, and fearful of sex with an unknown man. I was intrigued, too, by the bonds of female friendship which this story celebrates. Almaz's family may let her down but there is a sisterly friend who will rescue her.

There was no time for musing on the fate of Almaz and her family, however. Ato Mesele was already starting the next story, in which the main character was also a woman – a decorous, intelligent wife stamped from a conventional mould, whose weapons were more subtle than Almaz's, but no less effective.

The opening of the story was similar to the one I'd heard in Bahir Dar, about a wife pursued by a vile seducer who wants to take her from her husband. But in this case, it is the wife who takes the initiative.

Once there was an ignorant man who had a clever wife. Although they were different, the couple were happy, but they had a rich neighbour who desired the ignorant man's wife.

'You don't deserve this woman,' he said to the ignorant man. 'Divorce her, and give her to me.'

The ignorant man refused, but the rich man forced him to refer the matter to a judge.

'Why do you say this man is ignorant?' the judge asked the rich man.

'Ask him what you like,' the rich man replied. 'He won't be able to answer.'

The judge, who was afraid of the rich man, turned to the ignorant man.

'I'll ask you two questions. The first is this: how many stars are there in the sky? And the second is this: where is the navel of the earth?'

I can't answer, the ignorant man thought in despair. I've lost my wife.

'Take your time,' the judge said. 'Come back tomorrow and give me your answers then.'

The ignorant man hurried home. That night, he stared at the sky, but he couldn't count the stars.

'What are you doing?' asked his wife.

'I must tell the judge how many stars there are in the sky. And show him the navel of the earth.'

'Don't worry. I'll tell you how to answer,' said his wife.

The next day, she gave her husband a sack of wheat and a stick, and the two neighbours returned to the judge.

The ignorant man tipped out his sack of wheat onto the ground.

'There are as many stars in the sky as the grains of wheat

in this sack,' he said, 'and if you don't believe me, count them yourself.'

'And where,' asked the judge, 'is the navel of the earth?'

The ignorant man plunged his stick into the ground.

'Here,' he said. 'And if you don't believe me, dig until you find it.'

'You're no fool,' said the judge. 'You deserve your clever wife.'

'My wife is the clever one,' the ignorant man said proudly. 'It was she who gave me the answers.'

The judge and the rich man laughed.

'You see?' said the rich man. 'She's much too good for you.'

'I agree,' the judge said. 'Go home, you stupid man, and get ready to divorce your wife. And you, sir, prepare for your wedding.'

The ignorant man went home in great distress.

'My dear wife,' he said. 'I've lost you, and my life is ruined.'

'Did you answer as I told you to?' asked his wife.

'Yes, but they still want to take you from me.'

'Don't despair,' said his wife. 'Invite the judge and our neighbour for dinner. Then we'll see.'

When the guests arrived the next day, and the clever woman brought out the food she had cooked, the judge looked with disgust at the burnt injera she offered him and the rich neighbour looked in consternation at the feathers still sticking from the chicken in the stew.

'Keep your wife,' the judge said indignantly to the poor man, 'She's not worth having at all.'

As soon as the judge and the rich man had gone, the woman threw the burnt bread and the feathery stew away and served her husband the delicious meal she had prepared for him. And the man and his wife lived together happily for the rest of their lives.

I was to be told many stories celebrating the subtlety and cleverness of women. I began to wonder if they were tactfully offered to me because of my sex, or if the Derg's praiseworthy efforts to improve the status of women had made them politically correct. In the end, I decided that the reason was simpler. Such stories are popular everywhere. They belong to a lively sub-genre, which has many exemplars throughout the Middle East.

The clever woman, after all, has a distinguished pedigree in the mythical history of Ethiopia. The founder of the dynasty which ruled Ethiopia for two thousand years until the downfall of Haile Selassie was believed to be the son born of the union of King Solomon and the Queen of Sheba (presumed by Ethiopians to be the queen of Ethiopia).

This beautiful tale, familiar from the Bible, is much more interesting in the Ethiopian version. It is to be found in the Kebra Negast, or Book of Kings, which dates back at least seven hundred years and is one of the supreme treasures of Ethiopia's written heritage.

The Queen of Sheba's trading caravans were sent to supply materials for the building of Solomon's temple in Jerusalem. On their return, they so impressed the queen with their tales of Solomon's riches and wisdom that she decided to visit him herself. She marvelled at his wisdom and justice, and vowed to abandon her old religion and worship the God of Israel. Solomon was astonished by her beauty and intelligence, and wanted to produce a son with her. He invited her to a banquet, but over-spiced the dishes and provided nothing to drink. When the guests had all departed, he asked her to sleep in his tent. She agreed, on condition that he would not molest her. He promised that he would not, if she promised in return not to take anything from him without permission. They lay down on separate couches to sleep, but Sheba, crazed with thirst, crept from her bed and drank some water temptingly left nearby. Solomon, who had been waiting for this moment, leaped up and had his way with her.

Solomon gave her a ring as a parting gift, and Sheba returned to Ethiopia. Nine months later, she bore a son and called him Menelik. As the boy grew up, he wanted to know his father, and Sheba sent him off to Jerusalem with the ring as proof of his identity. When the time came for Menelik to return home, Solomon gave him an escort of the noble sons of Israel. Unable to bear separation from the holy Ark of the Covenant, they abducted it and secretly took it back to Ethiopia with them, installing it in the queen's capital in Axum, where it is said to exist to this day, kept away from all prying eyes in the church of St Mary.

The Queen of Sheba, writes Marina Warner, in her study of fairy tales *From the Beast to the Blonde*, 'mixes the fairy godmother and the fool, the enchantress and the houri, the wise woman and the witch, the Sybil and the granny.' That's a good starting point for considering the roles that women play in tales told in Ethiopia, and many kinds of truths are hidden in these prototypes. But the Sheba myth reflects a different kind of truth. The culture of the Amharas and Tigrayans of highland Ethiopia is a mingling of ancient Judeo-Christian influences from the north and east, and other even older traditions from the south and west, a state of affairs perfectly illustrated in the marriage of a Jewish king with an African queen.

Many more stories tumbled out of those closely written pages into my notebook that morning, through the medium of Ato Mesele's careful translations, but my plastic chair was hard and sweaty, and after a while I began to feel overwhelmed, as one does in an art gallery after looking at too many pictures.

'How can you understand all these things if you don't see them with your own eyes?' Ato Mesele said at last, and to my relief he proposed a walk in the countryside for the next day.

He came early to collect me and we drove out to a village called Ayn Alem (The Eye of the World). It was delightful to walk down a country lane, dodging big thistle plants, my sandalled feet stumbling on ploughed clods of earth. Mesele treated the place like a living museum, which embarrassed me at first, until I saw that the people he accosted didn't seem to mind.

He hailed the first woman we met and asked her to show me the loosely woven cloth with colourful ends that all the women wear round their waists.

'What do you call this in English?'

'It's a sash.'

'But in Tigrinya we have the same word! "Shash" means a cloth for your neck.'

'A scarf,' I said.

He was delighted.

'You see? You have taken the word from us.'[11]

The first house we came to was built of the usual cream stone, the blocks so cleanly cut that they fitted together with no need of mortar. A hedge of prickly pear ran round its compound, and a man was sitting in the roofed gateway. Ato Mesele asked if we could see round his house. He looked surprised, but politely waved us in.

Three elderly women, one wearing the cap of an Ethiopian Orthodox nun, were squatting over a tray of split peas, picking out the small stones. They looked up, but didn't seem startled

---

[11] Sash derives from the Arabic *shash* meaning the strip of cloth used to tie a turban.

by our intrusion. A couple of small children played in the dust nearby. Mesele made himself at home, showing me the raised manger at one end of the compound where the cattle are kept at night, the hollowed-out tree stump used as a mortar, the man's axe and the women's water pots. Boldly, he led me inside the house. The bed was a raised mud platform covered with a cow-skin and a blanket, and a few enamel dishes and baskets hung from the wall. Beyond the main room was a store, with sacks of tef and wheat, some jars and bundles of dry leaves. The cooking space was in another hut at the back. In it was the injera oven, a smooth round pottery tray embedded in a clay stand with room for a fire underneath. A pottery lid stood by to cover it during the cooking. Pots for wot (a spicy meat stew) stood by a separate fire.

Alongside the collection of water, foraging for fuel is another arduous task for Ethiopian women, and the resulting destruction of trees is one cause of the deforestation which has led to catastrophic soil erosion. Where trees are so scarce, as they are in Tigray, cow dung is the more common fuel (which sadly diminishes its use as a fertiliser), and the slightly acrid smell of its burning hangs over the farmsteads.

There were few spare belongings in this sparsely furnished home, and no clutter of ornaments or gadgets, but it had a comfortable feel of sufficiency and orderliness, with its well-swept floor and cheerful children.

'You saw that lady who is a nun?' Ato Mesele said as we walked back out into the lane. 'Many ladies who are old become nuns.'

'What about men?' I asked. 'They start the religious life as boys, don't they? Or do some older men become monks?'

His explanation was long and detailed, but I was once again baffled by the complexity of roles within the Ethiopian Orthodox

Church. The first rung of the ladder is the deacon, and boys start their training young, learning at ecclesiastical schools to read Ge'ez, a liturgical language which is no longer spoken and is understood only by clerics. Some deacons decide that the Church is not for them and move into other spheres of life, some go on to become priests, while others become monks.

The highlands of Ethiopia are dotted with monasteries. The most famous of these, Debre Damo, is on a spectacular flat mountain top with cliff sides so sheer that it can only be reached by climbing ropes. Women are not allowed to visit it, a fact I have always regretted.

We turned into a tala house.[12] This was a single-roomed dwelling with an earth floor finished off with a layer of smoothed cow dung which looked and felt as pleasant as cork. Two men were already sitting on stools near the door, which was the only source of light. Ato Mesele and I perched on an iron bedstead, and a woman brought us tala in pottery beakers. I sipped mine gingerly, afraid of bugs, but the drink tasted strong, sour, fruity and reassuringly alcoholic, so I thought, what the hell, and knocked it back.

This was a much better setting for stories than the upstairs office in the government building, and the atmosphere worked on both of us. We began to go over the stories Mesele had translated the day before, and he explained some things which had puzzled me. I have wished so often since then that I had asked more questions. There must be riches of hidden knowledge in these stories which I have not been able to mine.

'That was a good one, about the monks' blessing,' I said. We sat and mulled it over.

---

[12] Tala is a mildly alcoholic drink, a kind of beer.

A poor young man left his wife and child with his parents and set off to seek his fortune. After a long search, he found work in a monastery. He settled down happily. Years passed, and gradually he forgot his wife and child.

One day some young boys ran past the monastery, laughing.

'My son must be the same age as these boys,' the young man thought, and suddenly he longed for home. He went to the monks and asked them to pay his wages and let him go. The monks told him that he could either have his money, or their blessing. He chose their blessing.

As the first monk blessed him he said, 'Don't turn off the road. Always go straight on.'

The second monk said, 'When you are a guest, take whatever is offered to you.'

The third said, 'Control your anger and think before you act.'

They gave him a hundred silver dollars as a bonus, and the young man went on his way.

Soon he fell in with two other men. They urged him to leave the path and take a shortcut, but he remembered the first monk's blessings and refused. As he hurried on, he heard shouts, and looking back, he saw that the other two men were being attacked by bandits.

'The first blessing has saved my life,' the young man thought.

He came to a house as night fell. An old man welcomed him and offered to wash his feet. Ashamed to accept such an honour, the young man nearly objected, but he remembered the second monk's blessing, and let the old man wash his feet. A blind girl brought him food. He ate and lay down to sleep. But when the sun rose, he saw that the kindly old man of the night before had become an ogre with long sharp teeth.

'You are the only traveller who has accepted my hospitality, and so I did not kill you,' the ogre told him. 'Others have refused and are buried here, beneath your feet. I spared only this girl so that she could serve me. Take this sack full of silver dollars as your reward.'

'The second blessing has made me rich,' the young man thought.

He hurried away, and at last came to the church near his home. A crowd stood outside it, watching an old man and a young boy struggling together. Furious that a child would attack a greybeard, the young man ran forward to strike him down, but then he remembered the third monk's blessing and refrained.

'This old man is the boy's grandfather,' someone told him. 'Years ago, his son left home. Poverty and hunger have made him desperate and his grandson is trying to stop him from taking his own life.'

'The third blessing has stopped me killing my own son,' the young man thought, recognising in that instant his father and his son. He opened the ogre's sack and showed them the money, and amid general rejoicings let it be known that they would never suffer want again.

The heart of this story, with its classic fairy-tale structure, turns like so many others of its kind on the magical acquisition of riches, a compelling fantasy in the lives of countless millions struggling with hunger and poverty. But it is purely Ethiopian in its settings and details.

The monks in their small community are revered for their goodness, but there is a whiff of magic about them too. Since early times religion and magic have been in opposition in Europe, hostile to and suspicious of each other. In Ethiopia, the distinction is not so clear. Certain clerics are thought to have the ability to write spells against sickness or the evil eye. Some can give prophetic warnings to avert disastrous journeys or courses of action, as the monks do in this story.

I enjoyed the episode where the old man washes the young man's feet. Once, when I had been hot and tired at the end of a long day of running about the walled city of Harar in the sun, I was returning with relief to the shade of my room on the upper storey of an old inn. As I walked along the colonnaded veranda, a woman caught my arm. She led me to a stool, fetched a bowl of water, then knelt in front of me and began to wash my feet, massaging my soles and kneading my calves with strong, probing thumbs. We had no language in common and I sat in silence, profoundly touched, images from the Bible flashing through my mind. When she had finished she smiled and went away, and I felt more refreshed and renewed than after the sweetest sleep.

The silver dollars struck chords of memory too. The preferred unit of currency in Ethiopia until after the Second World War was the Maria Theresa thaler (dollar), always stamped with the date 1780.[13] People were so attached to these heavy silver coins that they adapted to the paper money minted by the Bank of Ethiopia with extreme reluctance. Although Maria Theresa dollars ceased to be legal currency in 1945, I would come across them from time to time in rural Ethiopia in the 1960s and I wish now that I'd collected a few. The Empress of Austria's heavy-jowled profile could hardly have been called beautiful, but it was reassuringly grand, and like those suspicious old farmers I preferred her dollars to the greasy, flimsy paper ones, which

[13] The Maria Theresa dollar was a heavy silver coin with a long and exotic history, which was produced in various European mints throughout the eighteenth and nineteenth centuries, and which fuelled trade in the Middle East, the Horn of Africa and the Arabian peninsula. It was the main currency of Ethiopia (along with bars of salt) until a new Ethiopian coinage was created in 1903.

stink of wood smoke and spicy stew.

Before we left the tala house, the proprietress showed us how she made her tala. She would tear up blackened bread, put it in water with fermented sorghum or barley and gesho[14] leaves and let it rest for some time to brew. I would have liked to hear her story. Her trade is not one for respectable women.

We left the tala house and walked on into the village. It wasn't a large place, and we soon reached its extremity where the drystone walls of the compounds met the fields beyond. A little girl, who looked no more than six years old, rushed out of a gateway, flapping her hands at us in distress, baring her teeth and giving high-pitched inarticulate cries. She seemed angry and afraid.

'She is a deaf,' Mesele said. He smiled at the little girl, who became more and more agitated, finally running across to where a baby was sitting at the edge of a field experimentally putting things into his mouth.

'Her mother is perhaps at the market, and she has been left to guard her brother while her mother is not present,' Mesele said.

We made reassuring gestures and backed away, but he seemed uncomfortable. I had been told several stories by now whose purpose was to raise a laugh at the antics of 'simpletons', or of deaf people, in which misunderstandings lead to farcical outcomes. It's only relatively recently that mocking the disabled in body or mind has become distasteful in our society. My father used to love telling a joke about two deaf men on a bus. Their conversation goes: 'Is this Wembley?' 'No, it's Thursday.' 'So am I. Let's go and have a drink.' While I agree that it's cruel to laugh at people with hearing difficulties, I wouldn't wish to be

---

[14] Gesho: *Rhamnus Prinioides*, or shiny-leaf buckthorn.

too solemn. I live with this problem. David's ears were blasted by big guns when he was a subaltern in the Royal Artillery (during an aberrant spell of martial ardour in his youth) and he is becoming increasingly deaf. The only way of dealing with it is to laugh at the comical misunderstandings that punctuate our days.

The houses were poorer at this far edge of the village. A gate made of a rusting piece of corrugated iron tacked to a rickety wooden structure creaked open as we passed it and an old man emerged, wearing a jacket which had been mended and patched so often that hardly any of the original blue cloth showed. He greeted Mesele in a friendly way and a minute later we were in his house. As before, Mesele made himself at home.

A loom was set up in a corner of the compound under a simple cane and leaf shelter. The old man climbed into it to demonstrate its working. The warp threads were hitched round pegs driven into the ground and the loom itself was so low to the ground that the weaver had dug a pit for his feet. He used his bare toes to lift the threads up and down as he threw the shuttle back and forth. The cloth he was making was about a metre wide, the warp threads a natural dun colour, and the weft threads bright white. I have never felt cloth as soft, warm and clinging as the hand-woven shammas of Ethiopia. Their quality ranges from the finest flimsy muslins used in women's scarves, to the heavy 'gabis' that farmers wear in the cold highlands, draped about their shoulders by day, and covering their whole bodies like blankets by night. I wrap myself in my old gabi frequently on cold winter nights in England, and there is nothing so cosy and comforting.

'Tell him that I had an ancestor who was a weaver in Scotland,' I said to Mesele. He did so. Neither of the men seemed impressed.

As we walked away, I wanted to ask Mesele for his opinion as to why weavers are thought to have sinister powers, and are generally despised, and why this skilled man was so poor, his house apart, on the margins of the village. But I couldn't find the words, and I didn't see how he could know the answer.

❖

That evening, Ato Mesele arranged a farewell dinner for me at the Castle Hotel. I arrived early and sat waiting for the others on a sofa in the entrance hall. A large number of middle-aged men came in and out of the dining room. I scrutinised each face as best I could while trying not to look too nosey. At first, when I had returned to Ethiopia, I had found myself automatically looking for my old students among the eighteen- and nineteen-year-old boys, forgetting the thirty years which had passed since I had last seen them. Now, more realistically, I looked for familiar traces in the faces of fifty-year-olds, but it was as ever a fruitless quest. Those ardent young men who had not fallen victim to Mengistu's terror had been scattered over different continents. In any case, they would all look quite different now.

Ato Mesele and one or two others arrived. His assistant came last. She was relaxed and much more friendly, and I was relieved. We parted amicably.

I was back at the hotel by 9 p.m. People don't stay out late in Ethiopia. Many are nervous of going out after dark, and the nightly curfews that have been imposed from time to time in periods of unrest create habits which are not easily broken.

The young man behind the reception the desk looked haggard.

'You are here every time I pass through,' I said. 'When is your time off?'

He looked puzzled.

'When do you have free time?'

He snorted.

'Free time? Never! I am here twenty-four hours, morning until night until morning. Even I sleep here on the floor behind the desk.' He leaned forward on his elbows. 'How many hours, do you think, a human being should sleep in the night?'

'Eight hours at your age. You need less when you're as old as me.'

'Eight hours! Eight!' he laughed ironically. 'You are right. I need it. But six is the maximum time I ever have.'

And he was indeed on duty the next morning, when I left for the airport.

A procession of women was marching past the hotel, waving flags, banging on drums and blowing horns.

'It is International Women's Day,' said my driver. 'Do you have such big celebrations in your country?'

THE HYENA KING OF AFAR

In the days when I roamed about Ethiopia in buses, on foot, on horseback and on the tops of oil tankers, my travelling companion was Mark Rosen, a wiry Norfolk man who was inured to physical hardship, hunger and thirst. He was tolerant with me, allowing me to trot at his heels.

By the time we travelled together, Mark had already walked from Cairo to the Cape. Since then, he has tramped across mountain ranges, deserts and jungles without fanfare, carrying with him the barest minimum, armed against difficulty and danger with nothing more than friendliness. He lived for years in remote parts of New Guinea as a teacher and headmaster, and now spends much of the year as the warden of a mountaineer's outpost in New Zealand's Southern Alps, sometimes seeing no one for weeks at a time.

On the rare occasions when we meet, I beg him to write the story of his life.

'Oh, you know those sorts of books,' he replies. '"Got up at dawn. Had a nasty time in the toilet." They're all the same.'

Having a nasty time in the toilet is an unfortunate fact of life in Ethiopia, and never more so for me than on my next foray, to the Afar region of Ethiopia. It was the beaker of tala in Tigray that I blamed.

The Danakil depression, where the Afar people live, must number among the earth's harshest inhabited places. Those who survive on its meagre resources deserve admiration for their powers of endurance. It's hotter here than anywhere else on the planet. The bare, gritty ground, scarcely relieved by scrubby thorn bushes, glitters with minerals. From a hillside one can look down on fields of white salt so dazzling that they hurt the eyes.

The fortunes of this region, like everywhere else in Ethiopia, have gone up and down according to the merry-go-round of climate change. Three and a half million years ago this must have been a friendlier place, for it was here that our little ancestor Lucy ('Australapithacus Afarensis') wandered about, foraging for her food. A million years earlier, Ardi ('Ardipithecus ramidus'), who could already walk without using her knuckles, still had the long arms that enabled her to swing about in the trees. The fossilised remains of these earliest of our grandparents attract palaeontologists to Afar. They scour the ground, pouncing on glints of light reflected off fragments of tooth or bone.

I visited the little skeleton of Lucy once in the museum where she lies in Addis Ababa, and unexpected tears started to fill my eyes.

'You're our mother,' I thought.

There can have been few individuals in each foraging group of those early hominids, and Afar (which was lush with vegetation then) is still sparsely populated. The Afar people live off their cattle, off smuggling and off the export of salt dug by hand from the surface area of the Danakil Depression. Their religion is Islam; their language is Cushitic. I'd like to think that the word 'Africa' derives from Afar, but no doubt there is another, more prosaic derivation.

The Afar have until recently been semi-nomadic, some living in permanent villages while other family members move about to find pasture for their animals, taking with them wooden struts and mats which are quickly erected into huts. These are small and flimsy, and look like nothing so much as upturned baskets, but they serve their purpose with admirable economy.

The world of modern education is penetrating Afar society very slowly. Few can read and write. People cleave loyally to their clans. Their natural enemies are the Issar, who live in and around Djibouti to the north, and while the Afar show extreme hospitality to those they choose to welcome, they have traditionally been hostile to travellers in their region. The Afar strike terror into the men of the highlands because of the widespread belief that an Afar groom must present to his bride the testicles of another man. Although they make no apologies for their ferocity, and killing for one's family or clan is admired, their reputation for indiscriminate castration annoys the Afar. Whether the custom of offering this grisly bride price was once universal or not, it certainly has ancient roots in the Near East as well as in Africa, as this verse from the Book of Samuel testifies: 'Wherefore David arose and went, he and his men, and slew of the Philistines two hundred men; and David brought their foreskins, and gave them in full tale to the king, that he might be the king's son in law. And Saul gave him Michal his daughter to wife.' (1 Samuel 18:27).[15]

I was violently ill during the night before I was due to travel to Assayita, then the capital of the Afar region,[16] and I was tempted to call the whole thing off, but this time I was not to go alone. The British Council was sending me in its own Land

---

[15] In fairness to the Afar, this practice was once common among other groups in Ethiopia also.

[16] The planned new town of Samara, built on the Awash-Asab highway, became the capital of the Afar Region in 2007.

Rover with one of their staff to accompany me. By 5.30, when the Land Rover rolled up to collect me, I had recovered enough to think that I might manage the journey, and I slung my little suitcase on top of the spare tyre at the back, and climbed up into the front seat.

The British Council driver was a tiny man called Dirije. I told him I felt like death, but he had a boil on the end of his nose and was sucking on antibiotics, so there was little sympathy to be had from him. The young British Council staff member, Michael Ambatchew, was sniffing dolefully. I told him I was as sick as a dog, but he responded that he had spent the weekend in bed with flu, so there was not much comfort from him either.

Addis Ababa had engulfed swathes of the surrounding countryside since I had lived in the city thirty years earlier, but once the swift red blush of dawn had turned to the blue of day we were beyond the sprawl and out on the open road, a slick of tarmac rolling across the land, uncluttered by streetlamps, barriers, speed limit signs or advertising hoardings.

We stopped for breakfast at Adama (once charmingly named Nazareth), where the road divides, one branch running south towards the Bale Mountains, the other striking north-east towards Somalia and the Red Sea. The town of Adama had exploded in size since I had last been there. A stop-over point for lorry drivers, its many prostitutes were falling prey in large numbers to Aids.

'Everyone is now here only for contraband,' said Dirije, whose English was approximate at best. 'Too much money is making everyone. Can buy here very cheap.'

Dirije had porridge for breakfast. An Orthodox Christian, he kept to strict rules of fasting. (There are 180 fasting days a year in the Orthodox calendar, including each Wednesday and Friday, as well as certain festivals and the whole of Lent.) Michael tucked into eggs. I nibbled at dry bread and drank a little tea, having decided to give my insides a rest.

Geology hits you between the eyes in Ethiopia, and especially here, where the turmoil beneath the earth's crust erupts to the surface, demanding to be noticed. The road north-east of Addis Ababa cuts through a region of black laval rock, too recently formed to have acquired a topsoil, although a few trees, their leaves unnaturally green, cling to life in a crack or two. Beyond this moonscape is another composed of tumbled masses of boulders, some as small as melons, others as large as cars. They look alien in this place, as if they belong in a ring of Saturn and should be hurtling round their mother planet in ever re-forming coils. Whirlwinds spiral up here and there, in wispy plumes.

Once past the volcanic spills, there was little cheer to be had on the road to Assayita. The sun beat down on the roof of the Land Rover, turning it into an oven. Only a little dead grass and some dry thorn bushes spoke of life. The few trees which had struggled to maturity had been hacked down, their wood turned to charcoal which lay in sacks for sale at the side of the road. Charcoal is widely used for cooking throughout Ethiopia, especially in the little braziers used to prepare coffee in the traditional coffee ceremony.

It seemed impossible to believe that people could eke out a living here, but occasionally we would see a woman walk out from nowhere into nowhere, or a man lead a camel through a cloud of dust. Once or twice we passed a few huts made of bent sticks covered with woven mats.

The road, so solid under our spinning tyres, was a life-support system, protecting us from the hostile world through which we sped. There were frequent signs of how much more hostile it had recently been. Burnt-out tanks and military trucks, relics of Mengistu's wars, lay tipped over like the corpses of scaly monsters. An oil tanker upside down, or a bus on its side, its windows smashed and its interior a mess of twisted seats, spoke of more recent disasters, while the scorch marks of near misses ran in parallel snakes along the tarmac.

I noticed that the telegraph wires were mostly down, the posts lying on the ground or tilted at angles, while the wires trailed in useless coils.

'Afar ladies is using wires to make his jewellery,' Dirije said with the derision of a superior highlander.

The colour of the land was fading to dun under the hot sun, trance-inducing in its monotony. The spell was broken by a construction scene as we came over the crest of a hill. Big yellow machines were levelling out and remaking the road. Diggers and trucks moved about, while teams of workmen stood around or squatted in whatever shade they could find. We were reduced to a crawl, becoming the moving kernel of a cloud of dust, as we were diverted down a rough track beside the existing road. Michael told me that a new capital of the Afar region was being built. Called Samara, it would soon return Assayita to the backwater it had once been.

Once off the main highway, there were seventy more kilometres of bumpy track before Assayita. Away to our right, a line of trees showed the course of the Awash river. They were a dingy grey rather than a refreshing green, no more than a strip of shadow dividing a mirage shimmering over the surface of the desert from the sand-coloured sky above. The telegraph wires were intact here. I half hypnotised myself by watching them rise and fall as we rode alongside. Vultures perched on the poles, though what they could find to scavenge I couldn't imagine.

Assayita came as a shock. I had allowed myself to daydream, as the wearing day had ground on, of a quiet room, a shower, and a comfortable bed, but it was clear that none of these would be forthcoming. A main street bordered with old-style Ethiopian houses, the grander ones with covered verandas in front, led up to the 'piazza' (the name given to the central square in all Ethiopian towns). Low buildings surrounded this expanse of uneven ground, whose surface had been worn to stone-like hardness by the pressure of human and animal feet. Ours was the only wheeled vehicle in sight, although there were many camels and donkeys resting from their day's work, lipping over piles of dry fodder.

Exhausted, Dirije drove the Land Rover into the courtyard of the only hotel in town which boasted running water and rooms with concrete floors. It was full. Messages sent from Addis Ababa had not been received, and even if they had been, no landlord would have been foolish enough to hold rooms in reserve for travellers who might never appear.

I had eaten and drunk almost nothing all day, and this news was a blow. We went in search of Mohammed Ahmed Algani, our contact at the Regional Educational bureau, to put our problem into his hands.

Mohammed lived in an area of new housing for government officials. This consisted of lines of six or seven small houses in parallel terraces painted a rich ochre. Each house had two small rooms, about ten feet square, and a tiny shower room and toilet. Behind, on the far side of a concrete path, was the little kitchen. These rear quarters were the women's world, where neighbours lived in intimate proximity.

Dirije frowned at this display of luxury.

'All is for post,' he said, conjuring up, in one scornful word, his opinion of those holding government positions. 'Post' was his shorthand for a lazy scrounger with his fingers in the till.

I climbed stiffly out of the Land Rover, stared at by a gaggle of children. Mohammed came out of his house. He was tall with a loose-limbed elegance. His nose had once been broken, his incisors had been capped with gold, his eyes were enormous and his lashes swept his cheeks. I became aware that I looked a fright. My hair was brittle with dust, my face streaked with dirt, my bush shirt and trousers dark with sweat.

Mohammed was courteous but distant, and I sensed that our presence was an inconvenience, that we were interrupting some business or process that was preoccupying everyone, about which we would never learn. I was afraid that our project would seem bizarre here, and that people would be looking for our ulterior motive.

Mohammed called for his little daughter. She didn't come fast enough, and he landed a stinging slap on her cheek. Then he sent her off to find his assistant, a more open-faced young man called Ousman. He earned my gratitude by offering me a shower in his house, which was in a parallel line of government quarters. After a pause, Mohammed offered the same treat to Michael and Dirije.

I kicked off my shoes and went into Ousman's house. Thin mattresses lay alongside three walls, and two men and a woman were sitting on them, leaning on bolsters. On the floor in front of them were twigs of chat[17] and bottles of Miranda and Pepsi.

My stomach was cramping again and I had no time to be polite. It was heavenly to be in that tiny clean bathroom with running

[17] A mild narcotic known as khat or qat in Yemen and throughout the Middle East, but as chat in Ethiopia. The leaves are chewed.

water. The shower was a sensuous pleasure, and I emerged in a better frame of mind.

A hotel had been found for us. It was no more than a ramshackle café with a row of mud rooms at the back. The floor of mine was damp and smelling of urine, and the only furniture was a rickety bed, spotted with the faeces of cockroaches. It was stiflingly hot.

'It's terrible,' I said to Michael.

'It's safe,' he said. 'There are locks on the doors. There's a guard. What's the problem? Look, you've got a ceiling fan.'

The light was fading, and our next requirement was supper. Mohammed offered to show us a restaurant, and we drove up through the piazza to stop outside a mud shack. We followed him down a narrow lane and he pointed through a picket fence. He couldn't come any further, he said. It was time to pray.

It was pleasant sitting in the restaurant, under the rush awnings which made the roof. A little breeze stirred the hot air. As the darkness deepened, a few 20-watt light bulbs hanging from the ceiling flickered on. I didn't want to irritate my digestion any further with the spicy stew on offer, and swallowed only a few mouthfuls of bread, washed down with a couple of bottles of fizzy liquid.

Exhaustion made me sleep that night, between runs to the foul latrine, and I was more or less functioning the next morning when, at eight o'clock, we arrived at Mohammed's office. This was a dusty, concrete room with three desks in it. A secretary sat at one, tapping slowly on a typewriter, pausing frequently to unruckle the six carbon copies she had scrolled into it.

The room quickly filled with other people: Ousman, who greeted us with a friendly smile, a small man with a white embroidered skull cap, a wild-looking individual with unkempt hair and an orange shirt, and a man with a pink and green striped towel wrapped around his head who was slowly writing Amharic letters into a child's copybook. We sat and waited. Others came and went.

'They want us to meet the director before they do anything,' Michael told me at last. 'He's in a meeting.'

But then, without any warning, the man in the white skull cap launched into a story. He was sitting beside Mohammed, who rested a hand on his shoulder to encourage him. The others leaned forward to listen and began to set up a chanting echo, repeating the last vowel of the final word whenever the narrator paused for breath. If they had been talking in English, it would have sounded like this:

'Once upon a time . . .'

'Aiee.'

'There was a beautiful Afar girl . . .'

'Urr.'

'And she was in love . . .'

'Uh . . .'

I had once been invited to a Caribbean church in London by a friend from Grenada, and I was reminded of how the congregation had cried out, 'Praise the Lord!' or 'Alleluia!' in antiphonal response to the preacher.

I brought out my tape recorder, ready to capture the story, but Mohammed waved his hand dismissively. There was a bustle by the door. The man with the wild hair summoned Michael, who followed him outside. He returned a few moments later.

'This guy is insisting that no one should tell stories unless they're paid,' Michael whispered to me.

'That's all right. Offer the usual amount.'

I was already groping in my bag. In Addis Ababa, we had agreed on an appropriate fee for the storytellers and had made out receipt forms for them to sign.

'It won't be enough. They make so much money smuggling contraband, they'll expect a fortune.'

I squared my shoulders, knowing that the one card I had to play would impress nobody. I made ready to stand up and express with regret that unlike the other regions of Ethiopia, Afar schoolchildren would not benefit from the books we were going to produce. Then I would sweep out. But unexpectedly the toing and froing and whispering in corners stopped. Mohammed held out his hand for the tape recorder, his long fingers beckoning. He frowned repressively at the wild-haired man and told the first storyteller to start again. A hush fell. The spools turned in the machine. I felt a thrill of anticipation.

And here is the story:

Four brave Afar brothers decide to enter the forest which is the abode of the fearsome hyena king. They are quickly surrounded by hyenas, and the king asks them who had given them the courage to invade his realm. The first brother claims that his courage comes from God, and that he fears nothing because the day of his death is written in God's great book. The second brother relies on his clansmen, who will take revenge if he is harmed. The third puts his trust in Mother Earth who gave birth to him and to whom he will one day return in burial. But the fourth brother foolishly tries to flatter the hyena king.

'I put my faith in you, the hyenas,' he says. 'I have hyena friends and I rely on their strength and goodness.'

The king accepts the explanations of the first three brothers and lets them go. But to the fourth brother he says, 'You're a fool to rely on your hyena friends. We're used to quarrelling among ourselves, and we'll be happy to fight over you.'

So the hyenas fall on the fourth brother and eat him.

This story intrigued me. Though Afars are uniformly Muslim, they retain some beliefs from earlier times. I would have liked to know more about 'Mother Earth'.

The story was greeted with approval. A spirit of competition took over, and even the wild-haired man, whose name was Akitoy, wanted to tell one. Mohammed was strict with them, listening to each outline before he would accept it as suitable. Then, when the story was finished, they would debate the moral until all agreed that they had got it right.

By noon the small office, crowded with men, was stuffy and very hot, but seven stories were in the bag. I had recorded them first in the Afar language, then Mohammed had translated them, again onto the tape, into Amharic. Later, Michael would listen to the Amharic version and dictate the English translation to me, which I would write down in my notebook. I could usually understand a little of the Amharic stories, enough to know get some idea of the characters, but not enough to follow the plot.

It was agreed, after some discussion, that the session could continue in the afternoon.

'But the office isn't right for telling stories. They want to go to their usual place,' said Michael.

'OK. Where's that?'

'Mohammed's house. They want to chew chat. I've got a feeling they'd appreciate it if you'd buy it for them. Best quality.'

Depending on how you look at it, chat is the curse or the blessing of the Horn of Africa. It's a shrub whose leaves, when chewed, produce a feeling of excitement, talkativeness and euphoria, followed by an irritable lethargy. In Yemen it is almost a national obsession, its cultivation using up forty per cent of available farmland. Afars too are enthusiastic users of chat, and many are heavily addicted, a state which can lead to paranoia and hallucinations. While on the plus side, chat provides some hours of pleasure and oils the social wheels in a harsh world, on the negative side it absorbs a great deal of productive energy, crowding out more fruitful pursuits and wreaking havoc on the fabric of society. The Ethiopian government has tried to ban the cultivation and sale of chat from time to time without success.

If I had a qualm about spending Her Majesty's Government's money on drugs, it was only momentary, and I shelled out a hundred birr, a large sum, to buy an ample supply.

We had all forgotten the existence of the director of education whose approval had earlier seemed so important, but suddenly he was ready to meet us. I was surprised to see, as we were ushered into his office, that all the chairs down the long table were occupied. At least one man was wearing camouflage battledress while another was an Ethiopian army soldier with the three pips of a captain on his shoulder. These were not Afars. It was obvious that they were a visitation delegation from the central government. The lack of room at the hotel was now explained.

There were no smiles. The meeting we were interrupting had been tense.

The man in the director's chair, at the head of the long table, was so young and insignificant looking that I offered my hand first to the man beside him, who refused it.

'He is director,' he said curtly, pointing to the youth.

This poor young man, harassed and sweating, waved us to a sofa at the far end of the room. We perched on it as I tried to explain our mission. It was clear that the director understood barely a word of English. The others did, however, and one, a bearded man with the pale face of a high-born Tigrayan, said, 'Cultural stories of the Afar people. That is good.'

We had been slotted into a pigeon-hole conforming to the

government's policy of encouraging the diverse cultures of Ethiopia's regions. We had been accepted.

As we left the office, Michael told me what he had just heard: the department heads of the entire Afar regional government had been arrested a week earlier and were now in prison, awaiting charges for corruption. The new director of education, who had nothing but a diploma in agriculture to his name and was twenty-four years old, was being inducted into his duties by the Tigrayan officials, who had come to impose some order on the affairs of the Afars. The Afar ministries had run through their annual budgets in three months, and had asked for more money.

Last night's restaurant, to which we returned for lunch, was more appealing in the daylight. The matting roof was held up by the trunks of trees, and the chairs and stools were cut roughly from pieces of wood, their lattice seats made of woven leather thongs. The owners would have been incredulous at the vast sums of money spent by designers in smart European resorts to create just such a 'natural' and 'authentic' style.

I needed the latrine at once, of course, and two girls pointed the way. A narrow alley came out into another, unroofed courtyard, and below this the ground dropped away. I found myself standing on a cliff looking down onto a wide plain. Just below me was a narrow branch of the Awash river, fringed with palms. Grass and thick-leaved vegetation grew beside the water, and further away, at the point where the green was already fading into the dusty brown of the desert, was a nomad camp of portable basket-work huts, with camels feeding nearby.

The latrine was at the edge of the cliff, and as I approached it, large black and white birds flapped heavily away. From here I could look along the edge of the escarpment and see older buildings teetering along the cliff edge. They looked timeless, like natural eruptions from the earth.

The latrine was a nice one, the concrete surrounding the hole clean and dry. Looking down, I could see that below was a channel with water running through it. I dropped my trousers and squatted. Life was improving. The large doses of Imodium I'd been taking, and the starvation diet, were slowing things down.

And then I heard a scraping, sliding noise below. I started up, my hair standing on end. Beneath me I caught sight of a scaly hind leg, a clawed foot and a tail half a metre long. A huge lizard-like creature was crawling along the channel. I let out a screech and burst out of the latrine, my trousers round my ankles.

The two girls from the restaurant had followed me and were watching, clutching each other and laughing. The ruckus brought Michael and Dirije running. I'd hauled up my trousers by this time and was trying to restore my dignity.

'It's only a Gila monster,' Michael said. 'A monitor lizard. They're all over the place here.'

The story spread round the restaurant and everyone thought it was indescribably funny.

That's it, I thought gloomily, plodding back towards Mohammed's house in the government lines. I've made myself a laughing stock on top of everything else.

About a dozen men were sitting on the mattresses set around the walls in Mohammed's house when we arrived. The bundles of chat, neatly rolled in flower-patterned cloths, were laid out on the floor. The men shuffled up to make room for us, and we sat down. I leaned back against the bolster and, just to show willing, nibbled at a stalk of chat. I had no intention of chewing it properly. The last time I'd chewed, my heart had raced with terrifying speed and I hadn't been able to sleep all night.

Everyone seemed happy. The tensions of the morning had melted away, and Michael's description of my encounter with the lizard had gone down well. The atmosphere worked on me more effectively than any number of stimulating leaves. I was light-headed already, and suddenly everything seemed tinged with a sublime aura. It was hot, but enough of a breeze wafted through the open window to keep us comfortable. The bright draperies fluttering round Mohammed's wife Fatumah, as she sat near the doorway with her little tray table of coffee cups, seemed exquisitely pretty. Maiyrum, her small daughter, squatted beside her, keeping an anxious eye on her father, while the baby, a chubby two-year-old known simply as 'Baba' waddled about, naked except for a vest that barely reached his belly button.

Mohammed's assistant Ousman was there, and Akitoy, the man with the wild hair, and the one with the skull cap and others from the office. I wrote down all their names, but as most of them seemed to be called Ahmed Mohammed, or Mohammed Ahmed Mohammed, I was soon confused.

They had been chewing for some time before we'd arrived and everyone was on fire with inspiration. Mohammed had dropped the guarded manner of yesterday. His gold incisors flashed as he smiled, his cheek bulged with its wad of chat, his hands sliced through the air as he talked.

He was in charge of the show. Stories were offered for his approval, and it was only on his nod that Ousman would stand up, pick his way across the tangle of legs, discarded chat twigs, bottles of water, ashtrays and coffee cups which littered the floor to hold the tape recorder to the next storyteller's mouth.

I kept my eyes on each storyteller as he spoke, nodding if they looked at me as if I could understand, smiling as euphoria washed over me. And in fact I could follow a little of the Amharic, enough, anyway, to know if the story was one I had heard before. Michael, a teetotaller, picked politely at a leaf or two of chat, and scribbled asides to me in my notebook from time to time. 'This one's got to be a trilogy.' Or 'This one sounds like a Russian novel', Or 'I think we've got a haiku here', making me want to giggle.

Some of the stories were long. The occasion demanded the full narrative treatment, but I'll shorten them here.

A prince sets out to find a clever woman to marry. He comes upon a girl looking after sheep, and asks if she had seen his lost camel.

'No,' she answers, 'but if he was blind in one eye, had no tail and was wounded on his right side, then he passed this way.'

The prince, astonished, asks how she could tell.

'Look,' she answers. 'Here is a bush eaten only on the right side. The camel who ate this must be blind in the other eye. And his droppings are all in one heap. A camel usually swishes his tail to disperse them. And he has rolled in the sand but only on his left side.'

The prince wishes to meet the girl's father, who is setting out on a journey, and decides to walk with him. On the way, the young man makes nonsensical remarks, making the older one think he is a fool, but when the pair return to the old man's hut the girl explains the meaning of the prince's words. He has been talking in riddles, which she is able to interpret.

The prince asks for the girl's hand and the marriage is arranged. When the time comes, the prince goes with a servant to the bride's house. They stop at a water hole to drink, and the servant forces the prince, on pain of being murdered, to switch clothes so that he can marry the girl in the place of his master.

The prince has no choice but to agree, give up his clothes and act the part of the servant. They arrive at the bride's house, where, oddly, everyone but the bride is fooled by the switch of clothes.

'This man is not my bridegroom,' she says, and to prove it she asks him three questions: What is the heaviest burden for a man? What is the sweetest food? What is the sweetest smell?

The servant offers a grindstone, honey and a scented herb for answers. The girl calls him a fool, and sets the same questions to the 'servant' prince, who replies that the heaviest burden is a promise, the sweetest food is what you eat when you're starving, and the sweetest smell rises from the neck of your baby son.

The deception is discovered and the girl claims the prince as her husband. They live happily for many years, but one day the prince is attacked by bandits. Before they kill him, they allow him to send a message to his wife, who deciphers the riddles it contains, and the robbers are duly caught and executed.

Riddles feature frequently in ancient stories. The folk hero Samson, round whom a cycle of stories revolves in the Book of Judges, sets this riddle for his companions: 'Out of the eater came forth meat, and out of the strong came forth sweetness.' None of them guess that the answer is the bees which have made their hive in the carcass of a dead lion, until Delilah wheedles the answer from him. Oedipus too must solve the riddle set him by the Sphinx, who, after all, was said by the Greeks to come from Ethiopia. The plot of Puccini's opera *Turandot*, derived from an old Chinese folk tale, revolves around the solving of riddles.

The others in the room enjoyed this story more than I did. I could tell that they delighted in the wordplay and puzzles, which I found irritating, distancing me from the characters. They sat chewing, open-mouthed, leaning forward from time to time to sip a fizzy drink or shake a coffee cup at Fatumah to be refilled.

From her position by the door, she would lean out from time to time and call to her little servant girl to fetch tea or another ashtray.

I suddenly noticed that Dirije, suffering perhaps from mild paranoia from the combined effect of chat and chewing being surrounded by Afar men, had pulled out a cross from under his shirt and was fingering it.

The next story was more fun.

A young man falls in love with a beautiful girl and sends his relatives to her father's house to negotiate the marriage. The father demands as a dowry all the young man's wealth in flocks, herds and camels. Crazed with love, the young man agrees. But now the couple have nothing to live on, so the husband goes out hunting every day in order to feed himself and his wife.

One day, the girl's father comes to visit while her husband is still out hunting. She had nothing to give him to eat. Embarrassed, she waits for her husband to return.

At last, she hears a noise outside. Another hunter is walking by, with a dead bushbuck slung over his shoulder. She begs for a leg of it, promising that her husband will repay him in kind. The hunter looks her up and down and sees how beautiful she is.

'I'll give you a leg of my bushbuck,' he says, 'but only if you'll make love to me.'

What can she do? She can't bear the shame of letting her father go hungry, so she agrees to meet the stranger later, after dark.

While she is cooking the meat her husband returns, having killed a zebra, so there is a feast for them all that night. As they sit eating, she hears a pebble rattle on the matting roof of the hut. She ignores it. A second pebble rattles on the roof. She smiles. When she hears the third pebble, she bursts out laughing.

'What's the matter with you?' say her husband and father.

'I'm laughing at three fools,' she answers. 'The first is my husband who gave away all his property so that he could marry me. The second is my father, who took everything from his son-in-law and then expects to eat when he comes to visit us. And the third is the fool outside, who thinks I'm going to sleep with him just because he gave me the leg of his bushbuck.'

There was a lull. Michael turned to me.

'They want you to tell a story.'

'I don't mind if I do,' I said, taking a swig from a bottle of fizzy water, and I launched into 'Beauty and the Beast'.

It would have been impossible to find a more appreciative audience. The men sucked air noisily through their teeth, sighed at the sad bits and smiled at the happy bits, their eyes glued to my face as I spoke. Michael translated sentence by sentence into Amharic, while Mohammed chipped in with Afar explanations from time to time. I noticed as I talked that some children had crept up to the back door of the house and were crowding round to listen, inching forward as more piled in at the back. Fatumah suddenly rounded on them and shooed them away. Stories were for grown-ups in these parts.

'What's the meaning of the story?' Mohammed asked, when at last, with sighs of satisfaction all round, Beauty had been united with her transformed lover.

'I don't know,' I said. 'It's a story.'

'That won't do,' said Michael. 'You've got to tell them what it means.'

'OK.' I thought for a moment. It was easy, really. 'It's about the power of love. Even an ugly person is beautiful in the eyes of the one who loves.'

This was approved of, and a discussion ensued which of course

I couldn't follow. It only ended when the next story began. It was clear that as the high of the chat intensified, the mood was becoming ribald.

There was once a married woman who took a lover. She couldn't get enough of him, and planned a way to keep him in her house. So she told her husband that her mother was coming to stay, and sent clothes and jewellery to her lover so that he would dress up as a woman.

Afar men are supposed to be very respectful towards their mothers-in-law, and are not allowed to approach them, so for the duration of her supposed mother's stay, the husband would have to stay outside and never enter the hut.

One day, when his wife had gone out to gather firewood, the husband needed his axe, and realised that it was inside the hut where his supposed mother-in-law was. He coughed politely but there was no answer, as the lover was fast asleep.

The husband decided to creep inside and take his axe without waking her, but when he stole inside, and felt under the bed for his axe, he saw that the sleeping lover had rolled over, and that something erect was sticking up from between his legs. At once he whipped out his dagger, pulled up the lover's dress, and with one swift cut sliced off the lover's offending member. Then out he went, with his dripping dagger in one hand and the lover's genitals in the other, to find his wife and cut off her head.

She saw him coming, understood the situation at once and began screaming, 'This is a curse! A curse!'

'What curse?' demanded her husband.

'I didn't like to tell you,' she said, 'but my mother's family have had a feud with a sorcerer and he's changed all the females into males, and all the males into females. And now look what you've done to my mother!'

'Well, I'm sorry,' the man said, 'but what was I to think? At least the curse hasn't affected you.'

They went back to their hut together to find that the lover had run away, and they lived happily together for the rest of their lives.

And the moral of the story, it was generally agreed, is that a clever woman can get her poor husband to believe anything. But for me, the joy of these two stories is the delightful impropriety, the terror one feels as the plot unfolds, knowing what ghastly retribution is surely in store for each of these dashing wives, only for them to turn the situation to their own advantage.

By five o'clock, the fountain of stories was beginning to dry up, and I could see that the effects of the chat were wearing off. It was time to go, and with reluctance I peeled myself off the mattress and shook hands all round with many thanks.

Ever since my glimpse of the river from the latrine at the top of the cliff, I had wanted to explore, so I asked Ousman if he would show me round. He looked surprised, but agreed, and now I realised how wonderful it was to have at my beck and call a Land Rover and a driver. I could never, in my present state and in that great heat, have walked so far.

Dirije had soon driven us out beyond the town. We passed a compound in which were piled mountains of sacks bulging with cotton, which had grown in the strip of irrigated fields along the Awash.

'What happens if it rains?' I asked. 'Won't all this be ruined?'

'It doesn't rain,' said Ousman.

We came down to the river and drew up beside a Bailey bridge. The stream was narrow here, but crocodiles lurked in it, and sometimes hippos came. We strolled a little way along the river bank. It was a pretty scene. Mature old palms and some other large trees shaded the river. The mud houses behind their wooden stockades had warmed to a pinky brown in the late afternoon sun. Flocks of sparrows bounced up from beneath our feet and egrets wheeled overhead. A train of three camels lurched past, led by a man robed in white with a bulky turban wrapped round his head and followed by a woman in bright, floating clothes.

After a hundred yards or so, Ousman, who had set a pace of crawling slowness, stopped and said that it was 'forbidden' to go on. I couldn't read his face. Was he puzzled by the whole concept of 'going for a walk' and embarrassed to be seen here with a foreign woman? Did this river bank have an evil reputation, which might harm his good name? Was there a risk of robbers? Were there supernatural dangers as dusk fell? As so often in Ethiopia, I was aware that a place which looked ordinary to me might have layers of meaning to the people I was with. A Palestinian friend once said to me crossly, 'You Europeans think you have the right to go anywhere you like, to wander round other people's countries, poke your way into their sacred places, trample on all their customs. The rest of the world has rather more respect.'

It was almost dark by the time we arrived back at our squalid hotel. I knew that I had to eat something or I would not have the strength for the next few days, and so walked back up to the restaurant with Michael and Dirije. I was greeted with delight by the girls, who acted out for me my horror at the Gila monster, and brought me a dish of plain spaghetti, cold and unappetising, but the safest option, all things considered.

And then, as we walked back across the dark space of the piazza, I was uplifted into a state of euphoria. The only light came from the teeming stars overhead and a few lamps glowing from the open fronts of the small shops which lined the square. The only sounds were the quiet voices of my companions talking in Amharic, a clatter of dishes from a far-off cookhouse, a grunt or two from a camel settled on its knees for the night and the scuffing of our feet on the beaten earth. I was alert to every passing smell and subtle alteration in the temperature of the warm night air.

I had never in my life been further away from all that was familiar, safe and comfortable, yet I was unafraid in this world so different from my own. I felt that I had slid back thousands of years, into one of the world's oldest cities: Thebes, or Babylon, or Mohenjodaro. The weakness I had felt in the last few days had gone and I was borne up with a sense that, although my sixtieth birthday was a mere three years away, I could accomplish anything from now on, and that no doors would be closed to me.

The exhilaration had gone by the morning. I was worn out by the heat and the dysentery that had had me on the run in the night, and I knew that once again I would have to be on the qui vive all day to avert a catastrophe.

It was market day in Assayita and herdsmen had come in with their animals from far and wide. Several were at other tables as we sat at breakfast in the little bar close to our hotel. They wore their hair in bushy clouds about their heads, and carried their daggers ostentatiously. Smaller, harder and more muscular than the townspeople, they stared at me open mouthed. Dirije, whose fast was so strictly vegan that he refused to touch even the honey which Michael and I were scooping onto our bread, shuffled uneasily and retreated to the safety of the Land Rover.

There was a dejected air of hangover in Mohammed's office when we walked into it a short while later. The usual crowd of hangers-on was there. I wondered how anyone made a living when they spent their days in Mohammed's office, watching such exciting events as the appearance of a secretary asking for a signature, or a message from the office of the director. It was clear that there would be no storytelling now. Mohammed offered to take me to the market. Michael and Dirije had gone off to track down a consignment of books donated some time ago to the Afar Region by the British Council, so we went on foot, forced to rely for communication largely on my rudimentary Amharic.

Our feet padded in the dust as we walked through the quiet back lanes of Assayita, passing domestic scenes of people and animals that would have been at home in the pages of a nineteenth-century orientalist's sketch book.

In the market place, the camels were on their knees, their wooden harnesses still on their backs, their noses in the air and their long-lashed eyes shut. A few men clad only in the traditional Afar loincloth were in evidence, but they no longer wore the cartridge belts bristling with bullets which I remembered from long ago, and I sensed that their dash and swagger had gone. The women looked duller too. None were now bare breasted, nor did they wear the once universal scarlet and orange striped sarongs in shiny cotton satin (I had hoped to buy some lengths to take home with me) and if it hadn't been for the black cloths tied over their oiled hair and the unusual brightness of their full-skirted dresses I would not have known they were Afars.

We walked past sacks of maize, displays of spices laid out on cloths on the ground, and a few piles of cabbages and tomatoes, but Mohammed assumed that there was nothing to interest me here, and was walking on towards the cattle market, which I supposed to be a more natural focus of interest for an Afar male.

Akitoy, he of the wild hair, had joined us by now. It was some way further on to the cattle market, past reed fences surrounding small mud houses. A few children called out 'Ferenji! Money!' but Mohammed rounded on them with such glares and contemptuous flicks of his fingers that they shrank away. I had the impression that he and Akitoy were beginning to enjoy themselves, relaxing in my presence. Akitoy detached from my hand the precious little tape recorder, which I carried with me everywhere, and looped the strap round his own wrist, letting it swing so that everyone could see it, to my considerable alarm.

Mohammed and I managed to converse in English, and I was surprised at how much he knew.

'Where did you learn?' I asked.

'At school. My teacher was American Peace Corpse.'

We came out at the top of a rise, and could see, at the bottom of a pebble-strewn slope, that the market extended for a considerable distance. Flocks of sheep and goats were nearest to us, with cattle and camels further off. Each small group of animals had a couple of herders minding them, and as we went down into the melee I noticed a group of these men squatting down, counting wads of money. Mohammed and Akitoy might be 'post', as Dirije would say, when they sat in the office in Assayita town, but here they were everyone's brothers. They made quite a progress through the market, greeting and being greeted. The men they talked to were curious about me and eagerly showed me the fine points of their camels (particularly their teeth) in case I might want to buy one.

Akitoy had walked on ahead, and I was anxious to keep up with him, worried about my tape recorder, but it was very hot and I could feel what strength I had ebbing away, so when Mohammed suggested that I might like to return to his house and rest there, I agreed with relief.

We walked slowly back up the slope towards the town. I watched out of the corner of my eye the languid, economical elegance of Mohammed's stride, which I could see was the best gait for covering the ground with the minimum of wasted effort in such heat. I knew, though, that I could never achieve it.

Mohammed exerted himself to point out places of interest as we walked. We passed the construction site of a new palace for the Sultan and a new mosque, a gift from the Saudi Arabians, who are sponsoring mosque building throughout Ethiopia.

'Derg bombed the old one. You know Derg?'

'Yes, I know. There was a war here, wasn't there, in the Derg time?'

He laughed, looking embarrassed.

'Weren't the Afar people fighting alongside the Somalis?'

'Yes.'

'Were you a soldier yourself?'

I had gone too far. His face froze and his pace increased. In any case, our conversation was struggling with the severe limitations of his English and my Amharic. We arrived at his house at last, none too soon for me.

'You are tired, Mrs Elizabeth?'

'Yes.'

'Thirsty?'

'Yes.'

He brought me a glass of water, but I didn't dare drink it, and said apologetically that I could only drink bottled liquid, then was embarrassed when the little girl servant was sent out to buy some.

I was getting used to Mohammed's house now. I gravitated naturally to my favourite corner, and leaned against 'my' bolster. Mohammed's daughter, Maiyrum, too, was losing her shyness of me, and when Mohammed pulled out a photograph album and began to show me pictures of his family, she peeped round at us from the bedroom door.

There were many pictures of the two children. I pointed to those of Maiyrum, but I must have mispronounced her name, because she called out suddenly, 'I'm not Mariam! I'm not a Christian! I am Muslim!'

'I would like to take a photograph of you, of your whole family,' I said to Mohammed. 'You, and Fatumah, and the children.'

His face froze. He turned back the pages of the album, detached a picture and reluctantly handed it to me.

'No!' I laughed, pulling out my camera. 'I mean I will *make* a photograph of you all.'

He smiled with relief and replaced the photograph. I noticed that there was a third child in it, an older one, a girl of about ten.

'She was my daughter,' Mohammed said.

The little girl had died a few months earlier. This was the only photograph her father possessed of her, yet he had felt that my request could not have been refused, that the rules of hospitality required him to fulfil every one of his guest's wishes. I realised how nearly I had blundered and wondered how many other misses and near-misses littered my path through Ethiopia. We agreed that the photographic session would take place later that afternoon.

The room had begun to fill with visitors, and when Fatumah produced a tray of injera and several dishes of vegetables, they all crowded round to eat. Maiyrum settled by the door beside her mother and wasn't invited to eat, but Baba, the toddler boy, had food thrust upon him from all sides.

'Come, Baba. Eat, Baba. Have more,' Mohammed kept saying.

When the meal was finished and Fatumah had cleared the dishes away, Mohammed showed me a slim book he had written, a guide to the Afar language for teachers. I leafed through it with interest. Afar was only then in the process of being written down. He looked pleased at my interest and asked about my husband and my sons. I tried to gauge, as I gave my answers in halting Amharic, what he must be thinking, how he must be surprised that my husband would permit me to travel so far in the company of other men, but his face gave nothing away.

He stood up suddenly and said he needed to go into town and I guessed that the hour for buying the afternoon's supply of chat had come. He suggested that I should lie down for a while, and I agreed with enthusiasm. Fatumah showed me into the bedroom, and I stretched out gratefully on the big bed which half filled the room, shutting the door firmly on a row of inquisitive children who had silently infiltrated the house and were staring at me, open-mouthed.

There was no furniture other than the bed, but a stack of suitcases and cardboard cartons rose up against the far wall. They gave a feeling of transience to the place, and I was reminded that the parents, or at any rate the grandparents, of this family had no doubt been nomads, able to carry all their possessions on the backs of a few camels. I had learned by now that Fatumah was Mohammed's first cousin. Christian Ethiopians have strict consanguinity laws, forbidding marriages between family members going back several generations, but among the Afars cousin marriage is favoured.

I dozed for a while, bothered by a cloud of flies which I could only keep off my face by spreading a hanky over it, and tense with anxiety about my tape recorder, which I had last seen disappearing with Akitoy into the camel market. Eventually, hearing his voice from the other room, I got up, and there he was. He handed it back to me, and though there was a nasty dent in the microphone, it looked unharmed. He walked me back to the hotel, chatting merrily.

I had asked Mohammed if it would be possible to go out of town to visit a village, and he had agreed to take me that afternoon. This was a little hard on Dirije and Michael, who had just returned, hot and thirsty, from driving round local schools to check on the books which had been donated by the British Council, but they good-naturedly agreed to the plan, and with Mohammed by now smiling and alert from his daily fix of chat, we set off in the Land Rover.

We drove quite a distance out of Assayita along the banks of the Awash, passing a huge plain of irrigated cotton plantations. The crop had recently been harvested, and soft mountains of snowy fluff rose from the middle of the fields. The extent of this green landscape was limited by the reach of the irrigation channels which radiated out from the mother river. Egrets, ibis, ducks, geese and a host of smaller birds with iridescent wings fluttered near the water. This lushness was in stark contrast to the desert beyond.

At last, Mohammed directed Dirije to turn off the road and he parked the Land Rover under a palm tree. From here we walked up a path below a high bank on top of which ran a channel of water. There were shouts behind us and we turned to see a policeman and several other men running up.

'So it's forbidden to bring ferenjis down here, is it?' Mohammed joked to them. Luckily they had recognised him, and their frowns turned to smiles as lengthy greetings began.

A leak in the water duct had made the path to the village quite muddy and I enjoyed the squelch underfoot. We passed a pen fenced with thorny branches in which cattle had already been corralled for the night. Their long-horned heads turned curiously as they watched us pass, their white and brown flanks pink with dust. Behind them, a range of distant hills was turning rosy in the lowering sun.

We came into the village, entering a peaceful, late afternoon scene. Some of the houses were permanent buildings made of mud, but others were nomad huts, surprisingly large when seen close up. Several women were sitting about outside, one nursing a child, another tending a fire, a third plaiting reeds to make a mat. Small children ran up. One dared to put out her hand to touch mine, then squealed and ran away.

A middle-aged woman with prominent cheekbones and deep-set eyes seemed to be Mohammed's relative, and greeted him with shoulder-to-shoulder embraces, then invited us into her hut.

The entrance was so narrow that even she, slim as she was, had to enter sideways. I had heard stories by now of leopards or hyenas stealing into huts by night. Were the doorways kept so tight to prevent an animal escaping from the hut with a victim in its mouth?

Once my eyes had adjusted to the deep gloom I could see that the hut had been expertly made. The framework consisted of thin branches, bent into hoops and neatly tied together with a covering of matting. A few possessions hung from the cross pieces: an aluminium ladle, a gourd sticky with honey, a fan woven from reeds and a milk pail of the finest basket-work, which the woman had made herself. She would line it, she indicated, to make it impermeable, but I didn't understand how she would do this. It was hard for me to take in the fact that this was her home. I felt that I was inside a living ethnographical museum.

It was surprisingly spacious inside the hut, which contained a large wooden bed frame, the mattress lying on an intricate lattice of leather thongs. The woman made me sit beside her while Mohammed and Michael stood about. I was full of questions, longing to ask this woman about her life, her family, her skills, and her opinions, but Michael said, 'Look, if we stay here we'll have to eat or drink something. We'd better go.' He was quite right, of course, but I couldn't help feeling that my diarrhoea was already so bad that another glass of infected water couldn't make much difference. However it was stifling inside the hut, the heat made worse by the cooking fire smoking beside the bed, so I followed the others outside.

A few other women had arrived to take a look at us. I tried to talk to them. They knew no Amharic and were shy, but I had sensed an opportunity. It was always hard in Ethiopia to make the men I was with understand that I wanted to collect stories from women, too. Here, on this calm afternoon, with the women at ease in their own village, perhaps something would emerge. I was about to ask Mohammed if he could ask them for a tale or two, when a man ran up followed by a woman muffled in cloths. His wife, the man explained, was suffering from an attack of asthma. Would we take her into Assayita to get her some medicine? She needed to go at once. Frustrated, I had no choice but to comply. In any case, Dirije wanted to rest.

I made my way back to the Land Rover. The woman and her husband were already settled in the back of it with a five-year-old child between them. The woman was lying back against the window with her eyes closed, looking drawn but breathing quite normally. Whatever was wrong with her, it wasn't asthma. I tried to dispel my disappointment at being dragged away so soon.

But the drive back into Assayita was memorable. The low sun had made every colour, so washed out in the heat of the day, glow with a final brilliance before night fell. We passed cattle being driven back to their villages from their day's foraging. The sick woman's husband pointed out one with a bleeding stump where one of its horns should have been and he and Mohammed began to discuss cattle diseases and their correct treatment, with interjections from Dirije. Cattle are the business of all men in Ethiopia, whether they are from the highlands or the desert.

I fell into a dream, wondering what it was about this place and these people that I found so fascinating. Was it their self-reliance? I certainly admired the skilful way in which the village people made their own houses, their utensils and implements from materials at hand, with little need for money. Then there was the direct connection between their work and their food supply. They rear and tend their cattle, then drink the milk and eat the meat. I could understand a little of the satisfaction this brings. Nothing gives me greater pleasure than cooking vegetables and bottling fruit I have grown myself. There was the binding loyalty of clan ties, the knowledge of genealogy, the confidence each child has in knowing who he is. There was a lack of hurry here, the days punctuated by small events and much conversation.

I was in danger of romanticising. The lives of the Afar are hard, hot and dangerous, especially those of the women. I thought of the things I value in my own world: freedom from the fear of attack, my independence as a woman, the notion of individual self-fulfilment, doctors, dentists, clean water, books, classical music, films, a cornucopia of varied and delicious foods and above all the sense of power I had felt so strongly the night before to forge my own way. And yet, underlying all these good things, I was aware of an unease, a sense of groping for what we in the rich world have lost.

We arrived back at Mohammed's house for the photographic session. A friend of Fatumah's, scandalised that Maiyrum had not been properly dressed for the occasion, was untying all the little plaits on her head and brushing her hair back into a ponytail, fixing this with a huge chiffon pom-pom according to the fashion of little girls in the Russia of the 1980s. This amused me. Russia had been Ethiopia's primary ally in the days of Mengistu and the Derg. They had left behind more than a trail of rusting tanks.

A few outfits were looked over and rejected until finally Maiyrum was ready in a red pinafore dress and white, embroidered blouse. Baba, who had been crawling around in the dust outside the house, wearing a little girl's dress, was stuffed into a pyjama suit, and at last the whole family was ready and posed, sitting on their bed, while a crowd of neighbours and children crammed into the room to watch and comment.

There's another thing I love about my life, I thought. Privacy.

The night that followed was so miserable that I still shiver at the thought of it. I had been unable to wash properly since the shower in Ousman's house, and I was dirty and smelly, my skin itching with prickly heat and the bites of bed bugs which I had caught during the previous night and squashed, smearing my fingers with blood. Mosquitoes whined about my room and the net over my bed had too many holes in it to provide proper protection. Stomach cramps drove me on frequent visits to the foul latrine, where I produced nothing but rushes of bowel water, returning on tiptoe for fear of puff adders, which were rumoured to lie out on the path at night. Worst of all was the loud conversation of a couple of men sitting a few yards from my door. I groped for my earplugs to try to block them out, and a cockroach crawled out of the box.

I lay in misery as the hours passed. Worse fears than snakes and insects loomed out at me, a host of old anxieties, troubles at home, fears for the future, doubts about the very foundations of my life. When the greyness of dawn finally crept in under the ill-fitting door, I got up with profound relief. Dirije and Michael were already stirring. We were on the road back to Addis Ababa by seven.

I had had a moment of profound happiness in Assayita, and a night of anguish. I felt I had left part of myself behind.

It was encouraging to see a little wildlife on the road – a few antelope, a jackal and a porcupine. But as the Land Rover hummed its way up the steep road towards the highlands, I could hardly bear to look out on the bare stumps of trees, hacked down by voracious charcoal burners. The police have the powers to stop charcoal being transported to Addis Ababa, in an effort to reduce the deforestation, but Dirije, knowing that our diplomatic number plates would protect him, stopped to buy some, to my intense disapproval.

The charcoal burner, who had risen to his feet as our car stopped, and was as thin as one of the tree trunks he had burned, did not take his eyes off me as he haggled with Dirije.

'You like this woman?' Dirije joked. 'How much would you give for her? Six sacks? Five? Four?'

He shook his head unsmilingly.

'You see how he thinks?' Dirije said gleefully. 'He would not give even four sacks for you.'

The man muttered something.

'What did he say?' I asked Michael.

'He said you wouldn't last a week out here.'

❖

It was heaven to be back in Addis Ababa. I went straight to the doctor who took a stool test then and there.

'Bacillary dysentery,' she said crisply. 'What on earth have you been doing? A simple antibiotic would have stopped it a week ago.'

⁘ 5 ⁘

TRICKSTERS IN GAMBELA

A few good nights' sleep, a whack of ciprofloxacin, draughts of clean water, a familiar diet and the kindness of my hosts soon put me on my feet again, and I was ready for more.

The prospect of Gambela, a region which I had never visited before, was particularly exciting. That part of Ethiopia had seemed impossibly remote in the 1960s. It occupied a 'here be dragons' corner in the imaginary map of my mind.

With the return of health came a surge of confidence. I could see, looking over my hoard of full tapes and notebooks, that this thing was going to work. I would have excellent stories for the Tigray, Amhara and Afar readers. I was already shaping them, working them into an English simple enough for young Ethiopian learners to cope with.

I checked over my kit the night before I left Addis Ababa. Those hours scratching my head over the oddments laid out on my bed in London had been worth it. A few more batteries, another cassette or two, and with the sand and sweat of Assayita washed out of my clothes I was ready to go.

Gambela is in the steamy far south-west of Ethiopia. A glance at a contour map explains much about this remote region, for it lies beyond and below the escarpment which has always defined highland, Christian Ethiopia, separating it from the lands of the Nilotic peoples to the south and west. Gambela sticks out like a blunt nose into the territory of the Sudan. Its major waterway is the Baro river, which feeds into the White Nile, and it is the traditional homeland of the Anuak, a tribe related to the Luo of Kenya.

Gambela is also home to many Nuer people. Strongly independent, the Nuer have resisted conquest down the ages. Their heartland is in Southern Sudan, but there are large communities in south-west Ethiopia too.

Like the Nuer people, the Anuak are lovers of cattle, and they measure their wealth by the size of their herds, but they also grow crops and eat fish from the river. I didn't hear stories of water demons in Gambela, perhaps because there are none, or perhaps because the river is so familiar and central to people's lives.

This region was briefly an outpost of the British Empire, administered by two no doubt hot and lonely 'customs inspectors', who exacted dues on the valuable coffee crop from Kafa, which was shipped on steamers down the Baro to Khartoum and beyond. Since those days, easier routes from Kafa to the north have killed off the trade on the Baro, and turmoil in Ethiopia has brought in settlers from the highlands as well as Nuer refugees from the long-running war in Sudan. This situation has been made more toxic by tidal waves of cheap and deadly weapons.

I emerged green of face and wobbly of leg from the plane onto the airstrip, a cleared space in a wooded area some five kilometres from town. No one was there to meet me, but the other passengers were keen to know who I was and what I had come for.

'What is your name?' asked a grey-haired man with white chin stubble and pebble-thick glasses. I told him.

'Mrs Elizabeth, we expected you two weeks ago. We have been in Addis for the last ten days. It is by good fortune that you did not come yesterday.'

Someone offered to take me to the hotel. The grey-haired man, whose name was Ogota, and who was the head of the Cultural Bureau, told me to take my rest and he would send someone to fetch me in the morning. The temperature was thirty-eight degrees, and I was happy to oblige.

The Ethiopia Hotel in Gambela has seen better days, but it has a certain charm. The bedrooms, dotted about under trees, are equipped with fans to stir the sluggish air. It was the hot season, and although the frangipani trees were in flower, filling the place with their heady scent, the garden was dry and dusty, and dead leaves crunched underfoot. I whiled away some hours that afternoon in the company of an elderly Geordie, Jim, who had come all this way to install a new engine into the river boat which he had sold to Gambela twenty-five years earlier. With him was his Ethiopian agent, a plump businessman from Addis Ababa.

I made some remark that was mildly critical of the Derg. The agent frowned.

'There's an Amharic proverb, "When an old tree falls, everyone runs to chop off the branches." People blame the Derg for everything! Things have changed. That's all there is to it. This new generation don't have any culture, they don't respect their parents like I respected mine.'

'Just like in England,' Jim chipped in. 'My wife, her domain is the house. She makes all the decisions there, and she leaves everything else to me.'

'That's how it should be,' nodded his agent.

It was too hot to argue. I took another slurp from my bottle of Coke, and kept my mouth shut.

❖

As Ogota had promised, a young man came to fetch me the next morning. He was a Tigrayan attached to the regional cultural office and was in the process of learning Anuak. A representative of the government in this remote place, far from Addis Ababa, he reminded me of those British colonial officers from half a century earlier.

Ogota was waiting for me in his office. Towers of files tottered on the desks in the rooms off the central corridor and typewriters were clattering. Ogota showed me some sheets of paper on which he had written a selection of proverbs for me, and explained that he had sent for a traditional musician who was even now on his way. It took a while to explain that it was stories I was after. I had come across this attitude before, and was coming to the conclusion that proverbs, riddles and poems were considered more 'literary' and were more highly prized than the humble folk tale.

'Stories are available,' Ogota said doubtfully at last, 'but only old people know them. We will go in search.'

The roads in Gambela are long, wide and clogged with tan-coloured dust. In the rainy season, water floods up from the river beds, bringing crocodiles on the hunt into town, but now we were able to pick our way across the stones of a dry wadi and walk up the hill on the far side. Small concrete houses had been built at the top of the slope by the Russian advisers to the Derg, but, like the British Empire, the Communist era was over and the houses were dilapidated now, surrounded by drifts of rubbish.

Ogota dived through a gap in a reed fence, and there we were in an Anuak settlement. Several women were sitting round a collection of jars, one of which was resting on three hearth stones over a fire. A tube from the top ran sideways into a bowl full of a thick white liquid from which rose a pungent smell. Even I could see that this was a home distillery.

'Arak,'[18] said Ogota, in his measured, dignified way, and I couldn't tell if he approved or not.

We found the men we were looking for at the end of a lane in another large open compound. They were sitting on a bench made of felled saplings, taking it in turns to draw smoke through a pipe made from a polished gourd with a long mouthpiece attached to it. Politely, they showed no surprise at my presence, and listened, nodding, as Ogota explained what I wanted. One began to speak at once, and I leaned forward to hold the little tape recorder close. I wanted to look round, to smile at the women and admire the way their huts were built, with a tiny veranda and small mud dyke round each one, but I had learned already that it was important not to distract the speaker, but watch with attention, as if I could understand every word.

'He has been talking about our traditional way of life,' Ogota translated at last. 'Years ago, he wants you to know that this is how we did things. Men lived outside the homestead, and women lived inside it. The women would cook the food and bring it to the men, and approach them walking on their knees. Then they would come back to fetch the dishes, or a boy would be sent to take them back.' The gourd pipe bubbled in the background as he spoke.

'Our tradition is respect, you see. Not only the women knelt when they came to the men, but the boys and girls too approached on their knees. It was a very good thing, because men could get what they needed. But the new generation! They don't respect

---

[18] A strong, aniseed-flavoured spirit.

their parents! If a father calls his child, he just stands there! He doesn't even say, "Yes, sir." Sometimes, he doesn't bother to come at all! You should write all this down to instruct our young people and teach them good manners. Then look what's happened with clothes! Years ago, our people didn't wear clothes, just a few animal skins. Now we all wear these silly clothes, and it's not healthy. Clothes carry diseases. Anyway, they're not necessary.'

The man's speech was punctuated by the regular thud of a pestle in a mortar as a woman pounded maize. The pestle was long and looked heavy. She hoisted it up with a double movement, making a skilful jerk as it reached her shoulders then bringing it down into the shallow wooden bowl with great force. She was very tall, and her arms were the colour of bitter chocolate.

'And there's another thing. We used to live in villages and protect ourselves from our enemies with our "adiang" – they were weapons made of sharpened wood. And we had shields of hippopotamus skins. The hide was so tough you couldn't pierce it with a spear. But now! There are iron weapons, and guns! People are too frightened to have a proper fight in case they kill each other. We used to have revenge feuds. If one person was killed, the killer would be caught and killed, and then his killer, like that. But since the downfall of His Majesty, all that has stopped. Maybe that's a good thing. But nothing's like it was.'

You grumpy old men should get over to the hotel, I thought, and have a chat with Jim. Plenty of common ground there.

People had been coming and going, sitting about and drinking the potent stuff the women dished out to them. I realised that I was in a kind of pub. I asked Ogota if making alcohol was part of traditional culture.

'No, and alcoholism is a very serious problem here.' He drained his own beaker. 'It dates from the colonial period.'

The British, I bet, I thought guiltily.

We set off again, the young Tigrayan Temesgen and I following Ogota through the maze of interlinked compounds, passing rudimentary market areas where a few women were trying to sell small quantities of salt, spices, a few garlic bulbs, onions and cakes of soap. We crossed a wide dry river bed. ('If there is a storm upstream, extreme care must be taken here, Mrs Elizabeth. The water rolls down with great speed and people are washed away.')

At last, Ogota pushed open a door made of a sheet of corrugated iron nailed to a framework of wood. This was the home of an old man who still bore the title Lieutenant from his days as a policeman.

'From the Italian period,' said Ogota. 'He has a pension.'

I couldn't quite do the sums and fit these facts together, since the Italians had left Ethiopia over sixty years earlier, but it was clear that Lieutenant Akwai Gora was indeed very old and comparatively affluent. He was sitting under a tree in an ancient wooden armchair, shiny with use, his gourd pipe hanging from a convenient nail overhead. Two women sat on mats near a fireplace nearby. A baby was feeding from one woman's breast. She lolled back against the roots of the tree and smiled at us. The other woman was peeling mangoes. The baby lost the nipple, sat up, burped, and reached for a piece of mango. He took it and dropped it, rolled it about in the dust, then ate it. I watched this approvingly. No child is healthy who hasn't eaten a peck of dirt, my mother had always said. If you grow up in Gambela, your immune system must need all the training it can get.

A very old deckchair was brought out for me, and I sat down gingerly, but it was sound, and I relaxed into it with gratitude, glad not to be sitting on the ground again.

Ogota explained our mission, and waved at Temesgen to hold the tape recorder to Lieutenant Akwai's lips. I had no idea what to expect, but this first story from Gambela was a wonder, and I retell it frequently to anyone who will listen. Here it is:

After the time of creation, God called the man and all the animals to him, and said to them, 'Come to me early tomorrow, when the morning star appears in the sky. I will give the best gift to the first who arrives.'

Secretly, he said to the buffalo, 'Come first, and I will give the best gift to you.'

The dogs overheard and ran to the man.

'Get up early, be first, and get the best gift.'

The man disguised himself to look like a buffalo.

God said, 'Who are you?'

'I am the foster child of the dogs, brought up by the dogs.'

God gave him spears.

The buffalo came. God said, 'Have you not come already? Who was it then, who came? I have given away the weapons. For you and the other grazing animals, all I have left is horns by which you can protect yourselves.'

And from that time on, the cattle have been subject to the man, who is the ruler, because he has the spear.

It was the mention of putting on a disguise which set my own skin tingling, for this story perfectly mirrors the blessing of Jacob by his father Isaac in Genesis chapter 27. In the Bible story, the blind Isaac wishes to give his blessing to his eldest son, the rough and hairy Esau, but Rebekah, mother of the smoother son, Jacob, overhears this intention, and dresses Jacob with goatskins on his hands and neck. Isaac embraces Jacob, believing him to be Esau, and gives him the blessing of the first-born, making him master of Esau and his heirs forever.

It's fruitless to speculate on the origins of stories, but I can't help it in this instance. Did this one come to Lieutenant Akwai Gora via the Bible, or was it unimaginably old, from the great soup of myth from which the Bible itself derives?

The old man had started his story by explaining that at the beginning of time, man and the animals were the same. They lived together and spoke in the same language. In industrialised societies, animals are either kept for food, eliminated as vermin, or elevated to quasi-human status as pets. A change in sensibility towards animals has altered human relationships with other creatures in modern times, encouraged in part by the green movement and televised wildlife films. But there is a more complex understanding of animals among peoples who are hunters, and who themselves can be hunted as prey. It's hard for us in our sanitised environment to imagine how it feels to be some way down the food chain. From childhood on, we experience bears, lions and tigers as cuddly toys or characters in anodyne story books. People such as the Anuak and Nuer live in close proximity to their cattle. They love them, and put themselves in harm's way to protect them from leopards and lions, who are superior in strength and speed, with formidable powers of camouflage and ambush. Such men respect the animal world, fear and admire it in a way that we have forgotten. I would be reminded of this many times.

Two naked little boys had crept up to listen to the stories. They stood motionless, their mouths open, oblivious to the fringe of flies sucking at their eyes, until they were shouted at to go away.

The Lieutenant was in full swing again, his second story longer than the first, and he needed to pause for deliberation from time to time as he told it.

'It's about the origin of the Anuak chiefs,' Temesgen said, when he had finished.

'Not chiefs. Kings,' corrected Ogota. 'Chiefs are also available.'

A man hid in a tree near where two women were catching fish. The women quarrelled over their catch, and the man called out from the tree to arbitrate. The same thing happened on the following day. The women told the people in the village about the man who had judged their quarrels from a hiding place in the tree. Everyone came down to the river and hid in the bushes to see what would happen. Again the women fished and quarrelled, and again the man called out his opinion. The villagers caught hold of him and took him back to their village.

On the way, he transformed himself into a white bull, then into a black bull, then into a bush with leaves and branches, and finally into a woman before resuming his own form.

He was given a hut to live in, but no food.

'If he is a true magician, he will feed himself,' they said, but they set the chief's daughter to guard him, and prevent him from falling into the fire. They told her to give him water, because he came from the river.

'Where's the mat to cover the water, and where's the stand for the gourd?' the man said. 'I can't drink from an uncovered gourd.'

She brought him a mat and a stand, and he drank. After a few days, she began to give him food.

The people said to her, 'He has drunk your water. You must take him into your hut.'

She did so, but when the morning came, the man had disappeared and returned to the river. The girl showed her father a necklace made of cowries (shells which resemble the female vulva) which he had left under her cow-skin.

'He took you but he didn't pay for you,' the chief said angrily. 'All he has given me is this necklace.'

The girl bore a son. His appetite was so voracious that no food could satisfy him. He grew into a man of gigantic strength and became the king of the Anuak people. No one knew his father's name, so they called him Ony-ya. From that time, the king of the Anuak wears the necklace of cowrie shells when he is crowned. He is called by his mother's name, but the people call him Ony-ya, which means 'the one who comes from the river'.

The importance of this story was clear from the way in which Lieutenant Akwai told it, and this was underlined when, having struggled over the translation with Ogota, we went back to the old man's compound to check that we had got it right. Several other elderly men were sitting with him by this time, and quite heated discussions erupted about one detail of the story or another. This is evident in my notebook, where there are many crossings-out and redraftings.

Ony-ya resembles heroes from many cultures. He is of unknown parentage, his mysterious father having the god-like ability to perform miracles, lay down the law and transform himself into animal form (like Zeus who also changes into the shape of a bull). He shares with Rostam and Sohrab, the ancient champions of Iran, an insatiable appetite and spectacular growth.

There is a clear boundary between religious and secular stories and writings in our culture, where tampering with 'scripture' causes upset. This story was one of a few told to me in Ethiopia which I sensed was quasi-religious.

There were shouts outside the fence, and someone called out for the Lieutenant to come. The guard at a nearby compound had drunk so much arak that he appeared to be on the point of death. Remedies were discussed, including tea, coffee and soup.

Ogota seemed uninterested in the outcome, and led me away.

Our next stop was the prison, where the governor was reputed to know good stories. The prison didn't look particularly secure to me. A metal gate was set into a breeze-block wall with broken bottles stuck on top, which surrounded a large compound. In the middle of this was a chest-high, flimsy wooden fence. There appeared to be twenty or thirty prisoners inside this rudimentary stockade. They flocked to the fence when we appeared, and hung their arms down over it, devouring us with their eyes. Their police guards sat in a row on the veranda, yawning. Some bright objects hung from a board. I couldn't see them clearly.

'Cultural decorations,' said Ogota.

'Jewellery,' said Temesgen. 'The prisoners thread beads to sell.'

The prison governor was not inspired to start telling stories, which didn't surprise me, and we went on our way.

❖

It was blisteringly hot.

'You have come at a bad season,' people kept telling me. 'Everything will be green when the rains have come.'

It was not the heat, though, that made our hours of translation difficult, but Ogota's English. This was sometimes clear, but at other times almost impenetrable.

'The trickster Achok blindfolded Lerro who is not present at this time, and told him some other thing far from that place,' he said the next afternoon, as we sat on the hotel veranda, my pen faltering as I wondered whether there was any point in writing this down.

I established after a while that by 'blindfolded' Ogota meant 'tricked'. But as this difficult session proceeded, I saw that

Ogota's thoughts were far away and he was speaking at random. His thick glasses obscured his eyes, and he became more and more silent. After a long pause, he sighed heavily.

'My child died two weeks ago.'

I thought I couldn't have heard correctly.

'Just, she died. I was in Addis Ababa so I was not watchful. I was not expecting it.'

I didn't know how to respond. Fifty years earlier, the death of my own small brother had dealt a wound to our family whose scar was still tender to the touch. I was mortified that this poor man had been trailing around with me when he should have been with his family, and I said so. He seemed surprised.

'No, it was a girl. Two and a half years. It was anaemia. The mother has a problem of ignorance. I was not there, and no understanding of the situation was possible.'

My father had had to go away during Alastair's last illness. I had a sudden memory of creeping out of bed and hanging over the banisters, drawn by the desperation in my mother's voice as she stood in the cold hall downstairs and spoke to my father on the telephone.

I let the silence go on, not knowing what to say.

'How many children do you have?' I asked at last.

'Now, five. Four are sons, aged fourteen, thirteen, eleven and eight. The last is a daughter, aged six. I have sent my oldest son to the village to look after the cattle.'

I urged Ogota to go home, but he would have none of it.

I had asked Ogota several times if we could find women to tell us stories. He hadn't liked the suggestion, but had agreed to try, and a while later we were settled with a group of women on cow-skins in the shade of a high reed fence in the compound of a well-made mud house, which was built up on a platform with patterns gouged out of its walls.

A baby girl, four or five months old, was feeding, working her fist on her mother's breast, her eyes half closed in bliss. I felt myself soften at the distant memory of my own babies.

She pulled away from the nipple and made the gooing, mamama noises that constitute the universal language of babies, while her mother smiled down at her and made the same noises back. I glanced at Ogota, but he had wrapped himself in dignity and his face gave nothing away.

The baby's familiar behaviour struck me so forcibly because the toddlers nearby, who were only a few months older, belonged already to a world so different from that of my own children. Crusts of snot clung to their nostrils, they embarked unimpeded on exploratory forays around the compound, and wore no clothes except for a string or two of beads. There were no nappies, potties, high chairs, toys and prams in their world. There were no smacks, and no tantrums. They moved among the group of women, who were grooming each other's hair with porcupine quills, exploring and learning, petted by all.

Ogota was getting nowhere in his request for stories. In fact, the woman were starting to mock him. Others were arriving. They crammed together on the cow hides, and the more sternly Ogota spoke to them, the more they stared at me and laughed, until a kind of hysteria took hold, and they held on to each other, gasping with hilarity.

I noticed that only the oldest woman was naked, except for a short loincloth. Most of the others wore polyester night dresses, sleeveless, long and loose to the calf. I had found these dresses startling at first, as I associated them with bedtime, but I was beginning to admire them. They looked practical, cheap and durable, and hung elegantly on the women's tall, slender bodies.

'Stories are not available,' Ogota said, giving up. 'They are making jokes.'

He looked disconsolate.

'There are a few which you haven't translated for me yet, from the last few days,' I said. 'Let's find somewhere pleasant to sit and work on them.'

He gave a rare smile, showing the gap where his four lower incisors had been removed, something I had noticed in other Anuak men, and we set off on another hot, exhausting walk.

This time, it was worth the effort, because we came out on the banks of the Baro, a sweeping stretch of life-giving water drifting north towards its junction with the Nile. It was fringed with old mango trees, whose glossy leaves cast a delicious shade.

People were busy here. Women were washing clothes and filling plastic jerry cans with water, hoisting them onto their heads then walking with perfect poise up the steep banks. Cattle were coming down to drink, wading into the water until it covered their knees and lowering their creamy heads to suck it in. Ogota waved vaguely along the bank and said that his house was nearby.

'Are you flooded sometimes, when the river is high?'

'Yes, and crocodiles enter my compound. They are malicious.'

It was here, by the river, that the ghostly British presence could be felt. The remains of looming warehouses were crumbling away among the trees. The legend 'PWD 1949' was inscribed in a section of disintegrating concrete rendering.[19]

---

[19] The initials PWD were stamped on public buildings all over the British Empire. They stand for Public Works Department.

Ogota led me through a fence into the warehouse compound. Most of the gaunt buildings were decayed beyond repair, the roofs tipping off and the brick walls caving in, but Ogota aimed for the only one that looked reasonably sound. In it was the office of the Gambela People's Liberation Front (GPLF). An old man was sitting inside the high-ceilinged room. He seemed to be expecting us and was nervous, but he embarked on a story at once.

I sat beside him, holding the tape recorder, which he eyed with suspicion. He waved his arms as he spoke. His wrists were as thin as billiard cues and his fingers as long and slim as a parrot's tail feathers. The skin on the back of his hands was a rich brown-black.

Achok and Lerro were cousins. Achok was a trickster but Lerro was a fool. Achok complained that both their mothers were old and useless, and should be killed. Lerro agreed. Achok took his mother across the river and hid her. Then he beat a log with a stick. Lerro heard him, thought he was killing his mother, went off, and killed his own.

Now Lerro had no one to cook for him, but Achok went secretly to his mother every day and she fed him. Lerro became suspicious, followed Achok and found him with his mother. He was enraged at the trick that Achok had played, so he killed Achok's mother and laid her body out on her cow-skin, putting a piece of dry porridge into each of her hands.

Achok came, thought his mother was sleeping, took the food from her hands and ate it. Then he noticed that she was dead. He tied her body into a cow-skin, as if for burial, and took it to the river.

'We must throw the bodies of both our mothers into the water,' he told Lerro.

While they quarrelled about who should go first, two girls

walked past. One was pretty, but the other was blind in one eye. Achok called out to them, 'Please fetch some water for these old women to drink.'

The girls fetched water and offered it to the corpse of Achok's mother, but the corpse didn't reply.

'She's deaf. Push her,' said Achok.

The girls pushed the body, which fell over.

'Ai-ee! You've killed my mother!' shrieked Achok. 'Now in compensation you must marry us.'

Achok took the pretty girl, and made Lerro marry the half-blind one. Achok's wife understood her husband's nature and refused to work, but Lerro's wife worked hard for him. Achok forced Lerro to exchange wives, but now it was Lerro's ex-wife who refused to work for Achok, while Achok's first wife worked hard for Lerro. Disgusted, Achok gave both girls to Lerro to be his wives. He wandered away and became a pariah, rejected by all because of his tricks.

I couldn't help expressing shock at the cruelty of this story. Humour, of course, seldom travels well. Perhaps I simply failed to get the joke. I realised later as I mulled it over that Achok was a member of a world-wide brotherhood of tricksters, including the mischievous Maori god Maui, Coyote in North America, Reynard the fox in Europe, Anansi the spider in West Africa, and our old friend Brer Rabbit. These lords of misrule bring chaos and disorder but in some mythologies they also initiate creation. Mavericks are staples of all forms of literature. They break taboos and provoke outrage. They live on the edge of society and fascinate us.

I had been told other stories about Achok and his vicious practical jokes. In one of these he persuades his uncle to catch the 'okok' (a spiny fish) by throwing himself into the river so that the okok's spines will stick into his flesh, to be picked off later. In another, he persuades his sidekick Lerro that honey can only be collected if the hunter is tied to a tree and allows the bees to sting him. Lerro falls for it, every time. Perhaps the very point of these stories is their extreme outrageousness. At least Achok is usually punished for his behaviour, either by banishment, or by suffering general disapproval.

Achok was not the only recurring trickster character in the stories I heard in Gambela. The wily Agenga, was a gentler proposition altogether. He was cousin to Aleka Gebrehana, or Nasruddin, rather than Maui or Coyote. His chief aim was to prove his superior cunning, particularly in contests with the king.

The king claims that no one can give him orders, but Agenga wants to prove him wrong. He goes to the king's compound and puts his shoes on the roof of the shelter, under which the king usually sits. The king arrives, and while everyone is sitting together, Agenga tries to reach his shoes. He doesn't dare stand in the king's presence, so he kneels, and stretches up his arms as far as he can.

The king asks him what he's doing.

'I'm trying to reach my shoes, but they're too high up.'

Innocently, the king stands up, takes the shoes off the roof and gives them to Agenga.

'You said that no one could give you orders,' Agenga says triumphantly, 'but I've made you do something for me.'

I don't know anything about the status of shoes in Anuak culture, but since biblical times they have been objects of desecration in the Middle East,[20] and in modern times the hurling

---

[20] 'Moab is my washpot; over Edom will I cast out my shoe; over Philistia will I triumph.' Psalm 108: 9.

of shoes at George W. Bush by the Iraqi journalist Muntadar al-Zaidi was a gross insult. Agenga's triumph in making the king not only sit underneath his shoes, but pick them up and hand them to him, seems to represents a victory indeed.

There was a curious coda to this story. When he had finished relating it, the storyteller said, matter-of-factly, 'This man was disturbed during the Derg and he was sent to Cuba and became mad there.'

It was in Gambela, more than any other place, that references to the modern world crept into traditional stories. I liked this attempt to give Agenga the flesh-and-blood presence of a real historical personage. It is the device used by storytellers the world over when relating urban myths.

In another Agenga story, the king genially challenges Agenga to get the better of him. 'If you can fool me, I'll give you my gun,' he says, bringing another touch of modernity to the story. The king then goes off to hunt for honey in the forest, whistling for the honey bird who will show him where the bees have made their hive. Agenga slips after him, then imitates the honey bird's call so that the king will follow him. But instead of leading him to a cache of honey, Agenga takes the king to the termite hills, where he falls into a thorn bush. 'I fooled you! Give me your gun,' says Agenga. The king demands a hearing before the elders, who find in Agenga's favour, and so the trickster gets the gun.

❖

The old man in the GPLF office embarked on another story, but Ogota cut him off in mid-stream.

'Achok story was good,' he said as we left the compound, stepping over the roots of a vast mango tree. 'The second one is bad. He confuses things. He was in my class at elementary school. Always a silly fellow.'

A whoop and a crash in the trees overhead made me look up. A colobus monkey in its black and white livery was hurling itself from branch to branch in death-defying leaps. I exclaimed with pleasure at the sight of it.

'There were many of them in the past,' remarked Ogota, 'but we used to shoot them.'

'Why?'

'To feed the leopard in the SPLA compound.'

'The SPLA?'

'Sudan People's Liberation Army. But the leopard killed a sheep and the captain shot it. After that we used the monkeys for target practice, but then we saw that only two were left and so we let them go. Now they are increasing. See? There are six. But take care, Mrs Elizabeth. They are mischievous and will take pleasure in urinating on you.'

Ogota's casual remarks had given me a glimpse into the seething cauldron of Ethiopian politics. The ambition of the post-Derg government had been to pacify the aspirations of the many ethnic groups within Ethiopia's historic borders by giving them some autonomy within a federation, hoping that, like the cantons of Switzerland, they would co-exist peacefully. But Switzerland is not surrounded by chaotic and violent states like Somalia, Sudan and Eritrea. The Swiss are not forced to compete with each other for access to water and pasturage, they have not suffered profound political upheavals in the recent past, they are not plagued by malaria, recurring famines and a huge arsenal of guns, and the population is literate and affluent. If a European comparison can be made, it should rather be with Yugoslavia in the last days of Tito.

Since my last visit to Gambela in 1997, the cauldron has boiled over. Fighting between the Nuer and Anuak brought in the Ethiopian army, who carried out brutal reprisals, principally on the Anuak, causing a reverse flow of refugees into the nightmare of Sudan.

Unimaginable changes are coming to Gambela, as they are to many of the regions of Ethiopia. Oil has been discovered. Indian and Chinese companies are buying up great swathes of land for mineral exploitation and farming. Under the assaults of ruthless development, the old stories will be more vulnerable than ever.

Ogota's laconic mention of the Sudan People's Liberation Army had made me even more curious about his own life, and he then divulged that he had been second in command of the Gambela People's Liberation Front during the time of the Derg, and had had to go into exile in Sudan. For five years he had worked as a waiter in the Hilton in Khartoum. (I could just hear him saying, 'No, Mister, fresh fruit is not available.') He had returned at last, and worked as a teacher before being appointed to run the Gambela Cultural Bureau.

'What was the best time of your life?' I asked him.

'Majesty time. I was at secondary school. I had many friends.'

❖

There was a dearth of bottled water in Gambela as the trucks supplying it had become bogged down somewhere on the road. The heat made thirst a constant worry. My options were to drink Coca-Cola, or resort to the brown, cloudy water in the bottle by my bed, which, the hotel barman assured me, had been boiled.

I've never liked sweet, fizzy drinks, and after a bottle or two I was sickened and twitchy with caffeine. There was no choice but to drink the hotel's offering.

I explained my problem the next morning to a senior government official, Okok Ojulo, as we sat in his air-conditioned office. Like a conjuror, he produced a bottle of Ambo water, the product of Ethiopia's own spa springs, and though it was salty with minerals, I gulped it down gratefully.

Okok Ojulo had started up from his desk as we walked in. He towered over us, a Nelson's column of a man. His actions were slow and thoughtful, as if, aware of his size and strength, he was used to taking care in case he blundered into something that might break.

'So you are from Britain or America?' he began.

'Britain.'

'I was in Birmingham for two years, then in Reading.'

I tried, but failed, to picture this Anuak giant striding down a Berkshire street.

He grasped the point of my project at once, and told me a charming tale of a man out hunting with his dog. It featured, as walk-on parts, some wild pigs, a waterbuck, a lion and a python, but sounded more like the true account of an actual expedition.

As he talked, I tried to puzzle out why his office was so bright, and realised that it was because the windows had been washed.

Later that day, as I trod back to my room, stirring the brittle leaves underfoot in the dusty garden, I found myself dwelling on Okok Ojulo's sparkling windows. I sat down on my bed and looked round, noticing the patina of dirt on everything: the crust of brown on the light switch, smears on the floor and sticky rings on the table, while the porcelain in the bathroom, visible through the open door, had clearly not been white for a long time.

It occurred to me that cleanliness is as much a cultural

concept as anything else. The Anuak compounds I had been in that day had been swept to such perfection that not a stray leaf or twig marred the expanse of beaten earth, while the walls of the round mud houses had been finished off with almost voluptuous smoothness. Cleaning meant sweeping here, rather than scrubbing. People in Gambela were not accustomed to shiny surfaces. They did not have (and would not have been able to afford) detergents and cleaning fluids. Their pots were made of rough earthenware, their furniture consisted of woven mats and low stools. Metal for domestic use is a relatively new material, and glass and plastic even newer. I knew that if I had suddenly found myself in the role of Anuak housewife, my casual attitude to fallen leaves and spills of wood ash would have put me in disgrace.

I was concerned that so far I had only collected stories from Anuak people (chiefly, I suspected, Ogota's friends), but that evening my first Nuer storytellers kindly agreed to come to the hotel bar to meet me.

I sat and waited for them. The TV in the bar was blaring out the crackling music of a popular Addis Ababa band, creating the wrong atmosphere for the telling of old stories. Outside it was very dark. There was no moon, and the lamps dotted about the hotel garden were dim, but there was enough light to make out the sets of white concrete seats and tables, and I settled at one of these to wait for them.

Rhamsi Shwoll and Gatwich Pal Monchek came silently through the trees at last, startling me. They sat down opposite me. A light flickered on in one of the nearby buildings and though it was still half dark I could just make out their faces. Raised bands of scars ran across Rhamsi Shwoll's head, and delicate whorls of dots patterned his cheeks.

'You do not have any scars?' I asked Gatwich Pal.

He explained that the scarification of boys, a traditional rite of passage for the Nuer, was going out of fashion, and his parents had decided against it.

We talked for a while. Rhamsi Shwoll spoke excellent English. He was in charge of the malaria programme in Gambela, a vital job, as a particularly deadly strain of the disease was plaguing the region. There had been an outbreak at Gibbo, and twenty-one people had so far died. Rhamsi was in the process of organising a team to take charge. As he described the symptoms I felt my toes curl. I had been careful to put on long socks to cover my bare feet, and had squirted myself all over with jungle juice.

Rhamsi Shwoll turned out to be a talented storyteller, and his tale of the sisters Ngap and Nyakwiy, the forest through which they walk and the shape-shifting man who pursues them, still brings me up in goose pimples.

There were three sisters. The eldest was married to a cannibal and lived far away in the forest. The second, Ngap, was beautiful, but lazy and selfish, and the parents' favourite. Nyakwiy, the youngest, was patient and kind-hearted, though her parents were cruel to her, using her back as a table on which to cut up their fish.

Nyakwiy went to visit her oldest sister. She was happy there, helping with the children. When at last she set off for home, her brother-in-law ran on ahead, and changed himself into a tree hung with fruits.

'Nyakwiy! Come and taste my fruit!'

'No. I have eaten all I need at my dear sister's house.'

He ran on and turned himself into a dish of dried fish and butter, with a spoon beside it.

'Are you not hungry? Taste me!'

'I have been well fed. I need nothing more.'

Ngap was jealous when she heard of Nyakwiy's happy visit. She too went to stay with the oldest sister. But she behaved badly, ate greedily and shouted at the children.

When she went home, her brother-in-law ran on ahead and once more changed himself into a tree.

'Ngap! Come and taste my fruit!'

'I will because I've been staying with a dirty cannibal, and eating dirty things.'

She ate the fruit and put some in her pocket.

Again he ran on and once more became a tasty dish.

'Come and eat me, Ngap!'

'I will. I come from a bad man's house and I am hungry.'

Her brother-in-law fell upon her and ate her, leaving only her head.

When Ngap did not return, her parents assumed that she had been killed by a wild animal. They arranged a marriage for Nyakwiy. On the wedding day, as everyone celebrated, the head of Ngap rolled in amongst them. It sang this song:

> *If I was alive, and I hadn't been eaten*
> *I would now be the bride, instead of my sister.*
> *I would have had cows, many colourful cows*
> *And my family would have been rich.*
> *Catch me now and bury me,*
> *So that I can die, once and for all.*

Perhaps it was the darkness all around us, or some rustling in the tree overhead, or the scream of an unknown animal down by the river, or even the velvety softness of Rhamsi's voice, but I felt a shiver run through me as he finished his story.

'You see,' he said, in a more practical tone, 'the meaning of the story is that children must be treated equally. The one the parents loved most, she was not well brought up and she died because of her stupidity.'

But it wasn't the moral of this tale which had captivated me. I wanted to know more about the brother-in-law. 'A cannibalistic man' Rhamsi had called him. 'Some kind of magician.' I tried out 'ogre' as a translation, but ogres are clumsy brutes with no powers of shape-shifting, and though they are cannibals, they lack the finesse of this villain, who rewards good behaviour and punishes bad manners. There is, too, in this story the classic fairy-tale motif of being devoured, a metaphor for sex. Ngap's brother-in-law (an incestuous touch, here) invites her to eat him; then, when she agrees, eats her himself to her own destruction.

We talked for a while about bringing up children. The elderly Anuak men had been much preoccupied with a decline in standards of behaviour. I thought of my own sons, who, without being told, had picked up a sense that one could not say certain words in front of Grandma or Granny.

But it was another instance of bad manners which Rhamsi Shwoll now wanted to discuss.

'There was a British man who wrote about us, the Nuer people,' he said. 'Evans-Pritchard. He said things about us which were not true. Do you know his book, Mrs Elizabeth?'[21]

I had heard of the eminent anthropologist, but knew little about him and had not read his books on the Nuer. Was the great man prone to blunders, after all? My husband, David, had once met him. Evans-Pritchard had recounted an incident

---

[21] E.E. Evans-Pritchard's studies of the Nuer (*The Nuer*, *Nuer Religion* and *Kinship and Religion among the Nuer*) were published in the 1940s and 1950s and are classics of social anthropology.

during his time in Syria, when Britain and France, two rival empires, were jockeying for position. A touchy French official had accused Evans-Pritchard of fomenting trouble among the Alawites. As a friendly gesture, Evans-Pritchard had sent the man a present – a valuable Arab knife chased with silver – but the Frenchman had been insulted, concluding that he was being invited to commit suicide. Would Evans-Pritchard have been surprised that modern Nuer people, educated and sophisticated, were reading his account of their culture and being angered by it? In the 1930s, when he was doing his fieldwork in the Sudan, he could hardly have foreseen the huge social changes that would affect the peoples about whom he had written.

It was the turn of Gatwich Pal to tell a story.

At the time of creation God was very near to the people, but he was constantly pestered with conflicting requests.

'I want to sleep late today,' one would say. 'Please let the sun rise a little later.'

So God would hold back the sun.

Another would complain, 'I need the light. Why did you delay the sunrise?'

Later in the day, a woman might be walking in the heat, and she would say, 'Please God, this heat is tiring me. Let the sun set.'

And God would make it set right away.

But another would say, 'I need to finish my journey in the daylight! Raise the sun up a little bit for me, until I reach home.'

God became confused and didn't know what to do. And then the fox, who was clever, said to him, 'God, you are too near the people. You are God, not a human being, and you need to keep your place. Stay away, and only give us some blessing from time to time. Your creation is your creation and you should not be disturbed.'

So the sun remains as it is. Setting and rising, day by day.

I liked this story. I detected an echo from the third chapter of Genesis, the evocation of a golden age, when the Lord God walked with Adam in the Garden of Eden in the cool of the day. It made me think, too, of the mechanistic prayer of the Evangelical world in which I had grown up, which had consisted, more often than not, of a shopping list of requests to the Almighty. I used to wonder, when the superintendent of our Sunday school prayed for fine weather for the annual expedition to the seaside, whether my mother, a keen gardener might not be praying for rain at the same time. I would speculate on which of them would win. This story, in all its absurdity, struck me as a profound comment on the shallowness of so many prayers.

My plane was not due to fly until the following afternoon. Ogota and Temesgen called for me as usual in the morning, but I could see that I had exhausted them with my voracious demand for stories. I was tired too, fed up with the heat, sick of sweet sodas and dodgy water and longing for a proper drink. We decided with mutual relief that I had enough stories for the time being, and walked back down towards the river.

A crowd had gathered to watch a crane which was slowly progressing across the bridge.

'You see how fine the bridge is?' said Temesgen. 'It was built by the Derg. And the airstrip. They did everything for these people.'

But Ogota frowned.

'New bridge? New airstrip? It is all for facilitating troop movement as a means of oppression.'

Nearby a part of the bank had been fenced off. Inside it was a square-hulled iron ship beached above the water line. It looked ancient, a rusting wreck, posing for a star role in a film of *The*

African Queen, but the head of Jim, the Geordie engineer popped up from inside, and I heard the sound of others working in its metallic guts.

'See that thing?' Jim called out, pointing to the crane. 'She's going to lift my new engine into her. Come and take a look.'

The new engine, painted a startling yellow, was sitting on the bank. It looked incongruously smart beside the rusting hulk of the old ship, but Jim seemed happy enough. He stood with his stomach billowing over his belt while the crane came to a stop beside us and its hooks were lowered into the ship to lift out the old engine.

'First time I saw this thing,' Jim said, 'I was coming over the bridge into Gambela, and someone said, "There's your ship." Couldn't believe him. But when the river rises after the rains, she'll float off fine. She'll be chugging up and down for years yet.'

'A very good old steamer,' said Ogota.

'Not a steamer. Hasn't ever run on steam. She's a motorised vessel.'

No one understood the difference but he didn't mind.

Dug-out canoes, some piled high with green and yellow mangoes, were darting about on the water, their occupants paddling as close in as they could to watch the operation. A short way upstream two naked men were fishing, one with a net and the other with a line.

'See that mass of green stuff out there?' said Jim, pointing to a raft of leaves on the water. 'Water hyacinth. Terrible stuff. Nearly choked Lake Victoria to death. We've just invented a machine back in Thurrock to chop it all up. It'll make good compost if nothing else.'

I murmured a compliment.

'That's us. If it floats, we can fix it.'

The crane was a having hard time of it, as the ropes kept slipping. When one of them snapped, we realised that the operation would take some time and walked back into town. I fetched my bags, said goodbye to Ogota and Temesgen, and went into the airline office. This was a mud house built up on a stone platform with double doors that were fully opened to give ventilation. The roof was of corrugated iron and the wide eaves provided a good width of shade. It had been put up in the days before air conditioning, when people had known how to make buildings in hot places tolerably comfortable. It looked so old that I wondered if it had once been used by those British administrators, in their knee-high khaki socks and canvas shirts. The crackling radio in the corner seemed incongruous.

The flight was delayed. The plane had set off that morning from Dessie, in the highlands, and cloud had forced it to turn back. Air travel in Ethiopia is closer to the real world of weather and mountains and floods than it is in Europe. Schedules work erratically and bookings are notional. It is common to be thrown off a flight because someone more important wants one's seat. At last, after a long wait, there was a bustle outside, and I had to dash out in order not to miss the transport to the airport, a white 4 x 4, already crammed with people, including an airline official carrying the radio.

There was no sign of a plane when we reached the airstrip. The official opened the 'terminal', a corrugated iron shed, and went inside. We heard him shout and bang about, and he emerged a moment later with a long snake held at arms' length on a stick. Someone forced its mouth open to milk the venom from its fangs, then picked it up by the tail and flung it, writhing, into the undergrowth behind the shed.

Politely, the passengers asked about me and my business in

Gambela, and as the plane still hadn't arrived, begged me to tell some stories. I was just getting stuck into Ngap and Nyakwiy when a speck appeared in the sky and moments later the plane landed.

It was blissful to be released from horrid lurchings in the air and emerge into the cool, tangy atmosphere of Addis Ababa. I drank clean water till I thought I would burst, and wallowed in a hot shower.

'I'm getting soft in my old age,' I thought.

❖ 6 ❖

THE MAGIC COW IN
THE FOREST

My first visit to Gambela had been too short to gather enough stories for the two books of readers, and I hadn't managed to meet any storytellers from the Komo, Majangir and Opo peoples. Another visit was needed, and six months later I was on my way back to the far south-west of Ethiopia. This time, I was hitching my little wagon to a larger British Council expedition. Dirije, the diminutive driver, was to take a party of six of us in the British Council Land Rover, including Michael Ambatchew in the invaluable role of translator and facilitator.

Instead of swooping over the country in one long flight, we took two days over the journey, slowly dropping down off the cool highlands into the heat below. Dirije suffered as his European passengers opened the windows to let the air rush in and cool us down. He considered this unhealthy. Terrified of draughts, he piled on sweaters and an anorak, tying the hood as close as he could under his chin, muttering with disapproval whenever a window was adjusted. As the temperature rose into the 30s and then the 40s centigrade, sweat coursed down his thin face, and he took to emitting pointed hollow coughs.

My spirits lifted as, on the second day, the road wound downhill through thickly wooded country. I'd become increasingly depressed by the devastation the landscape had suffered in the three decades since I'd first travelled in Ethiopia: acacia forests reduced to arid wasteland, fields once thick with lilies grazed to nothing by cattle, 'national parks' unguarded and denuded of all their game. Here, at any rate, a little wilderness seemed to be left. As we reached the bottom of the escarpment and began to drive along the bank of a fast-flowing river, whose chocolate-coloured water was thick with silt from the eroding highlands, we passed a man, the first person we had seen for many miles. He was immensely tall and walked with a grace I had rarely seen, his slender limbs seeming only loosely jointed, and his skin a dark purple-brown. Highland Ethiopia was now truly behind and above us. We were back in the land of the Nuer and the Anuak.

Dirije must have been half dead with heat exhaustion when we pulled up at last outside the familiar Ethiopia Hotel. Ogota was waiting for us there. We greeted each other like old friends. I had never seen him so animated before. He clasped my hand in greeting and his face, usually so calm and dignified, dissolved into a grin. I beamed back at him. We would discover more gems of stories, I knew. I couldn't wait to start.

Supper that night was steak à la Bismarck, a favourite dish in government hotels. It consisted of a chunk of beef topped with a fried egg, mercifully accompanied by vegetables. As we lingered over a nightcap in the hotel bar, a man came to sit beside us. I barely looked at him until, after a while, he leaned across and said to me, 'Mrs Elizabeth, you don't know who I am?'

I hadn't recognised his face, which had filled out with an unhealthy puffiness since I had last seen him, but I recognised his soft, musical voice. It had made my hair stand on end as he had conjured up for me, in the creepy darkness of the garden, the cannibalistic ogre who had eaten the foolish Ngap.

'Rhamsi Shwoll!'

'Yes. You do remember. Have you brought my books?'

I smiled, pleased with myself.

'Yes. I have a big box of books to donate to the library here.'

He scowled.

'Not those. The books for me. I have been waiting for them for so long. Evans-Pritchard.'

'We talked about him. I remember. Did you ask me to send you his books?'

'Yes, yes! I have been waiting all this time!'

'I am very sorry, Ato Rhamsi.' I was contrite. 'I won't hide the truth from you. I forgot.'

He smiled unexpectedly.

'If you forgot I forgive you.'

He began to talk about the malaria programme and everyone listened in, fascinated. There had been a recent outbreak in an outlying district and twenty-one people had already died. He needed to get a team together to eradicate the mosquitoes.

At that moment, he felt a mosquito brush against his hand. He killed it deftly and held it up.

'My enemy. The female anopheles. Every forty-eight hours she will suck your blood, and deposit her infection in your veins.'

We all shuddered and began to pull ineffectually at our sleeves, trying to stretch them down our arms, then fished out bottles of repellent and slapped it on.

'You told me some wonderful stories last time I was here,' I began hopefully, 'but I need some more to make up my readers. I was hoping . . .'

'Hope is a good breakfast but a bad dinner,' he said, and stood up to go. He was unsteady on his feet and I realised that he had spent a long evening in the bar. 'And anyway, time is golden.' He began to laugh, but it was a melancholy sound, and I heard him, still laughing, as he walked away through the trees in the garden.

❖

My first task the next day was to revisit some of the storytellers I had met before to check that the versions of their tales that I had written for the books were accurate and met with their approval. We called first on the old Lieutenant. Months had passed since I had last stepped in through that bulging straw fence, but it seemed that I had been away for only a few hours. The same chair was in the same place under the tree and the same group of women were sitting on mats smoking their water pipes. Then I saw that the baby, whose babbling had so charmed me, was now a sturdy crawler. Time had passed, after all.

Ogota decided that memories needed refreshing, and taking my tape recorder he began to play back the stories which the Lieutenant had told us. At the sound of his own voice emerging from the machine, he jumped with surprise, and those within earshot laughed and leaned forward to listen. I glanced at my watch, concerned at the time this was clearly going to take, but everyone was enjoying the tape so much that I hadn't the heart to hurry things along. Eventually, Ogota began to explain the point of our visit. Taking the English versions I had made, he translated them back into Anuak, sentence by sentence. There were smiles and nods, but when it came to the story of the man from the river, who had become the first Anuak king, smiles faded and eyes narrowed as everyone concentrated.

An old man, who had settled himself commandingly in the Lieutenant's usual chair, was the only one who had a serious objection, which he emphasised with raps of his stick on the ground.

'He is saying that his clan history is not sufficiently represented,' Ogota said with a dismissive sweep of his hand. 'You can ignore him, Mrs Elizabeth.'

I let out my breath with relief. I felt as if I'd passed an exam.

'You have stayed all this time only in the city,' Ogota said as we left the Lieutenant's compound. 'This afternoon we will go out, into the rural area.'

I liked this idea, but I could almost read the thought bubble above Dirije's head.

'Government people, always wanting me to drive them around for their own schemes. What's this post fellow about now?'

'There are some security problems in the locality,' Ogota said, ignoring Dirije. 'It is customary to travel in the company of a gun. I will fetch my Kalashnikov.'

As the Land Rover's engine idled outside Ogota's house, several of his friends jumped into the back, arousing Dirije's suspicions even more, but I was glad of their company as we set out along the bumpy road. There had been an incident a year earlier, when four policemen and two airline officials had been murdered by shifta,[22] Ogota told me, pointing out the spot as we passed it. I looked uneasily at the head-high grasses waving at the side of the road, which screened whatever might lie beyond.

'Are there wild animals here?' I asked, imagining a lion or two bounding out of the grass and in through the window of the Land Rover, which I was keeping open in defiance of Dirije's muttered reproaches.

'Lions, yes. Elephants also.'

The road was a strip of tawny earth and stones between the walls of grass. A troop of baboons appeared ahead. Unbothered by the car, they ambled in front of us for a while, then turned away to disappear off the road. Once we passed a man walking

[22] Bandits.

quickly with a bundle of sticks on his head, and a little later I caught sight of a small, pot-bellied child, naked except for a string of beads around his neck, but he moved back into the sheltering grass and I wondered if I had imagined him.

Dirije let out a squeal and skidded to a halt. A python was lying on the road. Its back was bent at a sharp angle and it was clearly dead. Ogota, Michael and I got out of the Land Rover and stood looking down at it.

There is no creature at once so repellent and fascinating as a snake. Years earlier, I had been bitten in the foot by a sea snake in the South China Sea. Its poison had nearly done for me, and the pain is something I will never forget. But I had, oddly, been less afraid of snakes afterwards, and had learned to admire their beauty. There wasn't much beauty in this sad creature now. It was over three metres long, and quite fat. It lay inert, its once glossy skin dull with dust, but we felt conscious of the mysterious power it still exerted. Michael pointed out the curious claw that protruded from the underside of its body (the vestigial remains of a leg, apparently, which the male python uses to tickle his mate during courtship). I bent down to feel it. It was sharp. I let my fingers brush the creature's back in a stroke, almost expecting it to spring back to life. We left it to be dealt with by nature's undertakers, and drove on.

This area, Ogota told me, had been commandeered by the Derg during the 1980s for the resettlement of people from the famine-stricken highlands, but though they had left misery behind them, their troubles were only beginning. Poverty and famine had pursued them. Malaria must have accounted for many. Those who could had straggled back home to the cooler lands above. We were beginning to pass the homes of the ones who had remained: small houses edging the road beyond which cotton fields stretched away into the distance.

We stopped for refreshment at a roadside bar. Ogota disappeared into a village of grass huts while I sat on a stool to wait. A sad-eyed girl served me with sweet warm fizz.

'Where are you from?' I asked her.

'Wollo.'[23]

'Are your parents still there?'

'They are dead. I am here for working.'

'How old are you?'

'Fourteen.'

There is no protection for young girls forced to work in bars. Prostitution was this child's inevitable fate.

Ogota returned with three lanky men. They sat down on a bench under the eaves of the bar. A crowd had collected, and shyness overtook them, but one by one they cleared their throats and talked into the tape recorder, recounting more exploits of the wily trickster Agenga and his efforts to fool his king.

Ogota, sitting in the front seat of the Land Rover, nursing his Kalashnikov between his knees, entertained us with gruesome titbits of local news.

'Here, on this road. Three people, killed a month past by gunfire. Their hands and feet were bound with ropes. Up till now, the killers have not been found.'

Burnt-out buildings stretched away from the road. They had been put up, Ogota said, by the UN to house refugees from the endless conflict in the Sudan, but were empty now and had been torched.

---

[23] A highland region in north-eastern Ethiopia.

We arrived at Itang, a small town downstream from Gambela on the Baro river.

'We will go and report ourselves to the authorities,' said Ogota, unfolding his long limbs as he climbed out of the Land Rover with his curiously stiff movement. We followed him into a police station where an official behind a desk wrote our names down and studied them before granting us permission to proceed.

Itang was clearly a settler town. Its small, square, chikka houses, roofed in corrugated iron, were set behind wooden verandas in the Highland style. Some shops displayed bright cloths and scarves. In others, scarlet and blue plastic buckets rose in tottering piles beside displays of enamel pots and plates stencilled with flowers which, I was certain, would be stamped underneath with the words 'Made in China'.

Ogota left us at a crossroads and went off in search of a storyteller. He returned a moment or two later with his hand under the elbow of a young man who walked with the hesitant step of the blind.

'We will take his stories beside the water,' Ogota announced, guiding the young man into the car. 'The steamer also is there. You will remember it, from before when you were here.'

It was pleasant beside the river. Ogota directed Dirije towards a group of fine old fig trees. In their generous shade, men were carving out a canoe from a colossal log, their adzes ringing on the hard wood. Beyond them the river was slipping by, its toffee-coloured surface knotted with eddies and whirlpools.

'Too fast and deep for crocs,' I thought hopefully.

The 'steamer' was tied up at the water's edge and people were busy loading goods into its rusting hull. The mental camera shutter, which in this snapshot age we all carry in our heads, clicked away as I watched the scene. I felt as if I had blundered into the film set for a Conrad novel, or was leafing through an album of photographs taken by a traveller from a bygone age. Only the bright yellow paint of the boat's new engine, which took up most of the afterdeck, seemed out of place.

The storyteller was taken to sit on the roots of one of the trees and Michael, Ogota and I stood around him. A large crowd had collected by now and had begun to edge closer, those nearest pushed inwards by pressure from behind. The blind man seemed unsure what to do, and Michael, standing in front of him, could not coax him to begin. I watched, knowing there was nothing I could do to help. It was all wrong – the crowd, the sense of rush, the pressure on this bewildered man. There had been no chance to establish a rapport with him. I had barely had time to ask his name. It was no surprise that his few muttered stories were short and inconsequential. In his situation, I would have been hard pressed to think of anything to say at all.

❖

That night, back in the hotel in Gambela, I was woken by the sound of a gunshot and, my head full of Ogota's alarming stories of murders on the road, I couldn't get back to sleep. I gave up trying at last and got up as the sky was just beginning to lighten. Not wishing to waste the coolness of early morning, I decided to go for a walk.

The sun had barely risen when I walked out through the hotel's gates, but the wide, dusty streets beyond were already crowded with people. I walked towards the river. Several naked men were bathing in an inlet. Too embarrassed to go near them, I crossed the bridge and began to walk along a grove of mango trees on the far side.

'Cuba! Cuba!' shouted a troop of children, running along beside me.

The history of Ethiopia can be deduced from the begging cries of children. They must have been calling out 'Ferenji' to any foreigner since the early Middle Ages. In the 1960s, they had shouted '*Senora, caramella*,' harking back no doubt to the Italian occupation during the Second World War. Now, in the highlands, children would call out 'You! You! Give me pen!' or sometimes, 'What is your name?' which seemed to reflect the first lessons in their English primer. The bonds which the Derg had formed with sympathetic Communist countries had left their echo in the call of 'Cuba'. In one remote town I had detected the passage of a frustrated American Peace Corps volunteer when the kids called out, 'Fuck you!'

I ran into Rhamsi Shwoll on my way back to the hotel. He invited me to see his house and meet his wife. I followed him through a corrugated iron door set in a brushwood fence. About twenty long-horned cows, their smooth pink-brown and white sides glossy with health, stood waiting to be taken to pasture. Several women were washing pots in a corner of the compound which was so perfectly swept that not a single dead leaf littered the surface of the ground. The round house in the middle of the fenced space was a masterpiece of smoothed mud, its thick thatch trimmed in a fancy pattern at the edge. Rhamsi ducked his head to go inside and came out again with a chair. His little daughter, pretty in her yellow frock, bounced out after him and leaned against him as we sat and talked.

'I am not well,' Rhamsi said with a sigh. 'I am bitter in my heart. No one is concerned with the health of the people. They are suffering so much from malaria, but how can I go to help them without transportation? No one will provide us with fuel.'

He talked on about the frustration of his work while other children and young men appeared and stood about to listen, but although Rhamsi called and called, his wife would not emerge.

'She is not ready for guests,' Rhamsi said. 'She is not dressed.'

I realised that it was still barely seven o'clock in the morning, and felt embarrassed. It was far too early to make social calls. The evidence of a meticulous housewife was all around me in this perfectly kept home. I could well imagine that Rhamsi's wife would be reluctant to appear with sleepy dust in her eyes and her hair in tangles.

I was relieved to hear, when I got back to the hotel for breakfast, that the shot in the night had only come from the hotel's night watchman, scaring off a would-be thief.

❖

I had asked Ogota many times for women storytellers, and he had clearly been thinking this over, because when he came to pick me up in the middle of the afternoon, he announced that we were going out to a village where some women would be waiting for us. Michael was busy with the other members of the British Council team, so Dirije, Ogota and I set out on our own.

The road out of Gambela was bad, and Ogota, sitting in the front seat, directed Dirije down one lane after another with imperious waves, while the tracks grew narrower until the long grasses were sweeping the Land Rover's sides. A frown settled on Dirije's face, growing deeper, until at last he drew up at the edge of a deep rut.

'Ato Ogota. Cannot go. Puncture soon. No turn.'

Ogota urged him on. We were nearly there. The path would

widen out. There was no problem. Unwillingly, Dirije let off the brake and soldiered on.

Ogota allowed Dirije to pull up at last, where the track forked. I followed him down an almost hidden footpath, the soft golden grasses so close and so high that they met over my head and we were walking in a luminous penumbra.

I'm here, I told myself, now, in this strange and distant place, and I felt a stab of delight, a lurch of the heart, like the moment when one leaps from the diving board and soars through the air towards the water, or when the horse beneath one gathers itself for the jump.

The feeling was momentary, because almost at once we emerged from the thicket of grass into an open area, and the track, beaten hard by the passage of bare feet, wound through small patches of planted maize. Brushwood fences signalled the edge of the village, and once we were past them we came out into a large open space shaded by a magnificent fig tree. A group of women were sitting on its raised roots. They wore short loincloths wrapped around their hips, and beads around their necks, and their hair was cropped closely to their heads.

Ogota greeted them rather testily, I thought, and I remembered the last time he had tried to find women storytellers, and how they had mocked him. I looked around at the ring of faces, afraid that the same thing might happen, but then the realisation came that this was his own village and these were his own people, many no doubt closely related to him. It was only later that he told me I had been right. I wished that he had introduced me to his wife, but he had chosen not to, and I suspected that the encounter might have embarrassed him.

Chairs were brought from a nearby hut and we were invited to sit down. Dirije picked his up and moved it some distance away.

He watched the proceedings with a wrinkled nose and puckered forehead, looking both anxious and disapproving. I remembered how he had nervously fingered his cross in Assayita. He seemed to think that I had once again dragged him into the clutches of dangerous savages.

Ogota, on his dignity, was lecturing the women, encouraging them to tell stories, but they were beginning to giggle in embarrassment. I saw that I was too far away from them, sitting formally on the chair I had been given, so I kicked off my sandals, walked over to the tree and sat down on the mat spread out there, in the middle of the group.

'I want to talk to them myself, Ato Ogota. Will you translate for me?'

I didn't know what I was going to say until that moment, and then I saw that only one trick would work. I would have to set the ball rolling by telling a story myself.

Why did I choose Little Red Riding Hood? I don't know. I was well into the tale of the lonely child walking through the forest with a basket of food for her granny before I knew what I was doing.

They listened with rapt attention, and then, as so often after the telling of a story, the question came.

'What does the story mean?'

How many treatises have been written on Little Red Riding Hood? The story has been picked over by Freudians, German romantic patriots and a multitude of others.[24] I swallowed, thinking rapidly. Then, looking around at this open space, at the cluster of small houses surrounded by the tall grass that hid so effectively the entrance to this village, I saw that there was no

---

[24] See *From the Beast to the Blonde* by Marina Warner (Chatto & Windus, 1994).

need to go into the dark history of werewolves, or Freudian fears of sexuality. When the story was first told, it must have been in places similar to this, in small settlements surrounded by forest in which lurked bears and wolves, just as lions, leopards and hyenas prowled not far from this remote village. The simplest meaning of all, forgotten now in the tameness of Europe, was still relevant here.

'The story means,' I said, 'that it's dangerous for young girls to walk in the forest alone, because there are wild animals that might attack them.'

There were intakes of breath and murmurs of assent.

'And,' I went on, putting a slightly more daring toe into the whirlpool of interpretation, 'girls should be warned not to speak to strangers who try to give them presents and lead them away from the path because who knows what will happen to them?'

This went down well too. I saw that the ice had been broken. The women began consulting each other, pointing first towards this older woman, then towards that one, until at last someone cleared her throat and began, her voice high-pitched and cracked. I shuffled across the mat towards her, my tape recorder in my hand, and she made room for me, not minding that I held the machine to her lips.

Her story was a long one, and as she spoke I enjoyed myself looking around at the ever-growing crowd of women and small children congregated under the tree.

The women were of all ages, from young girls up to grand-mothers. They talked quietly to each other as the story pro-gressed, passing round a hubble-bubble pipe made from a gourd. Burning charcoal glowed in the metal saucer balanced on top, on which strong-smelling plugs of tobacco were balanced. The smoke must have been harsh because most women burst out in fits of coughing on the first draw. I began to notice that many chests rattled and that the infants, too, seemed affected. One small boy, naked except for a string of black and white beads round his neck, lay passively in his mother's arms ignoring her dangling nipple, his eyes half shut, and when he coughed his little body arched in pain. I thought of Ogota's daughter, who had died only a few months earlier. I worried for a moment about infection. TB was a problem here, I knew.

A young woman sat directly in front of me. A pattern of faint raised dots radiated out from her spine around her waist. The sun, dancing through the broad leaves of the tree overhead, brought out the delicate coppery sheen on her shoulder blades and the deep purple shadows under her arms. I was aware of the smell of her body. It was good and homely, the natural odour of naked skin unpolluted by lotions, soaps and deodorants, free of clothing impregnated with sweat and other bodily emissions.

The story ended at last and another hand was held out to take the recorder. The session was away now. I didn't have to pretend to listen. It was late in the afternoon and the colours were deepening in the low sunlight. Motes of dust danced off the thatch of the huts close by. The air was tinged with the scent of smoke from cooking fires. The only sounds were the coughing of the smokers, the occasional cry of a baby and the husky voice of the storyteller.

I found my eyes drawn to the path leading out of the village. Every now and then more women appeared, walking into the clearing with water pots balanced on their heads. Soon the men would no doubt come, driving the cattle home from the grazing lands for the night. For some reason, the path fascinated me. It was the way out of here, down to the open space where the Land Rover was waiting. Dirije would negotiate the vehicle along the rough lane until we met the dirt road back to Gambela. Here we would join the tarmac highway along which we would soon be rolling back to Addis Ababa. And from there all routes were open to the continents beyond. Our early ancestors – the 'first man' and 'first woman' who had featured in so many stories – had come from this corner of the world. They had chosen to walk the path and leave, pushing ever further away to conquer new lands. They must have taken stories with them. Did remnants of those ancient stories survive in the strange similarities of tales from Europe, North America, India, China and even Australia?

Dirije was shifting on his chair and giving me meaningful looks. I waited until the next story was finished, then with the greatest reluctance got to my feet. We would have to go before darkness fell when it would have been dangerous to be out on the road. As I walked back down the path through the long grasses I felt as if I was leaving the real world behind.

Ogota and I worked on the translations of the stories that evening. Only one of them fitted into my preconceived idea of a true 'teret', and I was disappointed with the other three. But as I mulled them over, I came to see how much they revealed about these women's lives.

In the first and most brutal tale, a woman and her husband roam the forest with their children at the time of a famine. They are looking for food. The woman finds a dead animal and thanks God for her good fortune, but the man claims that he was the one who had found it, and declares his intention to eat all the meat without sharing any with his wife and children. He even refuses to allow her to fetch water from a well that she has also discovered, saying he will go himself. He counts the pieces of meat and threatens to punish her if any are missing when he returns. Filled with suspicion, he walks backwards towards the well to make sure she isn't taking any meat, but he falls into it. The women and children throw earth in on him to bury him, and eat the meat together.

In a second, very short, story, a father refuses to let a girl marry, saying that she must spend her life with him to care for him. She secretly meets a man from another place, marries him and becomes pregnant. She presents her father with the fait accompli, and he has no choice but to accept her marriage.

The third story consists mainly of a song, and is uncannily reminiscent of Little Red Riding Hood. A girl is delayed by the chores her grandmother has set her and cannot set out with the other young people who are visiting another village. Forced to walk through the forest alone, she meets a lion. She sings to him:

> *Lion, when you eat me, eat only my back,*
> *Leaving my front behind for Alang's sons.*
> *Alang's sons are playing the drum.*
> *Oguta Nyimaro is one of them.*
> *He cannot play the drum,*
> *so he did not go out to play.*
> *He will be eaten by the lion today.*
> *Go and eat him instead of me.*

The lion agrees, the girl safely reaches the neighbouring village and her husband and his friends spear it.

When the story ended, the narrator added: 'When the lion fell, it said, "Please, spear me again."'

He replied, 'Why? If you had eaten my wife, would you have eaten her again?'

The meaning of the girl's song is: eat my back, not my front, so that my husband will recognise my face.'

(I have to confess I didn't understand this, and the translation is probably faulty, but I offer it to you anyway.)

It was the first and longest story, a true 'teret', that gripped me most. I have found echoes of it again and again in other fairy tales from all around the world. The narrator's name was Ajulo Ogogn.

It begins, like so many tales, with a wicked stepmother. Wishing to rid herself of her predecessor's two children, she refuses to feed them alongside her own. The children's real mother had foreseen this problem, and before she had died had told her children to go into the forest where they would find a source of food. The children do so. They find a magical cow who gives them food, and they return in secret every day having eaten well.

Their stepbrother wants to discover the source of their food and insists on accompanying them one day into the forest. They try to put him off, but he uncovers their secret and betrays them to his mother.

Determined to put a stop to this, the stepmother tells her husband that she is pregnant, and needs meat. She badgers him until he fetches the cow from the forest and tries to slaughter it, but he finds the task impossible. The stepmother threatens to kill the two children unless the cow dies, and hearing this the cow consents to be slaughtered. It then proves impossible to skin the carcase, but at the threat to kill the children, the carcase gives up its skin. In the same way, the meat can only be cooked, and the pots removed from the fire, after the stepmother threatens death to the children.

The stepmother has won, and eats the meat. The children now have no source of food. They run away into the forest. The story now loses sight of one child and focuses on the older boy. He arrives at a village and falls in love with the chief's daughter.

She returns his love, and gives him a car so that he can easily drive back and forth to visit her. A hostile group want to kill the chief and attack the village during the night. The boy rushes to the chief's defence. The chief wants to know the identity of the stranger who has helped him. He calls a meeting and asks each of his daughters to point out her husband or her lover.

By this time, our hero is suffering from smallpox and is covered with flies, but the chief's daughter still claims him as her lover. The smallpox puts the chief off his daughter's suitor and he refuses to let her marry him. At this, the chief's head begins to swell.

'Your head will only reduce in size if you let me marry this man,' the daughter says.

The chief is forced to agree, and the couple are duly married.

It was the car, of course, that leaped out at me from this story. I should have been used, by now, to modern embellishments into what I still thought of as 'traditional' tales, but this one seemed particularly striking. The car made the story 'real', as if it had happened last week to a friend of a friend.

If you know your folk stories from around the world, you will make connections at once with other tales where the dead mother provides for her child from beyond the grave. A fish stands in for the fairy godmother in the Chinese version of Cinderella, first written down in the ninth century. A hazel sapling planted on the mother's grave does the job in the Grimm Brothers' tale, while in the Scottish story the agent is Rashin Coatie, a magical calf, who feeds and cares for the despised surviving daughter.

The wicked stepmother, of course, is a stock character in folk fiction the world over. My Aunt Nancy was so influenced by the portrayal of stepmothers in her Andrew Lang fairy tale books that she became convinced that her own blameless if emotionally cool – and impeccably Scottish – stepmother had sinister designs. She thought up dreadful insults to hurl at her, the worst being, 'You're – you're *English!*'

❖

The day still hadn't ended. Back in Gambela, Michael had linked up with Temesgen, Ogota's Tigrayan assistant whom I remembered from my previous visit, and they had arranged for us to make an evening call on a settlement of the Komo people, a relatively small group who speak a Nilo-Saharan language, are predominately Muslim and have communities both in Ethiopia and the Sudan. I could find out nothing more about them.

I hadn't been to this part of Gambela before. The houses were square, unlike the round huts of the Nuer and Anuak, and they stood in a maze of inter-connected compounds. As Temesgen and Michael peered around in the gathering dusk, trying to find the right house, a one-legged man with unkempt hair and wild eyes raged at us and shook his fist. I would have expected Dirije to be alarmed, but he only snorted, 'A graduate of the school of Mengistu Haile Mariam.'

Our Komo contact's house was at the far end of the settlement, and as we walked past the intervening houses women, squatting over the open fires where they were cooking the evening meal, looked up in surprise, then politely looked away again.

We found our man at last. His name was Sambo Likasa Haya, and he invited us into his house.

It was still very hot. The small room, dimly lit from a central light bulb, was stifling and airless, and after a moment or two, by mutual consent, we moved outside to sit on stools and catch the slight stirring of air which the breeze of evening was bringing our way. It should have been a delightful occasion. Sambo was an enthusiastic storyteller and I could see that Michael, Temesgen and Dirije were enjoying themselves, but I felt jarred to be back in this male-dominated world after the sweetness of my afternoon with the women. Once again, I was rushing too fast, being forced to abandon each session before it reached maturity.

Sambo's stories included a raunchy tale, not much more than a joke, about a bush-rat who wheedles his way into the good graces of a woman and ends up seducing her. I understood, when I heard it, why the men had burst out laughing. My favourite, though, was a love story with a tragic ending which could have formed the basis of a novel.

A widow, who had three grown daughters, fell in love with a man whose thigh had been broken so that he walked with a limp. His name was Shigosh. Knowing that her daughters would disapprove, the widow would go to a tree near where she lived and call him to her in a song with the chorus: 'Shigosh! Shigosh! Come to me!' Shigosh would hurry to meet her, singing in reply, 'Yes, I'm coming, yes I'm coming.' (In the rhythm of the Komo words the limp can be heard.) They would make love in secret under the tree.

The three daughters were furious to discover that their mother had a lover. They took bark from a certain tree and dipped it in water to make it slippery, then they laid it on the path. They climbed into the tree and the youngest, whose voice resembled her mother's, sang, 'Shigosh! Shigosh! Come to me!' and Shigosh sang back, 'My wife! My wife! Yes, I'm coming, yes I'm coming.' He rushed along the path towards the tree, slipped on the bark and lay helpless while the three girls jumped down from the tree and beat him to death. Then they fled across the river to hide from their mother up another big tree, and they called out,

'Mother, Mother, your lover is waiting for you.'

The widow came running and found her lover's body already covered with flies. Then she saw her daughters hiding in the tree on the far side of the river. She tried to coax them to come down, promising not to hurt them, but they refused to move. At last she took an axe and cut down the tree. The trunk fell like a bridge across the river. The two oldest ran across it to safety, but the trunk landed on the thigh of the youngest one and broke the bone, so that for the rest of her life she walked with a limp, just like the man she had killed.

I was touched by this unusual story. Physical differences from the ideal norm – all kinds of disability, in fact – are often associated with wickedness or stupidity in stories, and not only in Ethiopia. The dwarf Rumpelstiltskin, Jack's giant at the top of the beanstalk, misshapen ogres and trolls, witches with hooked noses and pointed chins, Long John Silver with his peg leg, Captain Hook with his missing hand – the list of fairy-tale and pantomime villains is endless, while Hollywood has instilled in us the belief that heroes must be handsome and heroines 'as good as they are beautiful'. But in this story the disabled hero is a man so attractive that a woman risks everything to have him as her lover.

Michael Ambatchew, aware that we had, through Ogota's contacts, focussed too closely on Anuak stories, had bustled about in his efficient way to find storytellers from other communities, and the next morning we did a round of offices, finding ourselves at last seated at a table with two members of the Majangir community.

This small group was semi-nomadic until a few decades ago. They farmed by planting crops on virgin land, moving on when the soil was depleted to a new area every few years. They supplemented their diet with snared fish and game. Their language, like Komo, is of the Surmic group, but they told their stories in Amharic.

'This is a really funny one,' Michael said later, as we worked on the English translations. 'It's about this mischievous guy, Lave, who thinks it would be a good joke to persuade his friend Wallock to kill his mother because the old hags cause them so much trouble.'

I couldn't find the words to respond. In spite of my attempts to see this tale in the wider context of tricksterism, I really couldn't abide it. I failed to understand why this story, identical except for the change of names to the Anuak tale of Achok and Lero, was so popular and universal. I never found a satisfactory answer.

Like many of my favourites, the second Majangir story begins in the golden age, 'when the world began', and man and the animals were friends and spoke with each other.

One day, the first men quarrel with the dog, and need someone to resolve their argument. They go up to the sky, a holy place where the spirits live. They see fire for the first time, and they like the beautiful warm thing. The dog lingers after the men leave, picks up a burning branch with her tail and runs off with it, bringing fire to the earth for the first time.

Some while later, the men and the dog are hunting together. They catch a buffalo, and want to offer some meat to the spirits. They put a piece of succulent fat into the dog's mouth and tell her to carry the offering for them. But the juice from the fat runs down the dog's throat and after a while she succumbs to temptation and eats it. She runs back to the men.

'Have you taken the meat to the spirits?' they ask her. She tries to answer but can only put back her ears and howl. The men use the fire she has brought from the sky and learn to roast the meat, but from that time on the dog cannot talk to them. The spirits have taken away her voice because she has eaten the meat that was meant for them.

There is a similar, well-known story from the Pacific Northwest of America, in which Coyote steals fire from malevolent spirits who live on the top of a mountain and brings it down to the people below. There is no return visit in this American story, and no punishment for the thief, but the parallels over such a huge geographical distance are remarkable.

The Komo and Majangir groups are small, but the Opo language and culture must be one of the most endangered of any in Ethiopia. Statistics in these matters are always suspect, but some estimate the numbers of Opo at around 3,500.

'There is only one Opo in Gambela,' Ogota told us. 'We are lucky if we can find him.'

We ran him to earth outside the Women's Bureau, where some seats were set out in the shade of a huge mango tree. His name was Duwal Pul.

Duwal's best story had a modern ring to it.

A group of landlords compete to produce the biggest harvest. One of the landlords is so cruel that if he loses the annual competition he executes some of his serfs. The serfs have had enough of this and plot to get rid of him. They invite him to their village. The landlord rides on his donkey with his serf host beside him, but a cord has been tied across the road. The donkey stumbles and the landlord is thrown. Now that he is on foot, he is more vulnerable. The serf leads him a long way round through the forest, where an ostrich, who has been trained by the villagers to attack strangers, kicks him to death.

I guessed that this story would have found favour with the authorities through the Derg years, but I wondered if more traditional Opo tales had been forgotten.

Living in scattered communities, their social networks based on clan structures, small groups such as the Komo, Majangir and Opo must be reeling from the impact of the modern world which has penetrated even this region with devastating consequences. They have had to establish settled villages and abandon their old semi-nomadic way of life. Their territories have been carved up between administrative regions. They find themselves living in close proximity with incomers whose ways are strange. Their languages are threatened. Most have abandoned their old religion and become Evangelical Christians.

❖

We still had too few stories from the Nuer, and that afternoon drove out to a Nuer village on the outskirts of Gambela. This consisted of neat round houses plastered, like Rhamsi Shwoll's, with perfect smoothness, and standing without dividing fences around an attractive compound. At one end was a long building with mud walls. A kind of clerestory ran the length of the building under the low eaves. The thatched roof was steeply pitched. A group of women in Red Cross uniforms were sitting on a mat under a tree, reading to each other. Another group, some way away, were gently beating a drum and singing. The atmosphere was peaceful, earnest and purposeful.

My religious antennae are finely tuned. They should be. In the seventeenth century my ancestors were fiery Covenanters. My father was a member of the Christian Brethren, and the director of a worldwide Evangelical organisation. My mother was a Presbyterian. My great-grandmother was a Jehovah's Witness. My older sister's husband was the nephew of an Anglican archbishop. My second sister's husband is a Lutheran pastor. My husband's brother is an army padre. One of my cousins is married to a Seventh Day Adventist. There are Methodists, Baptists, Sandemanians and one rebellious Roman Catholic dotted about my family tree, along with numerous missionaries and theologians. I could therefore tell at a sniff that this was a missionary village, and so it proved to be.

A year earlier, at the start of another story-collecting trip to Ethiopia, I had been sitting over my breakfast in an Addis Ababa hotel spreading honey on to a newly baked bread roll, unable to avoid overhearing the conversation at the next table. An American missionary had fixed a young Ethiopian with his piercingly blue eyes and was putting the squeeze on him.

'Now you tell me that you love Jesus, and that's simply wonderful, because I want you to know that he loves you. And it's to tell the people of your beautiful country of Jesus's wonderful love that I have come.'

I was surprised at the anger which swept through me as I silently prayed, 'Oh God, please give this man diarrhoea and send him back to whatever horrible place he comes from.'

I must have recognised in the young's man face an expression of the feelings I had so often struggled with in my early youth, when I had sat through gospel meetings trying not to meet the eye of the preacher as he held out his arms and implored us, sinners one and all, to come forward and accept the Lord Jesus Christ as our own personal saviour. It wasn't that I hadn't given it my best shot. I had tried, many times, to achieve conversion, squeezing my eyes shut and hoping that this time, at last, I would be saved, redeemed, transformed, born again. But it had never seemed real. It hadn't stuck. I only ever felt guilty and inadequate, out on the edge, excluded from the holy circle of the saved.

Now, though, having met so many of the new Evangelical Christians, I realised that this knee-jerk reaction would not do. I would have to think things through more carefully. It was stupid to be sentimental and protective of the old order in rural Ethiopia. The modern world, with its technology, weaponry, IT, and all the rest of it was roaring through the country like an express train. The spears and shields of the old warriors were as helpless against the Kalashnikovs and rocket launchers of the modern era as the old beliefs were proving to be against the zeal of Christian and Muslim missionaries. In any case, it would be foolish to romanticise the traditional ways. Life had been brutish for many people in the old days: subject to arbitrary government, at the mercy of slavers, with the constant fear of famine and disease, men and women (but particularly women) had few chances to improve their lot. Both Christianity and Islam were giving people mental, social and spiritual footholds as they puzzled out a route from their old ways of life into the challenging modern world. This process is as old as history and as unstoppable as the spread of flood water.

After all, I told myself, if the Romans hadn't brought Christianity in their wake when they invaded Britain, we might still be waving mistletoe about and depositing strangled bodies in peat bogs – a state of affairs no doubt regretted by some.

A handsome, friendly man was coming forward to greet us with his hand outstretched. This was the Reverend James Duot Dol, the pastor of this Seventh Day Adventist community. He had assembled a group of men to meet us. They were perched on a simple framework of branches, the struts hammered into the ground in the shade of a clump of trees and worn to a lustrous smoothness by hands and bottoms. They stood up to greet Ogota, Michael and me, unfolding their long bodies, and we shook a forest of hands. Then we perched alongside them on the branches, and silence fell.

'I have started to write a story down for you,' Pastor James began, in his careful English, his tongue rolling round the vowels and caressing the consonants in the soft, Nuer way. He looked down at his piece of paper. 'I was not able to finish it, owing to many interruptions.'

I assured him that the tape recorder would do the work, that we would like them only to tell the stories, in Nuer if they wished, or in Amharic, if they felt uncomfortable in English.

For a moment I was afraid that I'd shown a lack of appreciation of the effort the pastor had made. But he took the recorder and read his story into it, laying the paper down with relief when he had come to the end of what he had written, and giving the rest from memory.

'And that is why the hyena is a cripple up to now,' he finished triumphantly, beaming at me. 'It is because he swallowed the spoon.'

Silence had fallen. The row of men perched on the logs were shuffling their feet and looking at the ground. Ogota was underlining and re-underlining words in his notebook, as was his habit at times of uncertainty. Michael, having lapsed as he always did into Amharic, was urging the others to have a go.

A few did so, but the session did not light up until a man called John took the tape recorder.

'The is the story of the fox,' he said, and began.

The fox needs help to clear his field for planting. He goes to the dog.

'Have you invited my enemy, the leopard?' says the dog. 'If he is there he will kill me.'

'No,' says the fox, but then he goes straight off to invite the leopard, who agrees to come.

Next the fox asks the sheep to come and help him.

'Will my enemy, the hyena, be there?'

'No,' says the fox, and at once proceeds to invite the hyena.

The fox then begs the hen for help, and assures her that her enemy, the hawk will not be there. But of course, he also invites the hawk.

The animals ask the fox what he will give them as a reward, and he promises them a good meal. All arrive on the appointed day to do the work. In spite of their fears, the dog, the sheep and the hen work alongside their enemies, the leopard, the hyena and the hawk. They work hard, and when they want to rest they ask the fox for the food he has promised.

'Later,' he keeps saying. 'When the work is done.'

He holds them off until his field is harvested and they are all exhausted.

'Give us what you promised,' they say.

'I'm tired of your complaints,' says the fox. 'Look around you and find what you want to eat.'

So the leopard, the hyena and the hawk fall upon the dog, the sheep and the hen and eat them.

Uneasy laughter followed this story, and I noticed for the first time that one of the men sitting on the branches was not a Nuer but a man from the highlands.

'Does the story have a meaning? Is there a moral?' I asked.

Michael nudged me to be quiet. The stranger leaned forward.

'Yes, what's the moral? What's the meaning of the story?' he asked, frowning.

John smiled back at him innocently.

'It is to explain the proverb, "the working of the fox's field."'

'No. The meaning. What is the meaning?'

'Just a proverb, as I told you.'

The Nuer men were holding their laughter in with increasing difficulty, their shoulders shaking.

'What's going on?' I whispered to Michael.

'That guy, he's Tigrayan,' he hissed back at me.

I have to confess, I had not been listening with much attention. I'd been looking round and drinking in the prettiness of the scene: the thatched houses set on the bare swept ground, the women clustered round their drum, a few cows lipping over some grass inside a thorn fence. But there was a new tension in the men sitting around me on the branches. What had the story been about? Why was it so important?

The answer came at once. Divide and rule, I thought. The fox makes the other animals work for him, and consolidates his power by setting them against each other. John's story was not, as I'd assumed, a mild animal fable but a political allegory with a subversive message for modern Ethiopia. Faced with its power and the laughter of the listeners, there was nothing the Tigrayan could do but stalk away.

Fables have been used for such purposes throughout history. They pierce the complacency of the men in power and can inflict wounds against which governments are unable to protect themselves. The fables of Phaedrus are famous for their subtle criticisms of authority figures. In the Bible, Nathan the prophet uses a fable to trap King David into confessing his guilt over his affair with Bathsheba.

The session was clearly over.

'Enough. It is enough,' Ogota said, shutting his notebook and sliding his biro back into the breast pocket of his shirt.

He looked exhausted, and I saw that he was old and had a backache and was dying to go home. And suddenly, I was too.

❖ 7 ❖

MIGHTY QUEENS IN SIDAMA
AND WOLAYITA

Ethiopia is blessed with a string of glorious lakes which mark the course of the Great Rift Valley, one of the most spectacular faults on the earth's crust. Its northernmost manifestation is the Bekaa valley in Lebanon: the River Jordan, the Dead Sea and the Red Sea mark its course. Volcanoes smoke along its edge as it cleaves its way down through Africa, and the lakes which have formed in its southerly cracks are some of the deepest in the world. It peters out finally in Mozambique.

The most popular lake for weekenders from Addis Ababa is Langano, some two hundred kilometres south of Addis Ababa. Its waters are so heavy with minerals that bilharzia[25]is not a problem. I used to love camping on its shore in the 1960s. The fizzy feeling that Addis Ababa's high altitude induced in me would bubble out of my veins by the time I'd reached the water's edge, and I would become pleasantly comatose, able to sleep the long nights through.

Robin and Merril, the kind British friends with whom I'd been staying in Addis Ababa, had the use of a house on Langano's shores. They offered me a weekend's R & R in between story-collecting trips and I leaped at the chance.

---

[25] A water-borne disease caused by a parasitic worm which infects many lakes in Ethiopia.

I had expected changes to the landscape on the long drive south, but was unprepared for the devastation all around. The last time I had driven this way, decades earlier, acacia forests had stretched for miles on both sides of the road, the spiny twigs of the flat-topped trees meeting over the tarmac, so that one drove in a dappled green shade. Monkeys chattered in the branches and an occasional panic-stricken antelope ran foolishly on in front of the car. I had had to wait once for a straggle of secretary birds to strut from one side of the road to other. In the early morning, a python might be basking on the warm tarmac.

The trees had gone, along with the animals which had lived in them. Only their stumps stood above the dusty ground. The charcoal burners had consumed almost every last piece of standing wood.

There's no call for self-righteousness when contemplating the degradation of the environment by hard-up Africans trying to make a living. As I write this, I'm looking out of my study window into Richmond Park. Forty years ago, when I first walked the park, partridges would whirr up under my feet and skylarks hovered overhead. One could start a hare from its form. The influx of dogs has seen off the hares and the ground-nesting birds. The venison, harvested during the annual cull of deer, can no longer be labelled organic because of the pollution of dog faeces, at least a hundred tons of which are deposited annually on the fragile acid soil. The amount of traffic on the through roads has increased to the point where they carry as many cars as an urban dual carriageway. The ancient oak trees have fallen sick. An aeroplane descending towards Heathrow passes overhead every two minutes.

I was woken the next morning out of a restorative sleep by a scrabbling on the corrugated iron roof overhead, and emerged yawning into the first light of day to see a flock of pink-breasted pigeons take off and wheel away over the toffee-coloured water of the lake. The sun was rising above the hills on the far shore, splashing everything with fast-changing colours. Although the animals had gone, it was comforting to see the great variety of birds that remained. Within a few minutes, I had observed a flock of egrets, a pair of pelicans, a fishing cormorant and a little thing decked in iridescent blue and scarlet feathers. Later, six fish eagles were at work on the water.

Ethiopia is justly famous for its bird life. An astonishing 830 species have been recorded, and there are more than 20 endemic birds, found nowhere else in the world. Many avian visitors fly in from Europe on their annual migration south. They picked their route well, because unlike the hunters of southern Europe who slaughter anything that flies, Ethiopians do not hunt wild birds for food. The birds of Ethiopia have attracted a secondary migration of twitchers. They can be observed in hotels and national parks, binoculars at the ready. The ones I have met seem to be mostly in their fifties and sixties. They know their Abyssinian salty flycatcher from their Sidama long-clawed lark (which is more than I do) but seem strangely unaware of the humans that cross their sight lines.

Every compound in Ethiopia comes complete with a 'zabaniya', or watchman, and this one was no exception. He walked up to say hello to me while I was watching the feathered flurries on the lake and sat down for a chat. He spoke English of sorts, picked up after years of associating with foreigners. It was a good deal better than my Amharic, anyway.

I told him that many years earlier I'd often come to Langano to camp beside the lake. There were no designated sites then, just the wild open shore. Little boys used to come and ask for empty tins.

'They would say "korkoro, korkoro",'[26] I said.

He nodded.

'I am too say "korkoro, korkoro". I come to ferenji, ask for tin. They give me and I sell to some man and he give me money for my food.'

'Where was your village? Where did you live?'

'No, I am living here and there. My mother died when I am small, small,' (he put his hand down to indicate a toddler's size) 'and my father dead also. Just another mother look after me.'

'She was your relative?'

'Not relative. Another mother. I am getting for tins some money and I give to the mother for food.'

I had a sudden memory of little boys jumping around naked in the water, mock-fighting with their spears, showing off to attract my attention, then begging for tins. He seemed to read my thoughts.

'For clothes I have nothing, only a little cloth one ferenji give me. I tie here,' (he tapped his shoulder), 'and it come just to here.' (He pointed to his knee.)

'Some of the boys had spears.'

'Yes, I have my spear.'

'Did you hunt with it?'

'For fish. I am catching fish and taking to sell and then I am pay for my school. Up to sixth grade.'

I nodded, impressed.

'Then I come here for guard. Some people come sometimes before, break all the glass, come into the house, but when I am sleeping here, no more will come.'

I was remembering something else.

---

[26] Tin can in Amharic.

'The women used to come down to the fetch water from the lake,' I said.

I could see them in my mind's eye. They had worn colourful bead halters round their necks and leather aprons oversewn with cowry shells. Heavy brass bracelets had been clipped round their arms.

'They had very nice necklaces.'

'Jewellery. Yes.' He was nodding, and I could see he was remembering too. 'Not now. They don't like them now. You can see in the market sometimes is there.'

I remarked on how the women's clothing had changed.

'Mengistu, he make them put on the ferenji dress. At first they don't like it. But then they do. And now they don't like the old one. Old-fashion is now, you see.'

'They would come down to the water's edge and fill their big pots.'

'Yes!' He leaned forward and mimicked a woman carrying a pot on her back. 'But they see ferenjis here and they don't like. Ferenjis take photo.'

I examined my conscience but it was clear. I had never tried to photograph the women, though I hadn't understood how much they had disliked it.

We fell silent, both of us looking out over the lake. Then he shook his head, and laid one hand on the side of his face.

'Ai-ee! Thirty years ago! I a little boy. Maybe you give for me tin.'

I told him that I was collecting stories. He seemed excited by the idea, and said that his twelve-year-old daughter knew many because she had been told them in school. She would come later, when school was out, and tell me some.

That afternoon young Meskerem duly arrived. I looked at this sweet-faced child with interest. Her grandmothers had no doubt walked barefoot in their leather aprons to fetch their water from the lake. Her father had scrambled through a solitary childhood living on his wits, putting himself with admirable determination through years of school. She was wearing a smart school uniform and plastic shoes and she carried a bundle of books under her arm. Her fresh young skin glowed with health. She was shy and spoke her story in a whisper, while her father translated from Amharic into English.

It was now that one mystery was solved. The story of the bull's placenta, which had been and would be almost the first story I was told anywhere in the country, was indeed in an Amharic primer, and I might as well give it here.

An ostrich, who owns a cow, and a lion, who owns a bull, live together. They take it in turns to lead the animals out to graze. One day, the lion notices that the ostrich's cow is about to give birth. Although it's the ostrich's turn to look after the animals, he volunteers to do it, and tells the ostrich he can rest.

Out in the field the cow gives birth to a calf. The lion takes the placenta and stuffs it into the anus of his bull. Then he takes the animals home, and claims that the bull had given birth to the calf, which consequently belongs to him.

The ostrich objects to this nonsense, and calls a council of animals. All are frightened of the lion, and give the verdict in his favour, except for the fox, who claims to be in a great hurry because he has to run to help his father who is in labour.

The lion foolishly says, 'How can your father be in labour? He's a male!'

'In the same way that your bull gave birth to a calf,' says the fox, running away to safety. The lion chases after him, leaving the ostrich in possession of the calf.

Later that day I set off to walk along the lake shore, curious to see if I could identify my old campsite. I came upon two teenage girls sitting on rocks by the water's edge. One wore a cotton dress, but the other was in the old leather apron of her grandmothers. I greeted them and tried to walk on, but they jumped up and blocked my way. They came very close, held out their hands and said, 'And birr, and birr.'[27] They were smiling, but were too close for comfort. They began to pat and feel my bag, saying, 'Camera, money,' then plucked at my shirt, saying 'Libs, libs.'[28]

I started to feel scared. I turned back and walked fast the way I had come. They followed for a while, pulling gently on my arms, then stopped. They shouted after me as I hurried on. My heartbeat was raised and I was disturbed. I wasn't used to feeling frightened in Ethiopia. I don't know if they intended to rob me, or were begging a little too insistently, but I looked back with regret to those little boys who had danced about naked in showers of spray, showing off in front of my campsite, calling out, 'Korkoro! Korkoro!'

Awassa is a pleasant holiday town, set on the shores of Lake Awassa, south of Langano. It's brash, bright and lively with Addis Ababans sauntering about in fashionable clothes. Glamorous new resort hotels have now sprung up along the lakeside, but I remembered with affection the old Wabe Shebele government hotel, and this was where Dirije and Michael brought me at

[27] One dollar, one dollar.
[28] Clothes.

the end of our long drive from Addis. Oleanders, bougainvillea, jacaranda and flame trees cast a pleasant shade over the chalet guest rooms dotted about the grounds, with the lake's water glittering beyond.

In spite of the faxes and phone calls which Ato Mulugeta had made from Addis Ababa, there was mystification at the Regional Cultural Office when we went to check in. The wrong person had been contacted. He was a journalist of some kind, not a government official. He was out of town anyway.

We waited, looked hopeful, and made small talk. Someone came up to us. He had seen a letter floating round the office a couple of weeks earlier. He had wondered what it was all about. If we would only explain again what we wanted, he would be happy to help us.

Ato Aklilu worked with the speed of a magician, and very shortly afterwards he produced, like rabbits from a hat, two storytellers, one from Sidama, and one from Wolayita, exactly the quarry we were after.

The Sidama peoples, who may number around three million, speak a non-Semitic, Cushitic language. Squeezed by the dominant Amhara and Tigrayan culture to the north, and by the powerful Oromo in the south, their fortunes have waxed and waned over many centuries. Most people in the Sidama and Wolayita regions have relinquished their old belief in the Sky God, who ruled through an avatar king. Today they are more likely to follow Islam or a version of Christianity (Orthodox, Roman Catholic or Evangelical) than their old religion.

The Sidama kings were canny in their dealings with the

powerful emperors to the north, recognising that loyal fealty
was the most sensible course. Sidama was amalgamated within
the borders of Ethiopia in the late nineteenth century, and from
time to time since then successive Ethiopian governments have
carved up its territories into administrative regions, cutting
fresh pieces to make a new jigsaw, but the Sidama people have
retained much that is distinctive. Their round houses are famous
for their frills of layered thatch. Standing stones, which some
archaeologists date to before the Egyptian pyramids, dot their
landscape, and their oral culture is known for its richness.

The man who was going to unveil its treasures to me was
called Abebe Kebede. He was good looking and unassuming,
but his mild presence was overshadowed by the ebullience of
his companion, Yisihak Aldade, who was from Wolayita. Abebe
good-naturedly agreed to start telling us stories straight away,
but Yisihak was suspicious. What was our *real* motive, he wanted
to know. Who had *really* sent us? Was there a political slant to
all this? Were we trying to get him into trouble? He was happier
after a delicate financial negotiation had taken place.

There was only one place in Awassa where stories could
suitably be told and that was on the shores of the lake. We
settled ourselves on stool-sized rocks of pumice, common in this
volcanic region. Pebbles of the stuff were bobbing about on the
water.

The storytelling began. The two men took it in turns. Abebe
told his tales quietly, murmuring into the tape recorder. Yisihak
gave a full performance. He leaped to his feet and sat down again.
He made large gestures with his arms. He imitated the calls of
birds and grunts of animals. He sang the rhymes.

I relaxed against the soft pumice boulder at my back.
Kingfishers with scarlet beaks whipped past my nose. A flock

of starlings chattered in a bush. Leggy marabou storks clacked their bills as they hopped about their messy nests in the tree overhead. Further away, a family of colobus monkeys lolled on the branches of a fig tree.

One of the many stories that Abebe told still keeps me guessing, with its examination of the vexed relationship between men and women.

The key role is played by Fura, a famous queen in Sidama 'who taught women how to behave'. She told them not to be too obedient to men, but on the other hand to be shy to keep them guessing. Women should cover themselves from waist to knee to hide their private parts and make the best of their beauty to attract a husband.

Queen Fura was cruel to men. She would give them impossible tasks, sending one to fetch water with a sieve, and another to divide one of her hairs into six parts. She executed any man who was bald or short in stature. In order to survive, bald men wore wigs, and short men wore high heeled shoes.

The men were angry with their queen but hesitated to assassinate her, because she was a woman, and, after all, a queen. They captured a giraffe and persuaded her to mount it. They strapped her onto its back and it bolted away. The queen fell to pieces, her head landing in one place, her intestines, legs and hands somewhere else. And that is why, in Sidama, there are towns named 'Oun' (head), 'Leka' (leg), and 'Anga' (hand).

Queen Fura reminded me of the semi-mythical Queen Gudit (Judith), who was said to have stormed through the kingdom of Axum (in the far north of modern Ethiopia) during the tenth century, murdering its king and burning churches and monasteries. All kinds of disasters are blamed on the destructive rampages of this warrior queen, and priests in some Tigray churches still point to their sooty ceilings and blame her for the fires that blackened them. Gudit was traditionally thought to be Jewish but some argue that she was related to the Sidama people, who had a tradition of matriarchal rulers. She is the bad girl in the Ethiopian gallery of famous queens, scowling alongside the beautiful and wise Makeda (as the Queen of Sheba is sometimes called) and the shadowy Candace 'queen of the Ethiopians' (often confused with Sheba) whose eunuch was converted to Christianity by the Apostle Philip as he rode in his chariot, studying the Book of Isaiah.[29]

Unlike these powerful, legendary women, Fura is a sly, illogical creature, teaching girls to be disobedient yet bashful, and persecuting the bald and the short. Her gruesome fate seems like a joke.

The rest of Abebe's stories were so good that I would like to narrate them all, complete with their sound effects, but will reluctantly desist.[30] I must just mention the leopard who keeps eating the same mouse, which runs right through him and jumps out of his bottom, and the mother goat who sews the tail of a leopard to the tail of a hyena, and the dying father who promises to leave his precious shield to whichever of his three sons performs the kindest deed.

The Wolayita region, which stretches east from Sidama, is one of the most thickly populated parts of the country, and

[29] Acts, chapter 8.
[30] All Abebe Kebede and Yisihak Aldade's stories can be read on the Ethiopian Folktales website at www.ethiopianfolktales.com. Follow the links through to Sidama and Wolayita.

overpopulation, along with the vagaries of an uncertain rainfall, has led to severe problems of soil erosion and intermittent famine. But like Sidama, Wolayita has a long and proud history. The last of their kings, the Kawa Tona, accepted Menelik, the 'king of kings', in 1894 only after a long and bloody struggle. Polygamy is a tradition in this region.

The next day was a Saturday, and when the storytellers arrived at the hotel after breakfast for another session, Yisahak wrinkled his nose at the prospect of spending more hours sitting on the rocks by the lake shore. Since we had a car, he said, we should get Dirije to us drive up to Yirgalem, a lovely place, not very far away. He would take us to a Wolayita village and show us the rural life of the people.

I saw Dirije's eyes narrow with suspicion.

And, Yisahak added jauntily, he would have the chance to drop in and see his wife and baby son, who were staying up there on a long visit.

Dirije nodded, knowingly.

❖

Yirgalem was indeed a delightful small town, full of flowers, with handsome houses and a public library. Yisahak directed Dirije up a side road to a hot spring with a café attached. We sat here in the muddy little garden, drinking tooth-coating sodas, and shifting about from concrete benches to tubular steel chairs to stay in the shade as the burning sun moved across the sky.

There was an old king, began Yisahak, who married a young girl. She was happy at first, because being a queen she was given plenty of honey and fat to eat, but after a while she grew restless. Her eye fell on a servant, a handsome young man who had grown up in the king's household, and she began to think about him night and day. At last she made her move.

When he understood what she wanted, the young man was outraged.

'The king is like my own father,' he said. 'I would rather die than sleep with you.'

The queen's love turned to hatred. She went to her husband, and with a show of reluctance told him that the young man had tried to seduce her. The furious king wanted to execute the culprit at once, but the queen said, 'I wish to revenge this deed in my own way. Tomorrow is your birthday. Say nothing until then. Have a deep pit dug for his grave, then send him out to your soldiers and make them cut off his head.'

So the king commanded his soldiers to dig a pit outside the royal compound.

'I will send someone out to you tomorrow morning,' he told them. 'Whoever it is, catch that person and cut off their head.'

But the next morning, the queen, impatient in her rage, and wanting to see the execution, ran out of the palace before the young man had appeared. The soldiers seized her and made ready to behead her.

'Stop this! The king didn't mean me!' she protested.

'We have our orders,' they told her, and they cut off her head and buried her in the pit.

When the young man came out and heard what had happened, he was appalled and ran back to tell the king. At first the king was beside himself with rage, but when he had heard the whole story, he saw that justice had been done, and he married another woman and lived a long and happy life.

This ancient story appears not only in the Old Testament, but in the Koran. In the Bible, it is Joseph who plays the part of the

servant, and Potiphar's wife who tries to seduce him, snatching
his coat as he runs away and using it as proof when she denounces
him to her husband, who duly has Joseph imprisoned.[31] The motif
of the pit occurs earlier in the story, when Joseph's jealous brothers
dig a pit and leave him in it, to become the prey of wild animals.

My favourite version, however, is in the Koran. Joseph spurns
the advances of his master's wife and tries to flee, but she catches
his shirt and tears it from behind. When she accuses Joseph to
her husband, his advisors tell him to examine the shirt. 'If it's
torn from the front, he is guilty,' they say. 'But if the tear is in the
back, it's proof that he was trying to run away.' The master does
this, and realises that Joseph is innocent. He reproves his wife,
but doesn't punish her. Her reputation, however, is in shreds. In
order to rehabilitate herself, she invites the women of the city to
a banquet at her house, and gives them each a sharp knife. Then
she calls for Joseph, and when he enters the room, the women
are so astonished by his beauty that they start with surprise and
cut their hands.

'Now do you understand?' she says to them triumphantly.[32]

The story of Joseph in its various guises illustrates the
way in which a good story is put to use by different narrators
according to their own times and purposes. The story in the
Book of Genesis forms part of the long narrative of God's special
providence for his Chosen People. Joseph's adventures in Egypt
are engineered by God so that he will be on hand at the right
moment to preserve the Israelites at a time of famine.

A thousand years later, the Koranic version of the story
concludes: 'This [the Koran] is no invented tale, but a confirm-

---

[31] Genesis, chapter 39.
[32] The Koran, surah 12.

ation of previous scriptures, an explanation of all things, a guide and blessing to true believers.'

Fourteen centuries later, Yisahak rounded off his tale with this flourish: 'The moral of the story is that you shouldn't dig a pit for your enemy, or you might end up in it yourself.'

Now that he was launched, Yisahak was unstoppable. A 'Just So' story of how the tortoise got his shell was followed by a sinister account of hyenas feeding upon each other in a cannibalistic frenzy. Next we were treated to the tale (versions of which exist in many parts of the world) of a king's servant who learns a terrible secret about his master. Unable to hold it in, he whispers it to the river. Musicians cut reeds on the riverbank to make their flutes, and the flutes pipe out the secret.

The next story, with the dull title 'The Sheep and the Goat', sent my mind spinning back to my childhood, then forward again into my own sons' earliest years.

Why is it that small children become fixated on one particular book, and insist on it being read again and again? Apparently, the object of my first literary love was the Australian story *Jennifer Jane*. We embarked from New Zealand in 1945, en route for Britain on the SS *Akaroa*, an old-fashioned liner which still wore its wartime camouflage of battleship grey. My parents, older brother and two older sisters must have been filled with dread as we travelled from the golden land of our childhood to the dinginess of post-war London, and, presumably unsettled by the tension, I drove them distracted with my screaming demands to have *Jennifer Jane* read to me again and again. Was it comfort I was after? Was there something in the story that provided it?

My oldest son became obsessed with a story about a little boy who cuts his finger and is given a sticking plaster and a cuddle by the nurse. I analysed this simple tale, and concluded that it was a quite profound study of the Problem of Pain. I gleaned from this the idea that even small children seek an emotional release from a story, and it was this insight that set me off on my career as a writer of books for children. (Later, my younger son made me abandon this idea in favour of a generalised chaos theory. He became fixated on a Chinese propaganda children's book, printed on cheap paper with garish pictures, featuring The Little Red Guard and her kind uncles in the People's Liberation Army. By then, however, my career was launched.)

Both of the boys had gone through a phase of demanding that dreadful story, Chicken Licken, a tale of such repetitious dullness that I groan whenever I think of it. I was eventually reduced to hiding the book and pretending it was lost.

But it was a version of Chicken Licken that Yisahak now produced and it was a cracker, beating the insipid European tale hands down. I have had no difficulty in narrating this one again and again, and have told it to many classrooms full of children around Britain.

A sheep and a goat, tired of living with their master, run away to find good pasture and fresh water. They meet a lion who threatens to eat them, and they tell him that the sky is falling and he must run away at once. The lion believes them and flees. They pull the same trick on a leopard, a hyena and a fox.

When night falls, they are suddenly scared, and climb a tree for shelter. By ill luck, the four predators take refuge for the night under the same tree, and discover that each of them has been tricked in a similar way. They threaten vengeance on the sheep and the goat, who are cowering, terrified, overhead.

Unfortunately, the sheep has drunk so much sweet water from the spring that she desperately needs to pee. The panic-stricken goat sees that she really can't wait, and tells her to turn onto her back so that her wool will absorb the urine, but the sheep loses her balance and falls down on to the heads of the lion, the leopard, the hyena and the fox below.

'They were right! The sky *is* falling!' the predators cry, and run off to save their lives. The next day, the sheep and the goat walk calmly home again.

I liked this story much better than Chicken Licken, but when I had finished laughing, I began to wonder all over again at the way in which seemingly random themes crop up in stories so geographically remote from each other, and the mesmerising effect they have on us.

While Yisahak was performing, I had been becoming gradually aware of screams rising from the valley below.

'Do you think someone's in trouble?' I asked at last. 'Shouldn't we go and see?'

The others laughed at me. There was an exorcism in progress, they told me, at a holy spot on the stream that ran through the valley. It was a well-known site for the casting out of evil spirits. In the atmosphere that Yisahak had been weaving, this seemed a reasonable thing to be doing in the middle of a Saturday, and we left them to it and set off back into town.

'Here,' said Yisahak, tapping Dirije on the shoulder. 'Just five minutes. Please.'

He got out of the car and ran across to one of the houses that edged the road. Dirije, keen for a bargain, had spotted a market a short way away and went off to look for coffee, hopeful that, in this coffee-growing region, he would make a killing.

He came back a few moments later.

'Same price as in Addis! Too much is asking!'

A crowd of children had collected to gaze at me in their disconcerting way.

'Do they buy people in this town?' Dirije asked them, using the same trick he had pulled on the charcoal seller in Afar.

Their eyes shifted momentarily from me to him.

'Because it looks as if there is someone in this car that you want to buy, or you wouldn't be staring like that.'

They grinned and moved off.

'And the rural life you wanted to show us?' I asked Yisahak, when at last he returned from visiting his wife.

'What rural life?' He had forgotten his promise. I didn't blame him. The ferenji obsession with poking about in houses and villages which most self-respecting Ethiopians long to escape from must seem very odd. But now that we were driving through Sidama country, Abebe seemed to feel obliged to honour Yisahak's promise. He sat bolt upright staring out of the Land Rover's side window as we drove back towards Awassa.

'Here,' he said suddenly.

Dirije stopped the car beside a cluster of 'tukuls'[33], handsome round houses set beside a small stand of 'ensete' or false banana plants. A man was driving a pair of cows through the screen of slim eucalyptus saplings that edged the road into a small field of closely cropped grass.

Abebe addressed him in his cheery manner and the man jerked his chin towards the houses. Then he went on his way with his cows, as if he was used to visitations by sensation-hungry foreigners.

Embarrassed, I climbed out of the Land Rover, ignoring a derisive snort from Dirije, who clearly thought we were engaged in some kind of farce. I followed Michael, Yisahak and Abebe towards a pair of houses, whose narrow doorways were set

---

[33] The word 'tukul' is used by foreigners to describe the traditional round thatched houses of highland Ethiopia. It is not an Amharic word and is unknown to Ethiopians.

facing each other. I guessed that the inhabitants were members of the same family.

Abebe urged me to photograph the larger of the two houses, which I did, without enthusiasm. I had come increasingly to dislike the intrusion of the camera. I was only entirely comfortable behind the lens when I was attempting to take portraits and was sure that the sitter was enjoying the process and making an event of it.

The larger house was a solid construction with straight walls about fifteen feet high. An upturned jar crowned the apex of the central pole which jutted out above the smooth thatch. In the unusual style typical of Sidama, the thatch ran from the roof right down to the ground and was cut in layers, reminding me of an exotic dancer's skirt.

I was urged to go inside. It was so dark that my eyes needed time to adjust from the sunlight outside, and while I was blinded I was startled by a moo beside me.

'The cows live here,' Abebe said, tapping a shoulder-high wall which I could now see was made of thick tree trunks blocking off about a quarter of the living area. Peering over the top, I made out a calf which blinked up at me as it passed its pink tongue over its nose.

There was a flicker of pale cloth ahead and I made out the shape of a woman standing in the opening of a matting screen which ran across the back of the hut. She carried a baby in her arms, and looked so shy – terrified, in fact – that I felt more embarrassed than ever, and wanted to leave. But Abebe was enthusiastically showing off the poor woman's bed, the sleeping mat beside it, and the depression in the middle of the floor where a fire would be lit. This had been swept clean and no sign of ashes remained.

Abebe pushed me through the matting screen, behind which the girl had disappeared, to show me her cooking area. This was so surrounded by walls that not a chink of light could penetrate from the outside. Only the glow from a few burning sticks enabled me to make out a clutter of bowls and pans. It was as if the preparation of food was something which had to be hidden from lurking forces of evil.

Later, it occurred to me that there is a tourist opportunity for Ethiopians here. Everyone is fascinated by the minutiae of other people's lives. Early on in our careers as writers, when David and I were struggling to make ends meet, we hatched a plan to offer tourists an insight into a fantasy British home.

'We'll get out Granny's tea set and give them tea,' I told David. 'I'll make cucumber sandwiches and scones. They'll want to look round the house. We'll have to tidy up.'

'I'll sit behind a copy of *The Times* and harrumph,' David said. 'Pity I've given up smoking a pipe.'

'Yes, and we can the dress the boys in white sweaters and get them to dash in swinging rackets and calling out "Who's for tennis?"'

'That's no good.' David injected a note of realism. 'There's no tennis court for miles around. And anyway, they'd just stand there picking their noses. Are you sure we're pitching this right? Sounds weirdly retro to me.'

We were sufficiently desperate to work the plan up into something quite credible and I laid it before a friend who worked at the English Tourist Board. Luckily a royalty cheque came in, and we were able to forget the whole thing.

Years later, visiting our son William in China, we came across Mr Lee, an entrepreneurial tour guide who had had the same idea. He offered to show us 'the real China'. We spent the most fascinating day of our China trip following him in and out of a pig market, a primary school, a brick factory, a blacksmith's shop (and the family's home behind it), a barber's shop and a couple of Buddhist temples. At one point we found ourselves in an old people's centre being asked to entertain them with a song. (We gave them 'In Dublin's Fair City'.) The whole experience beat the Forbidden City by miles.

In Ethiopia, tourists naturally focus on the spectacular castles, rock-hewn churches and stelae, or stare at birds down their telephoto lenses while their guide beats off curious students and hungry beggars. They are missing an opportunity. Ethiopian tourism needs a few Mr Lees.

Yisahak seemed to feel that he had not quite matched Abebe's output of stories, and once back in Awassa, he settled down in the hotel garden to tell more. We had a strange but charming story of an arrogant flood, who tries to marry his son to the daughter of a lake, but disappears when the rainy season ends, so that his pride comes to nothing. Then we heard about the starving travellers who were reduced to eating a donkey, and how they dealt with the shame of this forbidden act. This was followed by the mouse deer who prayed for safety at the same time as the lion who was praying for his dinner, and how God managed the difficult feat of granting both their desires.

I was tired by now. I was content to sit in the shade, fanned by a soft breeze from the lake, and watch the birds.

When Yisahak had at last run out of inspiration, we said goodbye. It was five o'clock, an hour before sunset. I walked down through the garden to a flight of steps leading up onto the dyke, then down the other side to a concrete jetty. I strolled along it. Naked boys were diving off into the water, shrieking with joy as they crashed through the carpet of lily pads which matted the surface of the water close to the shore. Further out, beyond the lilies, a couple of men were fishing with rods. One of them pulled out a catfish as I approached. It was about a foot long, its mouth gaping open in its ugly whiskered face.

A drop of rain made a circle as big as a pound coin on the concrete in front of me and looking up I saw that indigo clouds had boiled up on the horizon and rain was sweeping across the lake, so I hurried back down the jetty, up and over the dyke and made it through the garden to my room, half soaked before I could open the door.

❖

Much later, back in England, one of Yisahak's stories came back to me on another drive, this time into London. It was a winter's night, and David was driving me to dinner with friends.

'I haven't told you this one yet,' I said. 'I'll see if I can remember it.'

A merchant, travelling with his goods, passed a crowd watching a sad spectacle. A farmer had yoked his slave alongside his ox and was beating them both mercilessly. The merchant was so moved at the sad sight that tears came to his eyes, but the yoked man, seeing his distress, called out, 'Don't cry for me, my friend. Everything changes, everything passes, and this sorrow of mine will pass too.'

The merchant went on his way, but a year later his rounds brought him back to the same part of the country. He remembered the poor man being beaten like an animal, and asked people what had become of him.

'God saw his suffering,' they told him, 'and made him a king. He sits in state in his house.'

The merchant was delighted to hear this, and wanting to see this change of fortune with his own eyes, he went to the royal compound and laughed aloud with joy at the sight of the poor man now enjoying a life of wealth and power.

The king noticed him standing there and asked him why he was laughing.

'I saw you when you were a poor man, yoked to the plough, and I am rejoicing at your happiness,' said the merchant.

The king invited him in to eat and drink, but as they sat together, he said to the merchant, 'Don't rejoice for me, my friend. Remember, everything changes, everything passes, and this happiness of mine will pass too.'

The year went round again, and the merchant returned eagerly, hoping to see the king. But when he arrived at the royal house, the people told him that the king had died, and another had taken his place. Saddened, the merchant went to visit the king's grave. A stone marked the place and on it was written: 'Everything changes, everything passes, and this too will pass.'

The following year, the merchant went once more to visit the graveyard.

'Surely that cannot change. That cannot pass,' he told himself.

But the graveyard had gone. It had been swept away in the new town plan, and a skyscraper stood in its place, rising fifteen storeys high.

The merchant, dazzled by the sun sparkling from the glass, looked up at it and said, 'My friend was right. Everything does change. Every-thing does pass. And even this will pass too.'

David bounced his palms off the steering wheel in appreciation as I came to the end of this story. We had been living through some turbulence in our own lives. My mother was aging and needing care. Our sons were striking out in life, moving ever further from us into university and careers. The adjustment for us both had been painful.

Yisahak's profound and beautiful story has never ceased to have meaning for us. We quote its mantra often to each to each other.

'Everything changes, everything passes,' David says to me, when the pain in my aging hips flares up.

'All this will pass too,' I remind him, when the frustrations of writing and publishing threaten to overwhelm him.

Thank you, Yisahak.

❖ 8 ❖

THE MAN WHO GREW FEATHERS
IN OROMIA

I had a favourite street in Addis Ababa. It's some time now since I climbed the flight of steps above the old fountain in the angle of a sharp bend in the road leading from Arat Kilo to Piazza, and I don't know if the bust of Haile Selassie still stands on its plinth against the hillside. On every visit, I checked to see if it had survived.

'My' street was long, and rose gently up the hillside. I would like to give you its name, but I can't. Streets in Addis Ababa may have had names, in some official sense, but nobody knew them or used them. Anyway, the wide verges were covered with grass and the fences behind them sagged under the weight of jasmine and roses. Through the flowers one caught only glimpses of the houses behind. They were some of the oldest in the city. Some tilted to one side, as if they were tired. The windows were sectioned into small panes, and the gable roofs were edged with frivolously carved soffit boards. I didn't need to go in through those peeling front doors to know what it was like inside because I remembered so well my own dear ramshackle house, in a street further up the hill, which I had rented in 1967 from an old lady connected to the imperial court. I knew that in these houses, too, the rooms would be cool and dim, with bands of sunshine penetrating the slatted shutters. I could feel under my palm the irregular surface of the whitewashed walls. The gardens were overgrown, I was sure, with clumps of flowering bougainvillea under which dogs scratched at fleas.

I never walked up that street without wanting to throw up my life in Britain, rent one of those houses, move in and step back through the decades into the magical years of my youth.

I'm not sure that I will dare to climb the steps to that street again. Addis Ababa is changing so fast that for all I know it has been swept away, the roses crushed under the wheels of bulldozers.

I was staying on my next visit in another lovely old house. Michael and Patsy Sargent had offered me the spare room in their official British Council residence. A large garden surrounded this roomy, comfortable bungalow. Patsy, who has an intelligent passion for trees, was a member of PLANT (Plant Locally and Nurture Trees). She was rearing thousands of indigenous Ethiopian seedlings in a section of the grounds. These would then be delivered to schools, embassies and the slopes of Entoto for planting. Now that the forests which once covered the country have all but disappeared, and the eucalyptus has spread everywhere, Patsy's work is an example of practical conservation.

My project seemed to be progressing well. Back in Britain, I had already finished the readers for Afar and Gambela and they were working their way through the production process. We had found an artist to illustrate them, and he was turning out delightful drawings in pen and ink. His name was Yosef Kebede.

Yosef came to the Sargent's house to show me the drawings he had done for the Gambela stories on the morning after my arrival. We sat out on the veranda and spread the pictures over the table. Working with artists is one of the pleasures of being a writer for children, and I leafed over the pages of Yosef's sketchbooks with delight.

Yosef was a handsome, serious young man, who seemed undaunted by the large numbers of drawings we were asking him to produce. He was shy in showing me his work, but he seemed almost pleased when I made a few suggestions and criticisms.

'No one says things like this to me here,' he said. 'How am I to learn?'

Later, remembering how I feel when my work is pulled to pieces by an editor, I was worried in case I'd gone too far, but Yosef turned out to be a professional, always turning out good work on time. His animal studies, in particular, jumped off the page.

It was one of his drawings of animals that we had to sort out that day. He had already finished the artwork for the Afar readers, which had been sent to Assayita for comments. The sheep were wrong, we had been told. They were Issar sheep. How could an Afar reader contain the sheep of a rival and enemy? They would have to be redone.

The work over, Yosef told me something about himself. His father had been an artist, he said. He had learned his craft before the revolution, and had travelled about the country painting murals in churches. Yosef had sometimes gone with him, and had helped him to mix his paints and prepare the surfaces of the walls.

Ethiopian religious art is one of the glories of Africa. The murals in the church of St Mary Axum were known to travellers in the early days of Islam. In churches both ancient and modern, saints, prophets and angels surge from the walls in a variety of styles which have changed and developed across the centuries. The roots of church painting might lie in Byzantium, with a grafting of Catholic Portugal in the sixteenth century, but the flowering is uniquely Ethiopian. The colours are basic: red, green, blue and yellow, with the figures outlined in black. Surroundings and backgrounds are painted in flat planes of glowing colour. The faces are round and unmistakeably Ethiopian, with huge expressive eyes. In some very early pictures the fingers and toes are elegantly elongated.

The most famous churches of Ethiopia are the rock-hewn marvels of Lalibela, followed by the cave churches cut out of the faces of cliffs in Tigray. These are rectangular, or in the basilica form. In the villages of the Christian highlands, churches are more likely to be circular. The central Holy of Holies, barred to all but the priests, is walled off from the rest of the church by an ambulatory, and it is here that the artists were usually set to work. Their purpose was to teach the illiterate about Christ, his mother and the saints. (I have seldom seen pictures from the Old Testament apart from portraits of the prophets.) The artist might have his personal style, but he would keep to the sacred traditions of his craft, supervised by priests.

Ethiopian secular art was alive and well in the 1960s, when I commissioned a large painting of the Battle of Adowa from an old artist in Lalibela. The triumphant Ethiopians, led by the Emperor Menelik in his lion mane headdress, chase the Italians to defeat across one wall of our London living room. I acquired it just in time. The revolution brought changes to every aspect of Ethiopian life, and the old art was swept away along with so much else. If Yosef had been born twenty years earlier, he would no doubt have followed in his father's footsteps, travelling from place to place with his pack of brushes and colours strapped to the back of a donkey. Instead, he went to the School of Fine Art in Addis Ababa, and learned to draw and paint in the styles admired in the West.

No one can visit Ethiopia, however, without becoming aware of the vibrancy of popular mural art. The scenes which decorate Ethiopian churches are reproduced in books on African art and crop up on Christmas cards in the West, but no one seems to celebrate the paintings on the outside walls of shops and the insides of bars, restaurants and garages. I had begun to notice them first in Gambela, when, looking for an artist to create the front covers of our readers, Michael Ambatchew had diligently trawled the bars and inspected the walls until he had found the very person we needed. In some cafés and restaurants, the walls and even the ceilings explode with colour. Swans glide across a lake of the deepest blue. A beautiful girl poses against a sunset. The red tin roof of a house floats above a garden of flowers. On the staircase, dogs dressed as people are grouped round a table engaging in an arm-wrestling contest. The most impressive, a bulldog, sits with his legs open displaying bollocks the size of tennis balls.

❖

It was Oromo stories I was after on this visit and the search would yield fascinating results.

Quoting statistics about Ethiopia is a mug's game. As the distinguished economist, Dr Berhanu Abegaz, points out, there is a tendency towards 'mindless duplication of erroneous numbers' which leads to 'a pyramid of prejudice'.[34] And stating the percentage of this or that minority within the whole population of Ethiopia is one of the trickiest traps. This is not

---

[34] 'Ethiopia: A Model Nation of Minorities' by Berhanu Abegaz (http://www.ethiomedia.com/newpress/census_portrait.pdf).

only because statistics are not always to be trusted, but also because ethnic identity in a country where minorities have long been so integrated is hard to establish. Who is an Oromo? Is it someone who speaks Oromiffaa? Whose mother or father is Oromo? A person who 'feels' Oromo? This should be easy for us in Britain to understand. Who, after all, is a Scot? Or is Welsh? How English do you have to be to be English?

Having covered myself with the above, I hope, I shall now daringly state that the Oromo probably make up about one third of the population of Ethiopia. Around half of Oromos are Muslim, and half are Christian, the numbers of Evangelicals rapidly overtaking the Orthodox, as elsewhere. Only a small number still adhere to their traditional faiths. The Oromo language is Cushitic. It is written in the Latin script rather than the Amharic.

The Oromo peoples expanded into Ethiopia from the south over many centuries. Their search for good land and water brought them into contact with the Amhara to the north and Somalis in the east. Living alongside each other for many centuries, there have been times of inevitable conflict, but also much assimilation and peaceful cooperation. The Oromo enjoyed a particular form of government, called the Gadaa system, but by the start of the nineteenth century different Oromo communities had established monarchies, which could negotiate more easily with the powerful Amhara kings, through tribute, trade and dynastic marriage. I would find echoes of these kingdoms in the stories I was told in Bonga, where the Oromo kings of Kafa had ruled.

A look at a modern map of Ethiopia shows how large the Oromo region is. It forms an inverted L shape, stretching almost to the Sudan border in the west, then curving round in an arc to meet the Kenyan border in the south, while a broad arm

extends north towards Djibouti. Although the headquarters of
the Oromo regional government are in Addis Ababa, which sits
within the Oromo region, it cannot be described as an 'Oromo'
capital. Any attempt, in fact, to untangle the population of Addis
Ababa according to its multifarious minorities would leave
better brains than mine bewildered.

I would make three attempts to capture the essence of Oromo
stories. The first would be in Addis Ababa itself, at the Oromo
Education Bureau. Later, I would travel down to Arsi, a bare,
windy plain in the south, to the town of Asasa. And lastly I
would find myself in Gebre Geracha, a small town in the north-
western part of the region.

It wasn't particularly inspiring, sitting in the offices of the
Regional Cultural Bureau, while Michael Ambatchew talked to
the officials in Amharic. I found it hard to break into their small
masculine circle, and had to wait until later to get some feeling
for the stories.

The bull's placenta was there of course, along with a dying
father advising his three sons, a Hansel and Gretel tale of
a wicked stepmother and her weak husband who allows his
children to be persecuted, and a story of mice evading mass
slaughter at the funeral of a cat. But I was intrigued by a story
entitled 'The Mother-in-law'. Mothers-in-law are famously the
butt of comedians the world over and it is usually the wife's
mother who takes the shrewish part. This story was different.

A man, his mother and his wife live together. The wife
constantly complains to her husband about her mother-in-law
and finally persuades him to kill her. The husband, reckoning
that his mother is old and will soon die anyway, finally agrees,
and sets out with the old woman towards a high cliff.

The old woman, realising his intention, begs him to take care when he throws her over the cliff in case he too should slip and hurt himself. Her son is so struck by her self-sacrificing love that he changes his mind, takes her home, divorces his wife and lives with the old woman instead.

A weekend loomed, and I took the opportunity to climb to the ridge of Entoto above Addis Ababa for a walk, hoping that by some miracle I would once more meet the old farmer who had set me off on my story quest, and ask him to tell me again the story of the ant. A young friend, Ayele, came up with me.

It's a steep climb to the top from the place where the minibuses stop, and I puffed my way slowly up the slope. There were no cliffs up here to endanger the lives of the shepherd boys. They sat about safely on boulders, watching their flocks graze close together, the spirit drummed out of them by their small, stick-wielding masters.

It was September – spring time in Ethiopia, after the cold and wet of the Big Rains. The grass was dotted with flowers. There were several varieties of clover, a kind of self-heal, some little vetches and the first of the gilded Meskel daisies.

Ethiopia and Eritrea are still astonishingly rich in plants, boasting 7,000 recorded species with over 400 endemic to the region, but whereas the declining numbers of indigenous mammals have stimulated international rescue programmes, the wondrous plants of Ethiopia are suffering dangerous assaults from over-grazing, climate change and the ploughing of marginal lands while all eyes are turned elsewhere.

'It's true, they are beautiful,' Ayele said, bending down beside me to look. 'I don't know their names. I haven't noticed such things before. There is an Amharic saying: "We have gold in our hands but we see brass."'

I saw in those perfect little life-forms, their hopeful faces turned up to the sun, an analogy for the stories I was trying to collect: precious, valuable things in danger of extinction.

'I feel like the Brothers Grimm,' I burst out to Ayele, then spent the remainder of our walk explaining what I meant.

❖

It was a long drive to Asasa, in the Bale Mountain region. This area of Ethiopia was once known for its ancient forests, rare plants and abundant wildlife but the loggers were already at work when I was there in the 1960s. A national park was created to preserve some of the natural treasures, but as elsewhere in Ethiopia policing has not been possible, and shepherds and herdsmen are irresistibly attracted to land which seems to have no owner.

In the days of the Stalinist Derg, collectivisation was the mantra, and small farms were swallowed up into huge communal fields. The sight of acres of ripening wheat was encouraging. Here, surely, was a crop that would satisfy the hunger of Ethiopia's burgeoning population. A few months later, however, when I passed this way again, tractors were ploughing this same land, and clouds of dust were spiralling up into the air, the topsoil blowing away.

❖

Asasa is a small town. The wind that scours the soil from the fields blows relentlessly through its dusty streets. The weather in Asasa was cold, but the welcome we received was warm, and I found myself soon after our arrival in the house of a storyteller, perched on a bed, squeezed between cheerful elderly men who vied with each other to tell story after story. It was not of course until later that Michael had time to translate them for me, and they were gems.

'Once there was a wise old man called Robele Megerra . . .' began Mohammed Kuyu, after much throat clearing.

The old man sees two dogs fighting.

'Someone must separate them, or the boys will fight,' he calls out.

No one listens, and the boys do fight.

'Stop them!' cries Robele Megerra, 'or the mothers will fight.'

And so the battles escalate. The mothers fight. Their husbands are drawn in. The fight becomes general, and spreads to the clans. Soon, there is a small war with eight men dead on each side. At last, the people come to their senses and the elders are called to resolve the conflict at the Guma[35] court. The compensation to be paid for such severe loss of life is so great that even the Guma court is nonplussed. At last, a wise man suggests the solution. Each clan should take its 'meta'[36] to the river, and throw it into the water. They should be reconciled and forgive each other.

The sacrifice of pride in the pursuit of peace is surely the message of this story. It should be inscribed in letters of gold over the doorway to every army headquarters and foreign ministry throughout the world. When I think, too, of the disputes that flare up in my suburban street, over car parking, fences, blaring music, defecating dogs and the like, I could wish that we had a Guma court to resolve things with its kindly wisdom.

The storyteller, Mohammed Kuyu, was giving me a master class in Oromo traditions. On he went:

---

[35] The Guma is a traditional Oromo court in which crimes are settled by means of payment rather than by capital punishment.
[36] A ceremonial silver necklace.

A man has two sons. He tells them that before he dies, he wants to see them settled in their own homes. They should return to him after a month, he says, to give an account of their progress.

The first son sets about cutting trees and building a compound for himself with many fine huts. The second son spends his time visiting and making friends, becoming a blood brother in this family and that, putting his lips to his new brothers' nipples to show that they have drunk from one breast, according to Oromo tradition.

At the end of the month, the brothers returned to their father.

'Have you built your home?' the old man asks the first son, who takes him to his compound and shows off his fine huts.

The father walks by each hut and calls out, 'Is anyone in there?' But no one answers.

'Who is going to feed me here?' he says. 'There is no one. Let's go home.'

He asks the second son to show him his new home. The young man takes his father to the first family who had adopted him. They slaughter a sheep and made a feast. They go on to the second family, and another feast is prepared.

'You did well, my son,' the old man says. 'Friendship and warmth with other people is worth more than an empty house, however splendid it may be.'

I found this story hard to take at first. In my Western way, I had rather approved of the first brother and thought the second one feckless. I had expected a different outcome, along the lines of the Aesop story of the ant and the grasshopper. I see now that this tale strikes at the heart of what differentiates African and European culture. Africans living in the West may groan sometimes at the obligations which their families impose on them, buckling under the expectation that everything they have earned or acquired is available to be enjoyed by a wide circle of relatives, but they know that their families with all their strengths and weakness are the bedrock of their existence. The fragmentation of European cellular society, where increasingly we live in units of one, making friends with the TV and the computer, is a sad contrast. I still gulp at this story, but I value it too.

Resolving conflict and forging bonds seemed to be theme in Asasa. Wedged between the soft shammas of the men on either side of me, I started to feel sleepy, and watched in a dream as the mistress of the house made her preparations for the coffee ceremony. The incense only made me sleepier, and I needed the stiff beaker of coffee when at last it came my way.

In spite of the emphasis on conflict resolution in the stories I was told, these are turbulent times in the Oromo body politic. Latent resentment against the dominant Amhara/Tigrayan culture to the north, portrayed by some Oromos as a long history of repression and cruelty, has given rise to a number of political organisations, chiefly the Oromo Liberation Front. Full-scale war was waged by the Oromos against Mengistu Haile Mariam, but the Tigrayan-led government which replaced the Derg is seen by some Oromos as an extension of an old colonial repression by the Amhara emperors. The armed struggle of Oromos looking for further self-determination is a thorn in the side of the Ethiopian government as it attempts to hold the country together.

When the story session had ended, I exploded from that little room like pent-up champagne from a bottle, and was grateful to Merga Debelo for suggesting a walk down through town to a stream where crystal water welled up between rocks, and a few women were still pounding clothes on the stones, in spite of the lateness of the hour.

❖

It had taken me a while to get to know Merga Debelo, the gentle, dignified man who was organising the collection of Oromo stories, but over the next few days, as we drove back to Addis Ababa, and then on to Gebre Geracha near the northern border of the Oromo region, he began to talk to me about the Oromo traditions, which he clearly carried close to his heart.

The Oromo way of government, he told me, laying the tip of one finger on my knee, was democratic. It didn't matter how rich a man was, he was considered the equal of any other. This 'Gadaa' government was still in operation in Borana, the southern part of the Oromo region. It worked on an age-banding system, the roles and responsibilities of each set of youths changing every eight years. The leader, or 'king', known as the Abba Gadaa, was also appointed for an eight-year rule, after which he gave way to someone else. Every male member of society had the right to elect and be elected.

Merga didn't need to spell out for me how different this system was to the hierarchical divisions of traditional Amhara society, with its emperors and princes, its feudal nobility and the near-serfdom of its peasantry. However, neither did he spell out the disadvantages of the old Oromo system, with its militaristic ethos and the status accorded to men who had killed.

Gebre Geracha was a typical small Ethiopian road town, its houses strung out some way back from the strip of tarmac running through it. There were several hotels, ranging from new, concrete buildings to tumbledown mud houses, the usual flocks of sheep and goats feeling the stony ground with their lips for any last blade of grass, ebullient children shrieking, 'Ferenji! Give money!', women carting huge pots of water on their bent backs, and above and around everything the softest, freshest, unpolluted air.

As I climbed out of the Land Rover to become part of the peaceful morning scene, I was struck by the sheer endurance of Ethiopians. Their climate is uncertain, their homes spartan, their food supply erratic. They have little extra money for clothes or medicines, they live under the shadow of political chaos, and nasty new diseases lurk to attack them. Europeans would be hard pressed to remain cheerful under such circumstances.

Merga took us first to visit an old man who was thought to know many stories. I knew as soon as my eyes had adjusted to the gloom inside his small house that our visit would be fruitless. Grass had been strewn on the floor in preparation for our coming and a young woman shyly handed round bottles of soda, but the old man himself looked from Merga to Michael to me with the vague, sweet eyes of senility. I knew that look. I wanted to sit down beside him, hold his dry old hand and tell him that everything was fine, as I had done so often, first with my bewildered father, then with my even more bewildered mother-in-law. Instead, I sat on the cow-skin which had been laid on the mud bench by the door while Merga leaned on the plastic sheet that covered his rickety table and Michael coaxed him to tell us a story.

He began to talk in a quavering voice, and even I could tell that the same tale was being told over and over again.

'He is saying how he has been ill, and his daughter died, and his son too, and relatives are caring for him,' Merga said at last.

The old man hadn't noticed the interruption and was beginning his story again. We stood up to go.

'Thank him very much,' I said to Merga, 'and say we were honoured to meet him.'

The old man struggled up from his chair as he noticed that we were about to go. He seemed to see me for the first time and gave a wide smile. He embraced me warmly, tapping his shoulders to mine in turn, three or four times.

Merga shook his head as we left the little house.

'It is very sad,' he said. 'Not only for him but for us also. He knew many wonderful stories. Who will remember them now?'

The next morning, after I had slept the sleep of the exhausted for nine hours in one of the less well-appointed of Gebre Geracha's inns, I sat over breakfast enjoying coffee, fried eggs, rolls and honey, and talking about marriage with Merga.

His own marriage had been arranged by his family, but he had insisted on meeting his wife first. He had fallen deeply in love with her, and never looked at another woman. They had five children, the oldest seventeen, the youngest two. Michael arrived at this interesting point, to take us off to meet the storytellers who had assembled already in the office of the local administrator.

In spite of these official surroundings, the atmosphere was convivial, and the five old storytellers, four men and one woman, greeted me with enthusiasm. Merga, in his tactful way, explained to them again the purpose of the project. His voice was barely raised above a murmur. I noticed again how a quiet voice expresses politeness in Ethiopia. The braying conversation of Europeans must constantly startle and shock.

Worku Debele was the first to begin. He had the bearing and dignity of an elder, and sat comfortably on his chair. Like the other men, he wore a thick shamma over his shirt and jacket. It was snowy white, with an intricate coloured border. His eyes were sharp and intelligent behind his glasses.

'A rich man had two sons . . .' he began. I settled back. The session was under way.

In Ato Worku's story, the rich man leaves all his cattle to his first son, and nothing to the second except for a brightly coloured rooster. The rich brother falls ill. The only medicine that will cure him is the meat of a coloured rooster. Generously, the impoverished brother slaughters his rooster in order to save the other's life.

The rich brother regains his health, but after a while feathers sprout all over his body. Terrified, he asks advice from the elders who tell him that he is being punished for his unfairness in taking from his brother the only thing he had. He must take a 'keleche' as a sign of forgiveness to his brother. If the wronged man spits on it, it means that he forgives his brother, who will be cured.

The rich brother does as he is told, the poor brother spits on the keleche and the feathers fall away. The elders instruct the rich man to give his brother one of his three stables of cows, and they live in harmony from that time.

Sibling rivalry is a rich seam mined by stories in every genre, starting right at the beginning with Cain and Abel, and there are parallels to 'The Man Who Grew Feathers' in folk tales everywhere. I need only think of the webs of love, jealousy, loyalty, irritation, kindness, generosity and occasional rage that bind me to my sisters to tap into the undertow of meaning.

I had never heard of a keleche before. It seemed to be another Oromo ritual object, like the silver necklace in the story of the dogfight. I filed the word away in the hopes that I would find out more about it later. Moti Wayesse, the next storyteller, another grand old shamma-clad elder, would bring it up again.

In his story, a man is so anxious about his pregnant wife and unborn child that he implores God to keep the child from being born so that it will become bigger and stronger. God answers his prayer, and before the first child is born, the woman becomes pregnant with a second. After another nine months have passed, the two boys are born together.

When the boys grow up, they quarrel over their father's inheritance. The first brother claims the larger share, on the grounds that he is older, but the second brother points out that they are in fact the same age. They put their problem to the elders, who find this a difficult case. After consulting the Abba Gadaa, the elders take the brothers to the edge of a lake and say to them, 'We can't reach a decision. It must be up to God. Dive into the bottom of the lake and bring up whatever you find there.'

The brothers do so. The second one comes up with a fish in his hand, but the older brother comes up with a keleche. And this is how the keleche came to the Oromo people, and why the older ones receive it instead of the younger.

'But what is the keleche?' I asked Merga.

He smiled.

'It is – it is a thing. For the king.'

There was no time for more.

On the journey back to Addis Ababa, Merga, picked up our conversation at breakfast and tried to explain to me the complexities of the Oromo marriage system. Not everyone takes the path which he had taken. The arranged marriage, with its complex ceremonies and exhaustive researches into genealogy (marriage is forbidden between blood relatives going back seven generation) is only possible for some. Poor people make do with elopements or bridal kidnappings, which are regulated between the families after the event. This may suit young couples where both the boy and the girl are equally keen (girls have traditionally married young, by their early teens, and boys before they are twenty), but in many cases girls are forcibly snatched while on the way to school, or fetching water for their mothers. They are carried off to their suitor's family and raped. A little later, the husband's family will seek reconciliation with the girl's, and a few token cows are paid over.

To be kidnapped in this way seals the fate of a girl. Once she is no longer a virgin, she has lost her chance of any other kind of marriage. Many young women accept the situation, settle down in their new family and get on with their lives, but like many other traditional institutions the modern age has made matters worse. The ability of the elders to control the practice has weakened. Young men may find that their brides don't suit them after all and abandon them. Their parents are unlikely to take them back and they have no choice but to become prostitutes. I have met and listened to stories of young women who have been kidnapped and abandoned in this way, and have visited a project set up in an attempt to change attitudes, so that this cruel practice can be ended.

In another Oromo tradition, a widow marries her dead husband's brother, who becomes responsible for the upbringing of her children. This was intended to be a sensible and compassionate solution to the difficulties of widows and their children, but with the advent of Aids, which has swept with devastating effect through Ethiopia, the practice often leads to disaster, for if the husband has died of Aids and infected his widow, she will go on to infect her new husband.

❖

Back at the Sargents' house in Addis Ababa, I found Patsy cooking. A party was in preparation. Ministry of Education officials as well as Merga and others from the Oromo Education Bureau had been invited to dinner.

Cross-cultural evening parties are tricky to arrange in Addis Ababa. People are reluctant to venture out after dark. There is the problem of what type of cuisine to provide. Dogs, which in European households are family pets and used to ambling amiably round the guests, are not gentle with strangers in the Ethiopian compounds they guard. But Michael and Patsy had long experience of making such parties go well. The party started early, the food was a mixture of Ethiopian and ferenji, and the dogs had been tied up.

Ato Mulugeta, the librarian from the British Council with whom I had reminisced about the old days, steered me towards a group of Ministry of Education officials.

'Elizabeth was a teacher at the Lab School here in Addis thirty years ago,' he said, looking expectantly at one of the older men, like a trainer hoping his tame lion will jump through its hoop. He had judged it right.

'But I was at the Lab School then!' a senior official said, and beside me I could feel Mulugeta rock backwards on his heels with quiet satisfaction.

The old Lab school student and I studied each other, trying to peel away the ravages of time. Regretfully, neither of us remembered the other. He had not been in my English class. But we spent a happy half-hour reminiscing nevertheless.

The Oromo Bureau staff were sitting together in a corner, their plates of beef curry balanced on their knees. They reminded me of a piece of unfinished business.

'The keleche,' I said, plunging straight in. 'It keeps coming up in the stories. What is it?'

They laughed and looked down at their plates, then started telling me about the Abba Gadaa system of government.

'Abba Gadaa wears the keleche on his forehead. It is a symbol of his authority.'

'Yes, but what *is* it? Is it made of wood? Stone? Metal? How big is it?'

They kept on laughing.

'Not wood. Not stone.' One of them pointed to his forehead. 'He wears it here.'

His fingers curved up and out to indicate a horn.

I remembered something I had seen earlier that day.

'I think I saw a picture of one in Gebre Geracha,' I began.

'It is not right to say Gebre Geracha,' they interrupted. 'Not the right name. "Kuyu" is the name of that place.'

I understood this. A tussle over names has been going on for a long time in the Oromo region where the Oromo and Amhara names for the same place coexist uneasily.

I described the picture I had seen. The figure of Abba Gadaa had appeared to have a white horn sticking out of his forehead.

'Is it a horn?'

They conferred, then nodded.

'Yes, a horn.'

'A woman says, "My husband is my keleche,"' said one of them, laughing again.

A fertility symbol then, as well as a symbol of authority. Was that why Merga, out of delicacy, had found it hard to describe it to me?

Merga had not been with this group. I went over to join him on the far side of the room.

'So the keleche is a horn,' I said.

He shook his head.

'No. The horn is a symbol only of the keleche. It is deeper. A deep thing. Hidden.'

'Can you describe what it looks like?'

He and the man next to him exchanged looks and laughed.

'It has nipples,' Merga said reluctantly. 'There might be nine, for an important one, or seven, five, three, or even one.'

'Is it big?'

'Different sizes.'

Ato Mulugeta, himself of Oromo origin, had joined us. He was fascinated by the subject, of which he knew nothing, and I left the questions to him, afraid of probing further than was comfortable.

I pieced together, in the end, that the keleche is a sacred object pertaining to old Oromo religion. It's made of a shiny metal and each group of four or five villages would have possessed one in the old days. A respected elder who knows its secrets keeps it hidden in his care and hands it on, not to a member of his family, but to another old and respected man. In some regions it's a band bearing a phallus, worn round the head.

'Have you seen a keleche?' I asked Merga.

Glances were exchanged again, and then he nodded.

'When? How?' pressed Mulugeta.

He answered vaguely that the keleche only appeared on two occasions in public: when there is a reconciliation ceremony, of the kind that had cropped up in the stories I had been told, and when a girl refuses to marry a boy. If he takes the keleche to her house, she has to submit to him.

I asked if women had any part to play in all this. They had a sacred object of their own, I was told – the ch'ech'u. This is a leather necklace stitched all over with cowry shells, which are symbols of the female genitalia. When the keleche appears in public, it dangles from the ch'ech'u. The ch'ech'u is kept by an old woman in a basket in her house, or buried in a pot in the ground. Its existence is kept absolutely secret.

'What happens if it's lost or stolen?' I asked.

Merga vigorously shook his head.

'Never by Oromo people. They would never steal it.'

I asked if the keleche or the ch'ech'u had magical properties. No, they said, they are cultural objects.

'Religious as well?'

'Yes, but belonging to the old religion. Secrecy was vital because if the authorities or the Church knew of these things they would destroy them.'

'The priests would destroy them?'

'Not if they are Oromo. Amhara priests. They will destroy them because they are not from the Christian religion.'

I enjoyed my evening of amateur anthropological sleuthing but I wasn't sure, when the party was finally over and I was climbing into bed in the Sargents' comfortable guest room, whether I was much the wiser. As in so many other areas of Ethiopian life, I was all at sea when it came to politics, and I remembered Michael Ambatchew's wise warning that politics had a great deal to do with a perception of the old customs. In the long centuries of imperial Amhara domination, the old ways of the Oromo had gone underground. With the growth of Oromo power and confidence, they are coming up once more into the daylight, but in the many differing Oromo communities, spread over such a vast area of Ethiopia, differences of interpretation are inevitable.

All I could be certain of were the stories. In their simple narratives of brothers, fathers, mothers and daughters, they have carried within them old ideas and ways of seeing the world, some spelled out clearly and some almost hidden, like the mysterious objects on which so much ritual and ceremony had always depended.

⋄ 9 ⋄

ECHOES OF BAGHDAD
IN HARAR

In a country of such extravagant natural phenomena, it seems appro-priate to call upon a geological analogy to describe them. If you imagine the different peoples, with their distinct cultures, languages and modes of subsistence as a series of tectonic plates, it's clear how the fault lines running between them are subject to earthquakes. Perhaps the most troublesome of all these zones of friction is the area where the settled, Christian heartlands of the highlands rub alongside the pastoralist, nomadic, Muslim lands to the east, part of which form the region of Somali Ethiopia.

Many Ethiopians wouldn't like this idea. They point out that their country has been unified for a long time, populations overlap, intermarriage has taken place over many centuries, and communities in Ethiopia have always lived side by side regardless of linguistic, cultural and religious differences. They are anxious, with good reason, that an emphasis on separate cultural identities threatens the very fabric of Ethiopia.

A glance at the history books reveals a long litany of skirmishes along the troublesome eastern edge of the highlands, where the coolness of high altitude gives way to the dryer, hotter plains of the Ogaden below. The most spectacular of these was the invasion in 1529 by Ahmad Gragn ('the Left-handed') who defeated the Christian emperor Lebna Dengal and swept through his realm, burning churches and monasteries with their ancient manuscripts and jewelled vestments, slaughtering the inhabitants and bringing famine to the survivors. Gragn's memory is still alive in the lands he conquered. He has become a bogeyman, acquiring in legend gigantic stature, a monstrous horse and enormous weapons. He was defeated finally by the Emperor Gelawdewos (Claudius) in 1543, with a little help from the Portuguese (Christofero da Gama, Vasco's son, was killed during the struggle), an early example of European involvement in internal Ethiopian affairs. Gragn is naturally something of a hero to the Somalis.

The Somali region was incorporated into the Ethiopian state by the Emperor Menelik at the end of the nineteenth century, but he could exert no more than minimal control. The Italians annexed it in 1936. The British ejected them in 1943, and tried to absorb the Ogaden into British Somaliland. They didn't give up the attempt until 1954. If you think this is complicated, I will spare you the ins and outs of the subsequent decades, in which liberation movements have taken on one regime after another. All-out war erupted when Mengistu came to power. The horror of modern weaponry, pumped first into Somalia and then into Ethiopia by the Russians, created dreadful suffering, unmitigated by medical aid. Mengistu prevailed, and the region was 'pacified' (a blatantly misleading description of the brutality of repression) but the fires were only damped down and not extinguished. They flare up from time to time, the chaos in Somalia itself feeding the unrest in the Ogaden.

Perhaps because it was absorbed into the Ethiopian empire so recently (and so imperfectly), the Somali region has less ethnic diversity than many other areas. Of the four and a half million people who live scattered over this vast area, over ninety-five per cent are Muslim and speak the Somali language. The region is plagued with a vicious strain of malaria, and tsetse flies harass the cattle in many areas. Worst of all is the increasing threat of drought, making life ever more miserable for this nomadic, pastoralist society, whose existence depends on cattle, more than three quarters of which died during 1999 and 2000. The old ways of life are increasingly unsustainable, and I thought of this constantly as I listened to the stories I was told, and wondered how soon they would be lost and forgotten, along with the world they so elegantly celebrate.

There are few creature comforts for the people here. Only a tiny percentage have access to electricity. Less than a quarter of the children attend primary school, and hardly any make the leap into secondary education.

I was looking forward to tackling the Somali region, especially as the British Council had arranged for me to visit Harar at the same time. I had last been to the enticing walled city, with its romantic history and unique culture, with Mark Rosen in the 1960s, and I'd always wanted to return.

I was to have a different translator with me this time. His name was also Michael, though he spelled it Mikhail in the Ethiopian way.

'You'll look after Miss Laird and bring her back in one piece?' Michael Sargent said, as Mikhail and I left the British Council office after our final briefing.

'I will do my best!' Mikhail cried. 'I will do everything in my power!'

Mikhail was twenty-seven, a handsome young man, tall and strong with charming manners. He had set his heart on being a vet, but had failed to get into the veterinary school in Addis Ababa. His plan was to persuade various uncles settled in the USA to help him through veterinary studies in America. In the meantime he had tried his hand at business and worked in an orphanage. He was at a loose end and relished the idea of our expedition.

The night before we set off for Harar and Somalia, I had hardly slept at all. A few days earlier, there had been an unpleasant incident on the road between Harar and Somalia, when a bus had been hijacked by Somali insurgents (or more probably, bandits) and all the passengers had been taken out and shot. I sweated most of the night, persuading myself that I was dreadfully ill with typhoid, malaria, meningitis, or all three combined, and only fell asleep when I'd decided to call the trip off and spend the next day luxuriating in bed. However, I woke with a start at 6.50, realised that the Land Rover was coming to collect me at 7, threw on my clothes, left a note for kind Michael and Patsy Sargent, whose guest I was, grabbed a banana off their fruit bowl and was outside the door waiting when the Land Rover arrived ten minutes later.

It was a relief, too, that the volatile Dirije was not to be my driver this time, but Tekle, whom I had always liked and trusted. 'Tekle' is short for Tekle-Haimanot, the name of a hermit-saint of the twelfth century, who, in the manner of an anchorite of the early church, stood on one leg in meditation for seven years until the other withered and fell away. The name is common among the sons of churchmen, and I guessed that Tekle's father had been a priest. He was certainly a pious man, but in a less showy way than Dirije. He made no display over his fasting and bowed his head only unobtrusively when we passed a church or a priest along the way.

Tekle liked to wrap himself in the dignity of a diplomatic driver. When talking of me to other people, he always used 'ersachew', the polite third person plural form. He would take the briefcase out of my hand as I entered an office building, and when on the road would imperiously wave people out of the way of the Land Rover, which he would have polished to an immaculate white before setting off. Once, I even saw him wag a finger at a policeman who had had the temerity to try and flag him down.

After a three-hour drive we reached the town of Awash, which had grown up around a railway station on the Addis Ababa-Djibouti line (currently being rebuilt by the Chinese). The original railway was built during the reign of Menelik, a far-sighted monarch who foresaw the importance of installing and controlling new technologies. French and British companies were involved in its construction, and the stations still retain a flavour of France, from the main terminal in Addis Ababa, known generally as 'La Gare', to the halts along the way. The station at Awash is a white, bougainvillea-clad immigrant from the Mediterranean, and its glory is the 'Buffet de la Gare', an old-fashioned station restaurant, whose cool dining room is a roofed patio walled only with climbing plants. I sighed with pleasure as I walked in. Nothing had changed for thirty years. The clock over the door still said 5.30. The tables had the same red-and-white checked cloths and the polished concrete floor was perfectly swept.

For many years, the manager of this oasis had been Madam Kiki Jean Assimacopoulous, a staggeringly old Greek woman with violently hennaed hair. She had already seemed ancient to me in the 1960s, and I'd assumed she had died years ago. I hardly glanced at the old woman in a long brown dress with a white kerchief bound round her head, sitting on a chair by the kitchen door. In the style of the classic Ethiopian coffee ceremony, a low square table stood in front of her, containing handle-less coffee cups. Steam was rising from a black, long-stemmed coffee pot, and incense smoke puffed from a brazier. As I walked past her, she said, 'Voulez-vous du café, Madame?'

I looked down into her sunburnt face, startled by her blue eyes. She indicated the chair beside her, and I sat down.

'Vous êtes française?' I asked her, hardly knowing what to say.

'Je suis grecque, Madame.'

She told me that she had been born in Dire Dawa in the 1920s, and had been running the buffet in Awash since the 1940s. She had survived the Italians, lived through their ultimate defeat, the return of Haile Selassie, the revolution, the various wars that had followed, and the installation of the new regime. For all this time, her life had been dominated by the arrival of the daily train. In the old days, it had stopped for an hour at Awash to enable the passengers to disembark and eat a leisurely lunch in the buffet. Now, I was not sure who the customers could be.

As she talked, her old eyes were fixed on me with almost painful persistence, and her thin hands waved about her face.

'Didn't you have problems during all those years of revolution and war?'

'Jamais. Rien. Pas de problème. Aucune problème.'

'But in times of war the government must have commandeered the trains for troops, and so on.'

She shrugged, raising her eyebrows and dropping her lids at the same time in an expression of weary cynicism.

'C'est normal. Au temps de guerre, c'est normal.'

We talked about the failure of the rains, which was threatening another round of hunger that year in Ethiopia.

'It is a catastrophe, you know? It will need a century to recover. A hundred years, Madame. And on top of that, I don't know why, the potatoes are very bad this year.'

We talked for a little while, then went back to our table, where Mikhail was already demolishing an enormous plate of shish kebab. He pushed his plate back at last and began to talk about his family. His mother was a nurse, he told me, and he had one sister.

'What about your father?' I asked casually, spearing a mouthful of chicken.

I was unprepared for the story that followed. Mikhail's father had been a soldier. One of the bright young men of Haile Selassie's last days, he had been sent to Sandhurst for his training.

'To the Royal Military Academy.' Mikhail was keen to spell it out for me. I watched his face, afraid that this story would end badly. 'There were two from Ethiopia. That other one, he won the – the honour something.'

'The Sword of Honour.'

'Yes. My father came home to Ethiopia, and they sent him to Harar to the military academy, to train the officers for the Ethiopian army. You know there is a famous military academy in Harar?'

'Yes. Go on.'

'Then there was the revolution and the Derg came. My father did not like some of the things they were doing and he spoke up loudly.' He looked younger as he spoke. He pushed back his round-lensed, slightly tinted glasses, and wiped some grease from the fancy beard cut close round his chin. 'They arrested him from our house and took him away and we never heard from him again, or found out anything about him.'

'So your mother was left alone with two small children?'

'Yes. She was very bitter. She is still bitter. Her father was a businessman. He had many trucks and drivers. The Derg said he was a capitalist and stole everything from him. His heart couldn't bear it and he died. And my mother and father, they were very close. They were in love.' He linked his fingers together. 'Like that. Before she married my father, her parents tried to make an arranged marriage for her with a colonel, but she refused, and married my father although he was only a lieutenant. They were always angry with her after that.'

Later, his grandmother had been arrested, on a charge of aiding and abetting the forces arrayed against Mengistu. She too was never seen again.

I understood the air of melancholy that clung to Mikhail. He had about him the kind of 'soul' so celebrated in Russian literature, a nostalgia for things lost, a sense of injury for past wrongs done to him. There was too, perhaps, the vulnerability of the adored only son of a lonely mother.

As we left the Buffet de la Gare, Madame Kiki had one last word for me.

'Have you heard,' she said, 'that the Red Sea has boiled and all the fish have died? On ne parle que de ça, ici.'

❖

The road to Harar is beguiling. It winds over a range of almost-mountains between which valleys swoop down and up again. In Europe motorways would have thundered along these valley bottoms, souring the air, but for hundreds of miles to the north and south of us there was no motorised road other than the one we were on.

In spite of its beauty, the road had its dangers. At one point we came round a corner to find a row of boulders lying across the road. Tekle exclaimed under his breath, and without slowing down manoeuvred his way between them.

'Shifta,' he said with a shudder.

We encountered few other vehicles, although there is a constant traffic of people and animals on Ethiopian roads. Children leaning against their sticks mind flocks of sheep and goats grazing on the verges. People make their way to and from the local market, their backs bowed under sacks and bundles. Occasionally, one passes an itinerant priest or monk.

I noticed how brilliantly coloured the women's clothes had become. Years ago, every highlander had worn white cotton homespun, which dulled down to grey as it aged. The women we were now passing were arrayed in purple, electric blue or emerald green dresses topped off with shammas in poppy red or shocking pink. I thought they looked wonderful and said so to Mikhail.

He looked down his long aristocratic nose.

'All this cloth comes from outside Ethiopia. From India or the Far East. It is better when we make it ourselves.'

Regretfully, I had to agree.

It's a long way to Harar, and I was done in by the time we arrived. Thankfully, there were rooms for us at the old Ras Hotel. Built in the 1930s during the Italian era, this venerable establishment had since the revolution been government run. It had high ceilings, shabby furniture, dim light bulbs and dozens of underemployed personnel. I found myself in an entire suite, with a bedroom, sitting room and bathroom, the furniture practically antique, but clean and comfortable. The only problem was the electric shocks that tingled up my arm when I touched a tap, and the lack of a plug in the bath.

'Sorry, David,' I said out loud, and told myself I'd run my packing past him next time.

Tekle had disappeared when Mikhail and I met for dinner.

He had a way of sorting out his own eating and sleeping arrangements on long trips, and it was only much later that I discovered what a cool operator he was.

There was nothing much to tempt us on the dinner menu.

'At least we won't get fat, eating here,' I said to Mikhail. 'There's a silver lining to every cloud.'

He didn't know the expression and I explained its meaning to him. He was delighted and made a joke of it, begging me to teach him more such witty expressions.

In an Ethiopia replete with wonders, Harar must be among the most glamorous places. From the time of the Middle Ages, it existed as a prosperous Muslim city-state, with its own Emir, its trade links with Arabia and its urban population of merchants ('Haderis') who spoke their own language, developed their own style of architecture and guarded their independence from the outside world.

Two European travellers will be forever associated with Harar. In 1855 the dashing nineteenth-century explorer, Richard Burton, was the first European to penetrate the closely guarded city in the disguise of a Muslim. He spent ten days there, having revealed his identity as an Englishman, and was received by the Emir and other notables. The city, he said, was 'the emporium of the coffee trade, the headquarters of slavery, the birthplace of the chat plant, and the great manufactory of cotton cloths.'

Twenty-five years later, Rimbaud, the French *'poète maudit'*, in flight from the chaos of his Parisian life, set up as a trader in Harar and began dealing arms to the Ethiopian Emperor Menelik, who finally conquered Harar and incorporated it into his empire in 1890.

Menelik installed his cousin, Ras Makonnen, as the governor of Harar. Ras Makonnen's son, Ras Tafari, was to become Haile Selassie, the last Emperor of Ethiopia. His birth name lives on among the Rastafarians, who revere Haile Selassie as a reincarnation of Christ.

There is something particularly alluring about an ancient walled city, and Harar, remote and isolated, set within its white walls on the green side of a hill, is a jewel. From a distance, it looks like a picture-map from a medieval manuscript, its minarets rising up from the closely packed houses in elegant white spikes.

Harar has not escaped the modern world. The old gates, once shut at nightfall, are never closed now, and a road cuts through one section of wall so that trucks and buses can rumble into the heart of the city, but most streets in Harar are lanes so narrow that two laden donkeys have difficulty in passing each other. There are doors here and there in the high walls which line these lanes. When you are lucky enough to pass one that is open, you gain tantalising glimpses of courtyards and old houses. Colours assault you in Harar: washes of turquoise, deep blue and plum red among the predominantly white walls, with vistas of the green hills beyond; and everywhere the fluttering clothes of the Haderi women, whose distinctive style features striped satin leggings, and full-skirted dresses covered with flowers and dots in shocks of purple on green, or orange on blue, or pink on yellow.

I was raring to go that first morning in Harar. Tekle picked Mikhail and me up in the Land Rover, which he had washed until it gleamed and its yellow British Council CD plates glinted. Everyone in Ethiopia knows the code for diplomatic vehicles. I could not have been more publicly British if I had leaned out of the window and waved a Union Jack. As it was, I felt we had arrived at the Bureau of Culture and Sport in some style, with

Tekle on his dignity, adding to our consequence.

They were ready for us in Harar. By now, the books of stories from Afar and Gambela had been published and sent on to them, so they understood what the project was about, and were keen to have their share in it. In any case, there was a sophistication here, a consciousness of the importance and value of their heritage, its oral riches included.

We were passed by the head of the bureau to his assistant, a pretty young woman called Nejaha. Luckily, she knew Mikhail, having been his classmate years ago, and this link stood us in good stead. In any case, Nejaha was ready to throw herself into the whole delightful business of collecting stories. Although she belonged to the exclusive Haderi merchant community, she was dressed in the modern style in jeans and a blue denim shirt, and carried a natty handbag on her arm. She took us into her office, where two storytellers were waiting.

As I might have expected, some of the first stories I was offered were immigrants from Arabia, featuring Abu Nawas, the scandalous wit of Baghdad, and Nasruddin, that rascally, earthy rebel, whose mythical exploits have been celebrated in stories from China to Zanzibar for hundreds of years. As I watched my first storyteller push back his white skull cap to scratch his bald head and run his tongue around the two gold incisors at the corners of his mouth, I saw in my mind's eye a caravanserai, a fire of camel dung in a courtyard under the stars, white-robed merchants sitting cross-legged over tiny cups of coffee as they entertained each other with these very stories.

When it was translated, my first Harar story did indeed run true to form. A wicked Qadi,[37] lusting after Abu Nawas's beautiful

---

[37] The Arabic for 'judge'.

wife, persuades the Emir to bury Abu Nawas alive so that he
can deliver a cloak to the Emir's parents who are suffering from
the cold in their afterlife. Abu Nawas agrees to carry out the
commission, and prepares a grave with an escape tunnel. He is
duly buried, creeps out through his tunnel, and returns to tell
the Emir that his parents are well.

'The only problem is,' he tells the Emir. 'Your father has fallen
in love with a younger woman and wants to marry her. He can't
do so unless a Qadi goes to him to perform the ceremony.'

The Emir, wanting to carry out his father's wishes, commands
that the Qadi be buried alive, and so he is – a just punishment for
the plot he had hatched against Abu Nawas.

The pleasure in these story cycles lies in the way in which
the stock characters are manipulated by the cunning hero. The
Emir (or sultan, king or emperor) floats in his power, Zeus-like,
above his subjects. His whims may be arbitrary, he may be led
astray by his passions, have the wool pulled over his eyes, and
be deceived by villains, but his decisions are final and ultimate
power rests with him. He is not to be mocked. The butt of the
stories is usually a corrupt vizier or judge, and the plot revolves
around the ways in which such figures can be worsted.

We are so used to satire that we no longer appreciate the
edginess of these stories. They flirt with sedition, and push at the
limits of how far the folk hero can go as he squares up to figures
of authority. There is always, after all, a tension between art and
the state. One might even pity the censor, whose efforts can so
easily backfire. When the film *Doctor Zhivago* was screened in
Addis Ababa in 1968, there was official panic at the impact which
the execution of a tsar might have on Haile Selassie's restive
subjects. Most of the film passed uncut, but the announcement
of the death of Nicholas II was thought to be too inflammatory,

so the censor simply cut it out. The bringer of the dreadful news appeared on the screen. He opened his mouth. Cut. He shut it again. There was much mirth at the censor's expense.

Nejaha felt as I did that the office was not conducive to good storytelling, and when our first narrators had begun to tire, she asked me tentatively if I minded going about on foot. The Land Rover, she explained, would not be able to negotiate the narrow lanes of Harar. She was pleased when I told her that I would love to walk around Harar with her, and we set off into the already hot sunshine, in pursuit of an elderly hajji, who had said we might call at his house.

Our way took us through the old horse market, where sheep staggered about, intoxicated after scavenging leaves of chat left over from the early morning's sales. We met the hajji coming out of a shop, carrying a little bundle tied in newspaper. He wore a pale beige suit, a sky-blue shirt and highly polished shoes, and carried an elegant cane; if it hadn't been for the turban wrapped around his head he would have looked like an escapee from the 1930s. He greeted me courteously in old-fashioned French. We made an appointment for later in the morning.

The old houses of Harar, hidden behind the high white walls which enclose their compounds, are approached through weathered wooden doors which are surrounded sometimes by carved or painted lintels and creak back at a knock. In the centre of the compound, there might be a flower bed containing a vivid scarlet bougainvillea, or rows of kerosene tins planted with canna lilies. At the far end of the compound, the facade of the house is often decorated with plaster mouldings picked out in bright colours.

Inside, the Haderis love of colour and their pleasure in display is given full rein. A raised platform takes up much of the room, with a higher level in the grander houses. This area is covered with rugs, while bolsters, often made of frilled and embroidered satin, line the walls, which might be painted pink, green or yellow. Niches are crammed with pieces of china, books and vases of plastic flowers. Pictures, photographs of family members, clocks and stencilled enamel dishes decorated with flowers crowd the walls, along with samples of Harar's famously intricate baskets. The frank enjoyment of decor in Harar comes as a relief after the rather more strait-laced approach to domestic comfort in the highlands.

By the time we arrived at the hajji's house, he had changed into more comfortable clothes, and was wearing a floor-length cloth wrapped around his waist, a V-necked sweater over his shirt, and a simple white skull cap. He was ensconced on his sitting platform, leaning against a pile of bolsters. Beside him bookshelves were crammed with books and pamphlets, a radio and a telephone were placed on a low table, and in a niche in the wall was a jumble of pill bottles. He had only to stretch out a hand to reach anything he required, and I remembered with a pang my father's study, with its clutter of an old man's comforts.

It was not surprising, I suppose, that the hajji's stories also relied on the exploits of Sheikh Nasruddin and Abu Nawas, but he recounted one famous old tale which I often think of at times when circumstances seem against me.

A rich man decrees that the one who would marry his daughter must swim out to an island in a lake and spend the night alone on a rock, without food or the warmth of a fire. A young man decides to make the attempt although the night is bitterly cold. To help him, his mother lights a fire on the shore. The boy keeps his eyes fixed on the distant light and the thought of its warmth gives him the strength to survive. But when he returns to claim his bride, the rich man accuses him of cheating.

Abu Nawas hears of this. He invites the young man and the bride's father to a feast. He slaughters a bull, puts the meat in a saucepan, and hangs it in a tree, away from fire. The hungry guests demand to know how the food can be cooked when it is so far from the fire.

'And how can this young man have been warmed by a fire on the far side of the lake?' retorts Abu Nawas.

His argument is accepted, and the young man wins his bride.

I had been particularly delighted to be in the hands of Nejaha because I guessed she would have greater access to women storytellers, and she did not disappoint me. She led the way down one of Harar's narrow lanes, and a few moments later I was in another enchanting Haderi house, my sandals kicked off, my back propped up against a hard bolster on the carpeted platform, while our hostess, Zaineba, nodded at Nejaha's explanation, then went off to get us some refreshments, saying that she needed time to think.

A little later she settled herself cross-legged beside us, arranged her shawl over her head and shoulders, tucked the skirt of her dress (decorated with a pattern of strawberries on a white background) around her legs, and launched into the story of Irit and Nurit, a tale of two sisters and all that befell them.

Although this story has much in common with that of Ngap and Nyakwiy, from the very different setting of Gambela, for some reason Irit and Nurit have lodged firmly in my head, and I often scratch away at the story, trying to glean from it an ever greater understanding of Zaineba and the world she inhabited.

The story starts in a common enough way, introducing us to Irit, the good girl, whose mother is dead, and her half-sister Nurit, whose mother is only too alive. Nurit and her mother are cruel to Irit. They make her grind hot pepper in the kitchen.

One day, the two girls go out to pick chat. A 'fairy man' asks the girls to give him some. Irit does so with kind words, but Nurit refuses and is cursed. The girls fail to sell their chat in the market, and Irit is blamed by her stepmother and thrown out of the house. A holy man comes along and invites Irit to live with him. He tells Irit to wake him if golden water comes into the house, but not to wake him if black water comes.

Black water comes. She doesn't wake him. Golden water comes. She wakes him. The holy man puts Irit in the golden water and commands the wind to carry her off and set her down on her father's roof. There she sits, spitting gold saliva.

Nurit finds the gold and looks up to see her sister on the roof. She asks Irit how her spit has changed to gold, and Irit tells her about the old man. 'Go to him yourself,' Irit says, 'and wake him when black water comes into the house.'

Nurit does so. When the old man is woken and sees the black water, he commands the wind to blow the girl to her mother's kitchen, and hide her in the ashes of the fire, under the pan.

In the morning, the mother comes to light the fire, and sees something move under the pan. She thinks it is a cat and curses it, but Nurit says, 'No, Mother, it's me, Nurit!'

Her mother is ashamed, because her daughter is black, and she hides her.

A man comes and asks for Irit's hand in marriage, but the stepmother gives her to a python instead. The python eats Irit, but when the bridegroom and the best man came to the house to claim her, the python spits her out.

Irit now becomes a happy bride, but the bridegroom and the best man cut out Nurit's tongue to punish her for her cruelty to her sister.

This Cinderella-type tale (even to the ashes of the fire) follows the usual pattern of girls wronged by sisters and stepmothers, who win all in the end, helped by the agency of a fairy-person, but the details continue to intrigue and puzzle me.

Spittle is a magical substance in many of the stories I heard in Ethiopia. Hair, both animal and human, is also frequently used in enchantment. In the case of both hair and spittle, the magician in the stories is usually a woman.

Since early times, in many parts of the world, matter produced by the human body has been thought to have magical properties. Spittle, blood, hair, nails and sperm are powerful substances. In the Egyptian creation myth, Atum creates Shu (air) and Tefut (moisture) from his spittle. In southern Europe, a compliment might be accompanied by a spit to avert the evil eye. Jesus restores a man's sight by spitting on his eyes. Samson's strength resides in his hair, and is lost when it is cut off. (Later, in southern Ethiopia, I would come across single pubic hairs with the magical power to make locks for doors.) Body parts can be used for malevolent purposes. In Malaysia, fifty years ago, I was warned to dispose carefully of my nail clippings in case they fell into the hands of someone who might use them to curse me.

The roof of the house features once again in this story as a place of magical import. Nurit's shame in turning black hints at a murky side of Harar's history. Haderi merchants, relatively light-skinned themselves, were heavily involved in the slave trade, and anyone with the dark skin of the sub-Saharan African was presumed to be a slave and despised. As for the python, I leave him to the psychologists.

I suppose I was a hard task-mistress that evening, keeping Nejaha until long after her working day should have ended. She and Mikhail sat with me under a tree in the garden of the hotel,

chilly once the sun had gone down. We struggled together with
the translations of the stories, until at last I let them go.

Worn out, I fell asleep as soon as I lay down on my bed, but
I woke in the small hours and lay listening to the whoop of the
hyenas on the hills outside the city walls. For the rest of the
night I drifted in and out of half-dreams, seeing in my mind's
eye the characters from the stories I had heard set against bright
snapshots of the houses and lanes of Harar. At last, the muezzin
sang out the dawn call to prayer, and the first lorries rumbled
out of the city. It was time to get up.

I don't remember if the moon was full that night, but there
must have been something in the air, because Mikhail had not
slept either. He came heavy-eyed to breakfast with a story
involving a key, which I couldn't follow. And later, when we
called once more on Zaineba, she told me that she too had lain
awake half the night, thinking about Irit and Nurit.

'The meaning of the story,' she said earnestly, patting
my forearm with her work-calloused hand, 'is that the one
who wishes evil things to other people will have an evil fate
themselves. That's true in life. Isn't it?'

I can no longer separate out in my memory the many houses
we visited in Harar, the rugs on which I sat, the cushions against
which I leaned, the cups of coffee I sipped, and the voices of the
storytellers rising and falling.

Two special places have stayed with me. We had met, early on
our second morning, a tailor and cloth merchant called Abdul
Rahman. He spent his days in a small booth with the front open
on to the street. Piled on shelves around him were bales of cloth,
and more were displayed on poles over his head. He was working
at his treadle sewing machine as we approached him, but he was
delighted with the idea of taking time off to tell stories. The

ordinariness of an everyday house was not for him. He wanted the splendour of the town's museum as his setting.

The museum in Harar occupied an old Harari house of the grandest sort. The platform, which took up perhaps half the main room, was big enough to seat a crowd of people. There were no newly painted enamel plates, plastic flowers or fancy clocks hanging on the walls, but a display of exquisite Harar baskets.

Abdul Rahman settled himself beneath a photograph of the last Emir, who gazed out from under a bulbous white turban. There were several of us now, including some of Nejaha's colleagues from the Cultural Bureau, and we found ourselves places against the cushions, careful not to disturb the carved Koran stands and framed Koranic texts on the shelf above.

Abdul Rahman was a gifted storyteller. I couldn't understand a word he said, but neither could I take my eyes off him. He used his voice as an actor might, changing it for each character, throwing out his arms in expressive gestures and singing the rhymes embedded in the stories.

As usual I had to wait until the evening before I could hear the stories for myself. It wasn't surprising that they turned out, on the whole, to have a flavour of the Arabian Nights. There was an upstart merchant who plots to marry the only daughter of a king (and succeeds), a clever wife who manipulates her lazy husband into making a fortune, a hapless prince cast out by a cruel father, a talking whale, a cruel sorceress, jinns, and many more besides.

Telling stories in the museum was fun but a little stagy, and it was a much simpler house that lives most strongly in my memory. News of my visit to Zaineba must have spread among the women, because the next day an elderly woman with thick lenses in her glasses came to Nejaha with an invitation. There was a gathering in someone's house, and they had stories they would like to tell me. She hurried off down a lane, clinging to Nejaha's arm, and I followed, enjoying the slap of my sandals on the irregularly cut paving stones, which had been worn smooth by generations of feet and donkey hooves.

The woman led us through a battered gate set in a whitewashed wall and into a small courtyard. The house was simpler than some I had visited. Whereas a satellite dish might sometimes be displayed outside among the canna lilies, or a fridge or TV might gleam in the corner of a living room, there were no such modern appliances here, but there was the usual arrangement of two-tiered platforms extending in an L shape around the sides of the room.

I could barely make out the rugs and cushions because the available sitting space was already occupied by a crowd of women.

'Someone has died,' Nejaha whispered to me. 'They have come to pay their respects.'

Mikhail, embarrassed to be the only male among these birds of paradise, felt duty bound to take the lead. He cleared his throat and explained our project to them. Everyone nodded, but said that they needed to pray first, as their ceremonial mourning had not been completed. I retreated to a corner behind the door.

There must have been nine or ten women on the main dais, which measured no more than six feet by three, two more on the step below, and three others on the short arm of the L. Their bare feet jutted out from the cuffs of their calf-hugging satin leggings as they buried their toes in the pile of the peach-coloured rug.

Making ready to pray, they lifted their gauzy shawls up over their heads, and stayed for a moment in silence. Then they shuffled into kneeling positions and their lips began to move. Murmurs filled the room. I saw that they were all making the same gesture, pointing with a forefinger, then flicking their other fingers back and forth as if counting something off against their thumbs. The murmurs intensified, echoed by the buzzing of flies around their heads.

My attention wandered to the rest of the room and I had time to take in the steep stair that led up to a mezzanine floor above. There was no more than a metre of height below the whitewashed rafters, and I guessed that this was a sleeping area. As elsewhere, the walls above the dais were decorated with framed Koranic texts, wreaths of pink plastic flowers and Harari baskets decorated with cowry shells.

'This is cultural interior,' Nejaha whispered to me, as she had done in every house.

'Cultural' is a catch-all word in Ethiopia. Injera is cultural food, the white shamma is cultural dress, the nose flute makes cultural music, and honey-mead – 'tej' – is a cultural drink.

The individual murmurs of prayer were merging into a kind of unison, and I saw that the old woman with the thick glasses who had brought us here was the leader, raising her hands in gestures which the others were copying. They were chanting now, the volume of sound increasing. Then it was over. Each woman picked up her neighbour's hand, kissed the back, then the palm, then the back again and, duty done, they turned their attention to me. I was beckoned forward and room was made for me on a small square of carpet. The first storyteller was ready to begin.

The woman was plump and far beyond youth, but she was still beautiful. Her forehead was high, her cheeks round, and her skin the colour of pale, milky coffee. A drift of yellow gauze covered her head and shoulders, underneath which she wore a velvet skullcap fringed with sequins. Many small rings pierced the rims of her ears, and from behind them dangled two stuffed velvet baubles the size of tennis balls which were overlaid with gold netting. Her top dress was made of heavy white satin dotted with green flowers, and round her neck hung a string of amber beads as big as plums, and another of ivory beads the size of coffee beans. A heavy silver necklace fell over her breasts. Her name was Ay Nuria.

She started with one word, chanted high and loud.

'Riori!'

'What does it mean?' I whispered to Nejaha.

'It is in the Harari language. I means "I see something."'

'Minteri? Mintesami?' the other women were singing back.

'What do you see? What do you hear?' Nejaha translated.

The ritual introduction over, the story began, but instead of speaking it, Ay Nuria sang it. The effect was like the intoning of a prayer after the antiphonal responses in an Anglican evensong. She finished each sentence with a long-drawn-out vowel, and the women sang the sound back to her in the same way that the Afar men had done in Assayita. After a while, though, Ay Nuria stopped singing, and began to tell her story in a speaking voice, using it like a musical instrument, changing the speed, timbre and rhythm to match the characters in the drama. She was a compelling storyteller. She thrust her arms out and waved them, threatening from time to time to knock the tape recorder out of my hands. Once or twice, another woman tried to interrupt her, to add something or contest a point in the story, but Ay Nuria swept all interference aside and surged on until at last she came to an abrupt stop and subsided against the hard pink cushion behind her.

I had watched her throughout, enthralled. We were all crammed so close together that I had no room to move my legs. The women's veils and skirts fluttered against my skin as I breathed in the mingled smells of spices, breast milk and perspiration which rose from their bodies. Now I put aside the tape recorder and groped in my bag for my camera, but when the women saw it they frowned and shook their fingers. Photographs would not be allowed.

I was ridiculously disappointed. I realised that I had been mentally looking at the scene in that small house, with its brilliant colours, vibrant faces and elaborate clothes as if through a viewfinder. For a moment I was almost panic-stricken, wondering how I would capture this scene and hold it in my memory. Later, as I thought this reaction over, I reproached myself for falling victim to the camera's tyranny. Filled with a kind of greed, a desire to grab something from these people and take it away for my private enjoyment, I had been distancing myself from them. For the rest of the afternoon, knowing I would have no photographs to look back on, I used my eyes all the more carefully, imprinting scene after scene on my memory.

That evening, when we sat once again under the tree in the garden of the Ras Hotel, I heard at last the story that Ay Nuria had told.

A brother falls in love with his sister and plans to marry her by force with the collusion of her parents. A little brother overhears them plotting and warns the girl. When the older brother tries to seize her she throws hot pepper into his eyes and runs away. She crosses a river and hides in a tree. A prince sees her and falls in love with her.

She says, 'If my spit lands on you and turns to gold, I will marry you. If not, I will not.'

She spits and hits the prince. The spit turns to gold, so they marry. One day, the parents and the older brother, poor and weary, arrive at the prince's house. The girl lets them in and gives them food, clothes and water. And so the story ends on a note of forgiveness and reconciliation.

Nejaha didn't approve of this ending.

'My grandmother tells the story in another way,' she said. 'The parents and the bad brother, they try to cross the river and the crocodiles eat them. Only the little brother lives, because the tree bends down and saves him. They don't come along begging at the end and get forgiven.'

She made me write her version down too, sure that it was the 'correct' one.

There had been time, during our days in Harar, to take in the tourist sites. The most popular is a nineteenth-century trader's mansion, known as 'Rimbaud's house', although his connection to it is not at all certain. It was in the last stages of disrepair when I had seen it in the 1960s, but it had now been refurbished, and it was possible to climb the stairs and go from room to room, looking out from the upper windows across the domes of mosques and the corrugated iron roofs of Harar, and sneak peeks into the courtyards of old houses.

It was time to leave Harar but I was sorry to go. Like my favourite street in Addis Ababa, Harar casts its own enchantment, and it takes an effort of will to shake off the spell and move on.

⁂ 10 ⁂

THE LION'S BRIDE
OF SOMALIA

Tekle was nervous about the next leg of our journey. It was on the road to Jijiga that the notorious bus hijackings and shootings had taken place. His normal practice was to leave early, as soon as the sun had risen, but he would not set out for Jijiga until he had spent some time at the bus station, where he could see with his own eyes that the buses from Jijiga were making it through the dangerous passes and could be satisfied that no incidents had taken place. His visit to the police station the night before had failed to reassure him. They had told him that the hijackers had been rounded up and summarily shot, but he hadn't believed them.

I was grateful to Tekle for his caution. I knew I could trust his judgment.

The road from Harar to Jijiga winds around a hillside from which you can take a last farewell of the lovely little city and watch its walls slowly shrink till they are out of sight. For all Tekle's researches, I could tell that he was still nervous. Usually quiet, he was talking loudly and fast, engaging Mikhail in a long soliloquy. The countryside grew wilder and the intervals between oncoming vehicles lengthened until we were the only car on the road. I felt my stomach tighten.

'See this bridge? This is where the bus was stopped. This is where they were murdered,' Mikhail said at one point, with ghoulish pleasure, and Tekle drew in his breath, sucked his teeth and shook his head.

The scene looked quiet enough to me. Beside a pool in the shallow river, just under the bridge, some women with black cloths wound round their heads were beating clothes against the rocks, watched by a few men squatting under the trees. But Tekle was taking no chances. He pumped on the accelerator and we roared past.

It was now that we entered a truly scary landscape. The hillsides rose steeply on either side of the road. Boulders lay in tumbled heaps or were piled in gravity-defying towers, as if arranged in play by giants. The scraggy trees were undamaged – a sinister sign. No one could have ventured here for some years to forage for firewood or burn charcoal.

Tekle had fallen silent.

'This certainly looks like shifta country,' I remarked, my voice coming out more squeaky than I had expected.

I hadn't meant to be witty, but in his nervousness Tekle guffawed in response. He was driving faster than usual.

Then suddenly a Land Cruiser was hurtling towards us. In its open back men in uniform were huddled round a machine gun on a central platform over which crouched a hooded figure. Behind this vehicle came another car with smoked glass windows.

'President of Somali Region,' said Tekle, reading the number plates, and he hunched further down over the steering wheel.

This is mad, I told myself. I'm risking my life, and Tekle's, and Mikhail's, for the sake of a few stories.

At last, the defile opened out into a plain, and when we had crossed this and climbed a hill to a busy village, Tekle threw his hands up, then smacked then down again with relief on the steering wheel.

'Shifta baka,'[38] he said triumphantly.

From then on, we fell back into our usual conversational pattern, with stretches of silence interrupted by a few questions from me, and the occasional remark from Mikhail, who dozed in the back of the Land Rover, leaving me to enjoy the landscape.

This was beautiful. We were now winding through low hills. Occasional camels grazed among the bushes, herded by young women in bright clothes. And then the road straightened and we were drifting down a sloping plain which was dotted with the basket huts of nomads.

I had only a scanty memory of Jijiga from my first visit in 1968, when Mark and I had hitched a ride on top of an oil tanker for the long journey across the Ogaden down to the Red Sea. All I could remember was a hot little town, a stopping place for lorries, with a few administrative buildings set along wide straight streets and a café under whose awning I had sat fanning myself in the intense heat. But David, my husband, had visited Jijiga in 1980 with a team from Swedish Save the Children. The region was in the grip of a war between the Somalis and the Ethiopian government, which was being waged with the utmost brutality. He had described to me a deserted town, the corrugated iron doors of the compounds swinging in the wind. Only the hospital was occupied, and there he had seen a baby on the point of death from starvation and a man partially disembowelled by a lion, who also had only hours to live.

No signs of those traumatic times were visible as we cruised

---

[38] No more bandits.

down the dusty streets to come to a halt outside the Hotel Africa, but I knew that every woman leaning against the lintel of her doorway, and every man greeting a friend with mutual shoulder taps, must bear inner scars of grief and loss.

It's 12 November as I write this. Yesterday, all over Britain, there were ceremonies at cenotaphs, wreaths were laid, poppies flowered in buttonholes and poems from the trenches were read on the radio. I thought, as I always do, of my great-uncles Andrew and John, who died on the Somme. But how many Ethiopians have perished in the unsung wars that still rend their country? And how do the ones left behind manage their grief?

The Hotel Africa was a pleasant surprise. It was simple but clean, and my little room had its own small shower and toilet attached. There was the usual noisy bar, of course, but it was some way down at the end of a corridor, and the inevitable tinny music was not loud enough to disturb me.

A picture covered the whole of one wall of the bar. Bridges arched over a river under a northern sky.

'But that's – Newcastle!' I said at last.

'Newcastle United. Very good football,' the bar owner said delightedly.

I tried to ask him how he'd acquired the picture, but he had already exhausted his store of English and spoke no Amharic.

I wasn't surprised, when we made our first call at the Somalia Education Bureau, that no one was expecting us. Luckily someone in the office had been a student in the school I had taught at in the 1960s and remembered me. All doors were opened after that.

The head of the Education Bureau, Moge Abdi Omer, decided to look after us himself. A clever, energetic man, I would soon learn that he relished a good story, and was so enthusiastic that I would find it hard to keep up with him. There was no question of resting and recovering from our journey. A start was to be made at once.

Moge didn't need to be told that offices are bad places for storytelling, and he led Mikhail and me into a garden, settling us under a tree, while he dashed off to fetch a teacher, who, he was sure, had a fund of stories to tell.

Moge was right. The teacher, crossing his legs and sitting comfortably beside us, launched into story after story.

I had been aware, at the start of our session, of childish voices chanting on the far side of a stone wall bordering the garden. A Koranic class was being conducted in the next compound. The chanting died away. A row of heads appeared above the wall, and then, through a breach in the wall, a trickle of children broke through. The trickle became a flood. Shyly they approached, clutching their battered learning boards on which Arabic letters were inscribed, then, with increasing boldness, they came nearer and nearer. Their whispers and giggles turned to chatter, then to shouts and laughter.

At first charmed, I began to feel irritated, as small hands patted my arms and touched my hair. The old schoolmistress in me was mentally wagging a finger and calling for discipline. No one else seemed to mind. Moge, holding the precious tape recorder to the storyteller's lips, seemed unaware of the increasing hubbub. The Koranic teacher, a tall, rangy man in a long loincloth, had perched himself in the crook of a tree, and was enjoying the stories. At last, when even the patient Moge was gently telling the children to hush, the Koranic teacher leaped down from the tree, and wielding the switch which he had been carrying under his arm, set about the children's heads with it. They let out screams and were quiet for a while, but soon were crowding in closer than ever.

Fortunately, the stories were suitably moral for such a young audience. They included the exploits of two thieves, Hirsi and Kabaalaf. One fills a sack of ash to pass off as flour. The other fills his sack with goat droppings to sell as coffee beans. They meet on the road to market and manage to palm their fraudulent wares off onto each other, only to be outraged when they discover the deception. However, they then join forces and steal from a poor old woman, pretending to be blind, but the food they take from her makes them ill. They fear they will die and repent of their evil deeds.

I recognised Hirsi and Kabaalaf. I'd met their counterparts – Atrasu and Amegag – in Harar; an engaging pair of crooks, whose trickeries lead, not to repentance, but to retribution through the agency of an avenging jinn.

My favourite story from this session was what might in Europe be called an urban myth. It was about a boy who was snatched away from his home by lions when he was four or five years old. The lion, so the narrator said, took the child back to his den and brought him up along with his cubs. The lioness wanted to eat the boy but the lion stopped her. He wouldn't leave the child with the lioness for fear that she would harm him, and when he went hunting, he carried the boy with him on his back. The boy rode the lion into the bush. The lion set him down while he hunted, and when he had finished the boy mounted him again and rode back.

'This happened in the Fafen area,' the narrator said. 'I have spoken to people myself who have seen this boy. He is now a big person and he tells everyone his story. The boy said he lived like this for two years. His lion was the king and the other lions used to come to his house and they would have a meeting, sitting in a circle and talking in lion language. Then after two years he took the boy and dropped him near his village and said, "Go home."'

Mowgli of course is the world's favourite feral child, but there are many such stories, from Romulus and Remus and their mother wolf; the bear child in late seventeenth century Lithuania; the Wild Boy of Aveyron first seen in France in 1797; and modern reports of children suckled by wolves which appear from time to time in newspapers in India.

As elsewhere in Ethiopia, our success in Jijiga depended on the goodwill of officials. I was always surprised by their kindness to me. The good reputation of the British Council as a donor of books and provider of courses for teachers helped, of course, and my own pedigree as a teacher in the time of 'His Majesty' always went down well. But I sensed, time and again, a kind of pent-up energy in these intelligent men – frustrated ambition, a desire to break free from the stultifying bureaucracy in which they found themselves. Of them all, Moge was perhaps the most eager.

It was at the home of one of Moge's relatives that the most remarkable stories came my way. He had taken me there at the end of a long and tiring afternoon. A nomad's round-roofed hut, its woven walls covered with a tarpaulin, stood in the compound, and beside it was a new house, a good-sized, square chikka construction. A curtain hung over the door. Moge pushed it aside and ushered me in.

I could see nothing at first in the windowless interior, but gradually made out mats lying on a lino floor which was patterned in a bright geometric design. The mud walls were hung with lengths of flowered polyester cloth. Someone turned a switch by the door and the bulb hanging from the centre of the room flickered on. Now I could see six women, with toddlers and small babies around them, lounging on mats set against the walls.

Moge's explanation of our mission needed several repetitions before everyone was satisfied that they had fully grasped it. In the meantime news of our arrival had spread, and more and more people had lifted the curtain over the doorway and slipped in to settle themselves against the walls.

The mistress of the house – Moge's relative, I presumed – was queen here. Her name was Fatuma Omer. A handsome woman with a scarf tied in a topknot round her head, she had been issuing orders to daughters and minions from the moment of our arrival. A kettle had been brought in. A tray of enamel mugs was set in front of her, and a brazier of glowing charcoals. She started the long process of the coffee ceremony, roasting the beans, sending them round to be smelled, taking them out of the dish to grind in her mortar, and returning with the coffee ready in the kettle. From time to time she threw a few grains of incense on the brazier, and smoke puffed out into the room in scented clouds.

At last the ice was broken, and one of the women told a story. When she had finished, she prodded a small girl, who looked no more than ten years old. The child shuffled forward, and without any shyness embarked on a long tale, her voice rising and falling as she half-chanted it.

The child's name was Ikran. I've narrated her story to many children, watched them stiffen with terror, then slowly relax and squeal with enjoyment as the plot comes to a satisfactory end.

The story starts in the same way as Hansel and Gretel. A widowed father marries again, and his wife refuses to bring up the five daughters of the first marriage. After much persuasion, he agrees to take them out into the desert and leave them there to die. In the evening, the frightened children see a girl returning to her house with her sheep, and they beg her for help.

She refuses, explaining that her mother is an ogress and will eat them. They plead with her, and at last she agrees to let them sleep with the sheep in the safety of their fenced enclosure.

The ogress returns to her house and smells the children, but her daughter distracts her. The ogress has earache, and tells her daughter to pour hot oil into her ears, but the oil is so hot that it runs into the ogress's brain and kills her.

The ogress's daughter marries and leaves the house to the five sisters, who manage to live by making bread and selling it in the market.

I had thought the story ended at this point, but it merged into what seemed like a different tale. I had often encountered this. Sometimes, a story turned into a veritable patchwork of loosely stitched fragments, with certain episodes offered in a kind of shorthand, in the knowledge that the audience would know that bit and would be happy to skip it.

The second part of the story echoes countless tales around the world of dragons guarding hoards of gold and luring maidens to their death, only to be vanquished by a fearless rescuer. In this case, the dragon is a snake living in a water hole near the children's house. The snake catches the youngest sister, but the oldest one rescues her and kills the snake, finding a pile of gold at the bottom of the hole. Now the sisters are rich and live happily together for the rest of their lives.

This was the first time I had encountered a Hansel and Gretel story, where the children are 'thrown away', as little Ikran put it, but I would hear several more versions. One even featured the familiar motif of the breadcrumbs set out to mark the trail, which are eaten by the birds. In every case, the abandoned children fall into the hands of a cruel being with magical powers, and rescue themselves through their own great efforts.

More extraordinary stories poured out of that family gathering. The one I shall never forget, one of the most remarkable I ever heard in Ethiopia, expresses in the most poignant way the terror of a girl-child, barely in her teens, facing her unknown bridegroom on her wedding night. She will have already have suffered a brutal and unhygienic circumcision, her labia excised with a dirty knife or piece of broken glass, and her vagina may have been crudely stitched, leaving only a small hole for the passage of menstrual blood. It will be slashed opened with her new husband's knife before he penetrates her. Looking ahead, she will soon have to face the terror of giving birth, which many young brides are too small to survive. This story, which I give in full, is truly a woman's story.

A man went to take some cows as a dowry to the father of the girl he was to marry. On the way, a lion leaped out and killed one of the cows.

'Who killed my cow?' said the bridegroom.

'A *real* man,' snarled the lion.

'You are not more of a man than me,' said the bridegroom. 'Fight me.'

They fought. The man pinned the lion down.

'You only won because you have a right arm,' said the lion. 'Tie it, and fight again.'

They fought again, and again the man won.

'It's not fair,' said the lion. 'You have a left arm too. Tie it, and fight.'

The man tied his left arm, and the lion won the fight and ate him.

Then the lion donned the bridegroom's clothes and went on to the village. The bride's party met him with songs and ululations. They took him to a hut. The bride, Fatima, came and sat beside him. They offered meat to the lion, but he would not eat it cooked, and wanted it raw. They showed him a bed.

'This is not for me. I sleep on sticks.'

They gave him sticks to sleep on.

Now the lion was alone with the bride Fatima. He took off his clothes and she saw his fur. She ran in terror to her father's hut.

> *My Father! My Mother!*
> *This is no man.*
> *I have seen his fur.*
> *You have given me to a wild animal!*

Her father was angry.

'Go back to your husband. Do you want to bring shame on us?'

'But Father, it's true! My husband is a lion!'

Her father agreed to a test.

'In the morning, the village will move in search of grass and water. Everyone will shout 'The time has come!' and begin to pack up their huts. If he doesn't shout like the other men, I will believe you.'

The lion had followed the girl and was listening outside her father's hut. She didn't know this.

In the morning, while everyone was still asleep, the lion came out of his hut and shouted,

> *Why is the village still asleep?*
> *When will the people begin to wake?*
> *The time to move has come!*

Fatima's father was angry with her.

'Your husband is a real man. You must obey him now.'

The lion said to his father-in-law, 'I will not move with you. I will take my wife to meet my relatives.'

He set off with Fatima. She led the camel, and the lion rode on its back. On the way, the lion became hungry and bit the camel's hump. The camel roared.

'Why is he roaring?' Fatima asked.

'He doesn't like your veil. Take it off and throw it away.'

She obeyed. The lion bit the camel again.

'He doesn't like your bracelets and your necklace. Throw them away.'

She had no choice but to obey. Again the lion bit the camel.

'He doesn't like your dress. Throw it away.'

Now Fatima was naked.

At last the lion called a halt. Fatima unloaded the hut from the camel and set it up.

'I will fetch my relatives,' the lion said. 'Wait.'

She was alone now. She thought, 'My husband has gone to bring other wild animals who will come and eat me. I can't go back to my family. They will not believe me, and will be shamed.'

She cut off her little finger and put it in the mortar. Then she ran away. She ran, she ran, she ran, and came to a lake. There she found a rope and climbed up into a tree in the middle of the water.

The lion returned to the hut with his relatives, the hyena, the leopard, the snake and all the other wild animals.

'Fatima! Fatima!' he called out.

The little finger in the mortar cried out loud, 'She is not here! She has run away!'

The lion ate the finger.

A rat said to the lion, 'I have seen your bride. She is in a tree in the lake.

All the animals followed the rat to the lake.

'Come down, Fatima!' they called.

'I will not. You must come to me.'

She let down the rope. The lion caught hold of it first. She pulled him up, but when he was only half way up the tree, she cut the rope, and he fell into the lake and drowned.

One by one, all the other animals tried to climb the tree to her, but she played the same trick on them, until all of them were drowned.

Now Fatima was alone again. A bird came. It had only one wing.

'I'm hungry, girl. Give me a date to eat.'

'I will give you a date if you will fly to my father's village and say to him, 'Your daughter, Fatima, is crying in the tree.'

She gave a date to the bird, who flew to the village on her single wing. She found Fatima's mother churning butter, and sang to her,

> *You, woman, churning your butter,*
> *Your daughter hides in a tree in the lake,*
> *And she cries, 'Ohe o byo, Hoge o bayo!*
> *How can you make butter, bad woman,*
> *When your daughter needs your help?*

'What is this stupid bird?' said the mother.

The bird flew to the father, who was sewing shoes, and to the brother, who was herding cattle. At first, they would not listen, but at last they all said, 'Let us go to the lake and see.'

They went to the lake and saw Fatima up in the tree.

'You, Fatima, come down!'

'I will not. You gave me to a wild animal.'

Her mother begged her.

'You are our only daughter. We were wrong. We are sorry.'

'I will not come down.'

The youngest brother prayed to Allah, 'Allah, fell this tree so that my sister will come down.'

Allah heard him and felled the tree. Fatima returned with her family to the village.

Her mother said, 'Fatima, help me churn the butter.'

'Where? Inside the house? No, I will do it only on the roof.'

She took the butter churn up to the roof, and while she was churning the wind came and snatched her up into the sky with the churn.

Her mother shouted, 'Wind! Take the girl, but leave my butter churn!'

The father shouted, 'Wind! Take the churn, but leave the girl!'

The wind dropped the churn and took the girl. It dropped her in the bush. She turned into two sticks. A boy found the sticks. He picked one up and tried to beat his camel with it.

The stick girl entered the camel. He took the other stick, and tried to beat his camel, but it too entered the camel. The boy ran home and told his father.

'Two sticks have entered the camel!'

'Are you telling the truth? If you lie, I will kill you.'

The father cut the camel's throat and opened its body, but he couldn't find the sticks, which darted about to hide from him. In a rage, he killed his only son.

The sticks flew out of the camel and up into the tree, calling out,

> *I made you kill your camel,*
> *Which gave you milk.*

I made you kill your son,
Your only one.

I cannot now look at Chagall's flying brides without remembering Fatima and her butter churn flying through the air above the village. But in spite of the surrealism of this story, the details in it are so grounded in the reality of the nomad's life that I can almost smell the camel dung fire and hear the cattle chewing their cud. It brings to life the bridegroom coming with his dowry payment to buy his bride and the dawn call to break camp and move to fresh pastures. It offers vivid vignettes of daily life: the churning of butter, the sewing of shoes, the wife leading the camel on which is piled the struts and mats of the family home.

The girl, terrified by her husband's nakedness, then stripped by him until she too is naked and thrown to the mercy of his hostile relatives, will have no sugary finale to her story. No prince coaxes Fatima from her tree. She takes the escape route of an Ovidian metamorphosis, and, in an echo of Daphne transforming herself into a laurel tree, she turns herself into sticks. The revenge she takes is not even against her own cruel family but against the first humans who come her way.

The bird in the story takes the classic role of messenger. (In another story Moge told me, a mother offers herself to be eaten by a cannibal in place of her son, and her breasts fly off and become birds. In this guise, she follows her son and passes messages that will save his life.) Perhaps because of their power of flight, birds act as messengers in stories throughout the world. Noah releases birds to bring back news of the subsidence of the flood. Angels, the messengers of God, borrow their wings from birds.

Stories flowed that evening in that small Somali house. Fatuma, smiling behind her brazier, threw handfuls of incense on the glowing charcoal until the atmosphere became so chokingly stuffy that I was afraid I would faint. I stood up suddenly, trying not to stagger, and blundered through the mass of bodies out under the curtain and into the fresh air.

'Are you all right, Mrs Elizabeth? Are you tired?' Moge said, following me outside.

'Yes, I'm tired,' I said cravenly. 'Very tired.'

And so that extraordinary story session came to an end.

That night, Moge took Mikhail and me to a restaurant, where girls in gaudy clothes, their mouths painted a garish red, smiled with desperation at prospective punters.

As I shut the door of my little hotel room at last and flopped into bed my head was spinning with too many impressions, too many people, too many stories.

'I'm homesick,' I thought with surprise, remembering the quiet study I share with David. At his end of the room he writes his walkers' guidebooks, leafing through archaeological monographs and local histories in search of gems to amuse his readers as they walk. At my end of the room, files and books spill on to the floor. Every now and then one of us gets up to put a log on the wood stove or take the phone into another room to answer it. We have a rule of silence except for emergencies. We see few people except for each other. Small experiences are shared and mulled over. We have grown so used to our quietness that we find too much company exhausting.

❖

Professor Ahmed Mohammed Ali, whom I met the next morning,

would have understood how I felt. An academic with a great knowledge of Somali history and culture, he thrust in front of me a stack of books, mostly in languages which I couldn't read. After a few minutes of misunderstanding, he grasped what I was after, and immediately told me a story about how the crow lost its white feathers and became black through flying too close to the sun as it tried to approach the Sun God, Wak.

'The Oromo also believed in Wak,' the Professor told me, 'as well as the Somalis. Before the coming of Islam.'

What happens to old gods when no one believes in them any more? I don't think they ever quite go away. The god Pan bequeathed his horns and cloven feet to the Christian Devil. Other Roman godlets morphed painlessly into saints. Wak still has some diehard adherents. No doubt he will live on in the new religions sweeping Ethiopia in some form or other.

That same day, I found myself in a room full of rural midwives. They had been gathered from far and wide to attend a training session in Jijiga. To find them we had had to go to the outskirts of town, dive through a hole in a thorn fence and knock on the door of a small whitewashed room.

There must have been about twenty-five of them, along with a baby or two, sitting on the floor of that small room. They were a jolly bunch of women, clearly enjoying each other's company. I tried to imagine, as I looked around the room, the births they would soon be attending, out in nomad camps, in smoky huts, miles away from the help of doctors. There would be no last-minute dashes to an operating theatre for the women whose labour they would attend, no incubators for frail mites, no resuscitation units. When I remember the agonies of my own birthings – but I won't.

My favourite memory of this session is sound effects. Try

saying this out loud, and you too will hear the hooves of a trotting horse.

Chellalam, chellalum, chellalam, chellalum.

Now say this, speed up a bit, and you will hear the horse galloping.

Collalum, collalum, clum, collalum, collalum, clum.

That evening, Mikhail and I went to the souk. It was late, darkness was falling, and by the time we reached the clothing souk, the stallholders were putting up the shutters on their booths. We hurried towards the last open stalls. Thirty years earlier, the women in Somalia had worn bright draperies in flimsy cotton which had been woven and dyed in Harar, the patterns on them stamped with hand-blocks. I had bought several lengths of this material, which I had squirreled away in my linen chest at home. A few months earlier, I had brought them out and divided them between my sons to decorate their rooms at university. Now I hoped to replenish my stock.

I was to be disappointed. The only cloth on sale was imported, mass-produced in the Far East, and mostly polyester rather than cotton. There were heaps of second-hand clothes and shoes, too. Later, I learned that these were the leftovers from our own charity shops. Bought in huge bundles, our cast-off clothing ends up dumped in places like Jijiga. I was saddened to see this. A viable local industry, drawing on skilled labour and using age-old patterns and dyes, has been destroyed.

Tekle's round face was woebegone the next morning when he came to pick us up at the hotel. He had hardly slept for worrying about bandits on the road back to Harar, and had already spent a couple of hours hovering at the bus station, trying to gauge the state of the road. Thankfully we made it through to Harar without incident.

I had left some stories with Nejaha in Harar for her to translate. We found her in her office, absorbed in a game which involved screwing up pieces of paper and balancing them on sticks while a colleague toiled away at the last of the stories. I tucked them into my bag. We set off for Addis Ababa the next day.

At the Buffet de la Gare, Madame Kiki was in a fretful mood.

'Encore pas de l'eau!' she complained. 'No water for the past five months. Everything's going from bad to worse. Eh, Madame, qu'est-ce qu-on peut faire?'

❖ 11 ❖

THE PORCUPINE MAN OF
THE BENI SHANGUL

Emperor Haile Selassie's titles included 'King of Kings' and 'Conquering Lion of the Tribe of Judah'. These were not empty boasts. The Christian emperors of Ethiopia always sought to subdue the smaller kingdoms which ringed their highland fastnesses, and did so with increasing efficiency under the great nineteenth-century emperor Menelik, who incorporated many an emirate and princedom into his empire. He and his successor Haile Selassie were indeed kings ruling over kings.

The old imperial system was brutally exploitative of the peoples on the margins of the empire. The feudal lords and governors who were appointed over them were virtually encouraged to enrich themselves at the expense of their vassals. In some areas, subject peoples were the victims of frequent slave raids.

The traffic in slaves continued into the middle of the twentieth century. Paid to their overlord as a form of tribute by smaller rulers, slaves were used as servants in the imperial household, were exported abroad or were given to powerful lords to work on their lands. I never forgot the sight of a black-skinned man with tribal markings on his cheeks running behind the trotting mule of his Amhara master on the pilgrim route to Lalibela.

One area which suffered particularly from the activities of slavers was the western side of Ethiopia where it borders the Sudan. These were remote, wild lands until quite recently, sparsely populated by numerous tribes speaking a variety of languages. Some were Muslim, ruled over by small kings and warlords who had become vassals of the Ethiopian emperors. Others were nomadic hunter-gatherers armed with bows and arrows. There were no roads into this region, and little contact with the outside world. The people had more in common with Sudan than with Ethiopia, although they were used to trading their ivory for salt, cloth and cereals with their neighbours to the east.

With the creation of semi-autonomous regions federated together under a central government, this part of Ethiopia became known as Beni-Shangul. Unlike the Somali, Tigray or Oromo regions, there was no unifying way of life, but a collection of different languages and cultural traditions. These have been drastically affected by the modern world. Pressure of population elsewhere has brought many new immigrants into this fertile area. There have been geological surveys to look for mineral deposits, a motorised road and an airstrip at Asosa, the new regional capital (not to be confused with Asasa in the Oromo region). Until recently, forest covered much of the land, but the canopy is now being destroyed along with the animals who inhabit it. The discovery of gold, copper, zinc and marble will soon no doubt complete the destruction.

Efforts have been made to settle the semi-nomadic hunter-gatherers into permanent villages and teach them the skills of agriculture. Immunisation teams have visited. Missionaries have been at work.

I was asked to collect stories from three of the many different peoples in Beni Shangul – the Gumuz, the Berta and the Shinasha. The Berta are the most numerous group, numbering about 150,000 in 1994. There were slightly fewer Gumuz, and many fewer Shinasha.

❖

Mikhail Negussie was to be my translator again on this journey, and Tekle was our driver. It was not slaves, gold or ivory that were on our minds when we set off for Asosa, but mud. The road to the west, the lifeline of the Beni-Shangul region, was as brittle as a hair which could be snapped at any moment. A few days of heavy rain, and the untarred surface beyond Nekemte was quickly churned into a morass in which trucks, buses and cars wallowed like beached whales.

The early morning weather was fine when we set out from Addis Ababa and the landscape was as usual so beautiful that in Europe it would have attracted tourist buses with their attendant clutter of cafés, petrol stations, souvenir shops and toilets. Here, there was only the long ribbon of tarmac, almost devoid of traffic, and a few people trudging along it to market. Once a bushbuck bolted in front of our Land Rover. It was the first time I had seen one, and I wondered how the poor thing lived, since every patch of grass was shaved down to green velvet by the cattle, and dogs ran everywhere.

By late afternoon we were nearing Nekemte, where we were to spend our first night. Tekle, unimpressed by the view, leaned forward over the steering wheel to look up at the sky, and following his eyes I saw curtains of rain sweeping across the hills towards us from the west. We shook our heads but said nothing, both hoping for the best.

The first night on the road in Ethiopia, away from the comforts of Addis Ababa, always demands a certain stiffening of resolve. Large provincial centres like Nekemte are well equipped with modern hotels, but after the comfort of the Sargents' spare bedroom and Patsy Sargent's cooking, I was feeling picky, and

I sighed at the dripping cistern in my little bathroom and the cockroaches scuttling around in the wardrobe. Lying down in the bed, I felt tiny feet investigating my back and knew I had caught a flea. I was too tired to hunt for it, and resigned myself to being its dinner. I had discovered years ago that fleas are wildly attracted to new arrivals in Ethiopia, but after a while they seem to go in for territorial elimination until only one or two are left in possession of your body, and if you can bear to make an accommodation with these as permanent residents you'll only have a bite or two a day to cope with. Even these become almost unnoticeable as your skin stops reacting to them.

I was more confident, too, that I would weather this trip better than earlier ones. I had invested in a water bottle with a filter. You could put the dirtiest water into it, the manufacturers claimed, squeeze it through the carbon fitting at the top, and out would come pure drinking water. I had a supply of ciprofloxacin just in case the runs returned, and had acquired a better mosquito net too.

By the time we were sitting down to breakfast the next morning, Tekle had already reassured himself on the state of the road. We made the decision to go on, and were off by seven o'clock.

Mikhail was in a chatty mood. We talked about snakes.

'There were so many around Harar when I was a child there. We used to play with them, then we killed them and hung them from the trees because of the old saying, you know?'

'What old saying?'

'That if you leave a dead snake on the ground it will eat the earth and come alive again.'

Among the grasses at the edge of the road, sky-blue teasel flowers were dotted among the glinting Meskel daisies. These flowers had, in my youth, made sheets of gold across great tracts of the country at the end of the Big Rains in September. Now, thanks to the explosion in the populations both of people and cattle, they could only survive in the few remaining patches of unused land.

We passed Ghimbi, a pleasant small town, but I could sense that Tekle was worried. The tarmac had petered out by now. Heavy clouds pressed down on the hills and no traffic was coming from the opposite direction.

Trouble came on us without warning. We rounded a bend in the road, and looked down on a sea of mud. Two lorries were already floundering in it, the mud rising in waves of toffee-coloured goo over their wheels. Tekle clapped his hands to his head and pulled up. Mikhail jumped out of the Land Rover and ran ahead to see what was happening.

'There's a way through,' he said. 'We can do it, I'm sure we can.'

I should have gone to look myself. I should have taken into account Mikhail's youth, inexperience and love of adventure. Instead, I let him persuade Tekle, not following their quick Amharic debate, and we drove on.

A short while later, we ran into the next mud slick in which were embedded a dozen or so labouring lorries, their drivers fruitlessly revving their engines as they tried to extricate themselves, but succeeding only in sending their wheels spinning.

It was no good, other drivers came up to tell Tekle. The road was a morass for the next fifty kilometres. Some people had been stuck for days.

'That's it. We're turning back,' I said to Tekle.

He grinned, relieved. He had let Mikhail persuade him at the first sign of mud, he said, against his better judgment. He whipped the Land Rover round with a spin of the wheel and we set off back down the road towards Ghimbi. But we had turned too late. The first slick was now jammed with flailing lorries. In the half hour since we had passed that way, fifteen or twenty of them had slid down into the mud. There was no way past them. We were stuck.

There was no point in worrying about the situation. We could do nothing but wait. It was quite pleasant at first. A few country children with perfect teeth and huge smiles begged from me in a desultory fashion, the smell of their mothers' spicy cooking rising from their outstretched hands, but they ambled away when Tekle told them off. The clouds had cleared and the sun was well up. It was too hot to sit in its full glare, but I was happy perching on a bank in the shade of a tree, counting the different species of wild flowers among the close-cropped blades of grass and casting glances towards a young man sitting nearby, craning my neck to see what he was reading. It looked like a religious tract.

But as the day wore on, patient acceptance became harder. More lorries had arrived. Some pushed forward, trying to overtake those already stuck, only to slither to a halt in the ever deepening bog, creating a worse jam.

The hours passed. We had a packet of biscuits and some old bananas between us, and fortunately, several bottles of water. Occasionally there was a flurry of excitement when, after huge efforts, enough mud was dug away from a lorry's wheels to enable it to escape to the top of the next rise amid shouts of encouragement, but another lumbering vehicle would immediately take its place and the long process would begin again.

By half past three in the afternoon, Tekle's normally smiling face was puckering with anxiety, and I was beginning to find

Mikhail's cheeriness a little irritating. At that point, it began to rain. Most of the drivers and their passengers dashed to the cabs of their vehicles to take shelter, but some went on standing out in the open, ignoring the water sluicing out of the sky with the force of an emptying bucket.

'No Ghimbi, no Nekemte tonight,' said Tekle. 'We must stay here, in the car.'

I looked round the Land Rover, assessing how the three of us could arrange ourselves for the long night ahead. Thanking Providence that I had had the foresight to bring a sleeping bag, I resigned myself to fasting for the next twenty-four hours at least.

It's not as if I haven't done this before, I told myself, remembering a night long ago in the Ogaden when the chat-smuggling truck in which Mark Rosen and I were passengers had stuck so deeply we'd had to wait it out until dawn and then walk miles to the nearest village.

'We have time,' Mikhail said brightly. 'I will give you a lesson in Amharic.'

Sourly, I turned the offer down.

A new arrival had drawn up behind us. It was an ancient army lorry, Russian-made and painted khaki. I scowled as it forced its way past the logjam ahead, spouts of mud and water shooting up from behind its massive wheels.

Every man for himself, I thought. If you're big enough and ugly enough here, you get to push ahead, no matter who else is in trouble.

But then, when it had reached the head of the queue, the battered door of the lorry swung open. A man jumped down. He attached a tow rope to the front of the first truck in the queue, leaped back into his cab and revved his engine. At that moment,

I realised that the first three trucks were roped together. The driver of the Russian lorry was attempting to free them all at the same time.

He nearly made it. Amid shouts of encouragement, he gained a few metres of ground. The three trucks jerked along behind him, then he slithered sideways until, tilting dangerously, his lorry was embedded in a deep rut.

That's it, I thought. We'll be here for a week.

'Let's walk back to Ghimbi,' Mikhail suggested.

'Not till it's stopped raining.'

'Ghimbi ten kilometres from here,' said Tekle. 'It is dark soon. Too many bad men. Lions.'

Mikhail gave in.

And then, magically, the situation resolved itself. The Russian lorry backed out of its ditch. The tow ropes were reconnected. Engines roared into life, and all four vehicles lurched to the top of the hill. The rain stopped. Someone in front signalled us to take our chance. Two other small four-wheel drive vehicles were ahead of us, and I watched them, heart in mouth. The Russian lorry had rolled off into the twilight. If any of us smaller fry stuck, there would be no one to drag us out.

The first car, hesitating at a crucial moment, did momentarily halt, but a crowd of volunteers, already plastered in mud from head to foot, leaped to the rescue and pushed. It lurched but staggered on.

It was our turn. Tekle revved the engine. I shut my eyes and prayed. A few minutes later we had made it through the bog and to the top of the rise.

As we drove back into Ghimbi, I thought about the resource-fulness of Ethiopians. There are no emergency services at the end of a telephone line. People must rely on themselves or the goodwill of strangers. I was sorry I had been short with Mikhail. He had been doing his best to keep my spirits up.

A meal of injera and spicy wot was a treat after the rigours of the day. Tekle found rooms for us in a little inn, but the fence of its forecourt was too flimsy for his liking and he took the Land Rover off to the police station to lock it up for the night. My respect for him had risen even further. He had shown his courage on the road to Jijiga, but today he had kept a cool head, and brought us through safely.

Mikhail and I went with him to the police compound, where a muleteer's three animals were being allowed a glorious roll in the dust. As we walked back into our little hotel's forecourt, we saw a small boy kicking at a kitten. Mikhail let out a yell, grabbed the child, then squatted down and gently told him off. Released, the boy ran away. I thought with regret of how unwilling adults in Britain now are to engage with unknown children. I was ashamed to remember how I had recently hung my head and hurried past a group of nine year olds, who were holding another child against a wall and taunting him. The memory still fills me with shame.

The generator in Ghimbi had broken down and there was no electricity in the town. It was hard to make out our little hotel. My room, opening like the others onto the courtyard, was a cube with a door and an unglazed window covered with a wooden shutter. A bed and chair made up the furnishings. The landlord gave each of us a two-inch stub of candle. As it was only eight o'clock in the evening, too early to go to sleep, I asked for another piece. He gave me one as a great concession, but told me there would be no more after that, and returned to cutting up his candles.

A single candle flame gives a surprising amount of light, and

I positioned mine carefully out of any draughts to make it last longer.

'There's much to be thankful for,' my mother used to say, nodding fiercely, when difficulties came upon her, and I did feel grateful. We were safe indoors, and not out in the mud on the open road. There were a few fleas, but no mosquitoes in my room. We had had a good meal and I had no diarrhoea.

My second candle stub guttered suddenly and went out. The batteries in my torch were low, and I wanted to keep it for emergencies, so I lay in the dark and waited for a few hours till sleep came.

I woke with uncanny timing at 5.49, a minute before my alarm was due to go off. We were on the road by half past six. Tekle had already retrieved the Land Rover, washed and polished it, and we set off for Addis Ababa in our usual style.

❖

It was a year before I was to make a second attempt to reach Asosa, and when I did so it was with a different team. Michael Sargent had been posted out of Ethiopia, leaving the reader project in the hands of his successor, who had other priorities. On my future visits to Ethiopia there would be no welcome to the director's residence. The British Council Land Rover and drivers would not be spared, this time, for a mission that was now low on the new director's list of priorities.

But we were pressing on. Nine little books were already in print: two for Afar, two for Gambela, two for Oromia, two for Amhara and one for Tigray. The Somali and Harar ones were written, and the pages laid out and designed. Michael Ambatchew was efficiently co-ordinating the printing and distribution, and the British Council deputy director was supportive.

This time, we were taking no chances with the road. We were to fly to Asosa, leaping over the labouring vehicles on the ground below in one easy swoop.

I met my new translator at Addis Ababa airport. His name was Mesfin Habte-mariam.

'He is famous, you know,' I had been told. 'He is a funny man. A writer. Every one knows him. He talks on the radio.'

Mesfin and I went upstairs to the battered café in the old airport to get acquainted over tea and cakes. The waiter was wearing the yellow jacket found in all government hotels and restaurants, a relic of the Derg's Stalinist passion for uniformity. It was stretched tight across his waist, and he was in high spirits although it was only 6.30 in the morning, holding his tray aloft on the splayed fingers of one hand like a maitre d' in a cartoon. His cheerfulness was infectious and I felt my own mood lighten. Looking at Mesfin over the rim of my tea glass, I had a good feeling that we were going to get on.

Mesfin's face was creased like that of an actor who has exercised it fully in a repertoire of expressions. He sat with easy grace on the bent cane chair, studying me frankly. His wavy hair was cut *en brosse* above his square forehead. He had the yellowed teeth and husky voice of a life-long smoker and wore his shiny brown suit with such an air that it might have been cut by Armani. He was not thin, but there was not an ounce of spare flesh on him. His moustache was greying, and I guessed with some relief that he was about my age. I foresaw that we would have sympathy with each other's lapses of energy and middle-aged ailments.

He clicked his fingers to summon the waiter with the air of one used to frequenting cafés, and there was in his demeanour that touch of melancholy of the aristocratic Amhara.

'My grandfather,' he told me, 'was Armenian. You see how I look like an Arab? The hair? Not curled, but waving. And pale skinned, you see. He worked for the Emperor Menelik – I mean my grandfather.'

We swapped information about our children. He had five, between the ages of six and twenty-four. His wife was ill, and he was worried about her. I fondly showed him pictures of David and my two sons. By the time the plane was ready to take off, we were comfortable with each other.

In the place of Tekle and the trusty old Land Rover, the British Council had put our expedition into the hands of a private company, with a young driver who wore a snazzy baseball cap and designer jeans. A greater contrast with Tekle would have been hard to find.

For once, as I travelled about this remote region, I felt more experienced than my Ethiopian translator. Mesfin, a city sophisticate who had seen little of his own country, exclaimed at everything.

'Look, Liz. A bus! How did it come so far? And there are shops! The children! Just like kids anywhere.'

Of all the officials I had worked with – voluble Daniel in Bahir Dar, dignified Mesele in Tigray, the rascally Mohammed in Afar, Ogota with his pebble-thick glasses and Kalashnikov in Gambela, Nejaha with her crimson nail varnish in Harar, energetic Moge in Somalia, urbane Merga not quite explaining the keleche in Oromia – it was Dires Gebre Meskel, the Regional Cultural Officer of Beni Shangul, whose company I would most enjoy. Grey hair bubbled over his ears, and when he smiled his eyebrows lifted into the creases on his forehead as he stole sideways looks to catch my reaction. He had the typical Amhara trick of pulling down the corners of his mouth whenever he wished to sound judicious or give a cautious slant to what he was saying. I sensed that, like so many men of his generation, his life had been full of frustration and hardship, but whatever had happened to him he seemed to have reached a place of acceptance.

We had barely arrived in Asosa before Dires magically produced two elderly Shinasha farmers who happened to be in town, having walked for days to attend some kind of ceremonial occasion. I arranged a little party for them in the tea house of our hotel. The landlady put on her best dress and brought out her coffee tray and brazier, along with flasks of tej and a good meal of injera. The two old men settled themselves on a bench, ready for a treat.

Dires leaned forward, plying them with tej, like a teacher encouraging his star pupils to perform, while they held their bulbous glasses out at frequent intervals for refills. Mesfin was enjoying it too.

'You must have some of this, Liz,' he kept saying. 'It's really good stuff.'

The atmosphere became convivial, if a little less coherent, but I was disappointed in the stories. Familiar elements from Afar, Harar and Jijiga were shaken around like shards of colour in a kaleidoscope to emerge in new mosaics.

'They were married,' the storyteller would conclude, scratching his close-cropped head with hard-horned nails and rapping his stick on the ground. 'They lived happily ever after. This is what we have heard from our forefathers.'

They ran out of inspiration at last. Outside in the street a procession of chanting, white-clad people was winding its way along to the church of St Mary, whose monthly festival was occurring that day. The spell of our story session was broken. The farmers rose unsteadily to their feet and we parted after some long speeches of goodwill.

There's something about being at the end of a road, far away from any known place, which induces a kind of light-headedness and sense of unreality. Mesfin felt it as much as I did that evening. He was in a rollicking mood as we ate a dull supper of stodgy pasta at the government hotel.

'I have to tell you this joke about writers. It's for us!'[39] he cried. 'A writer, he died and went to heaven. "You can choose," they told him. "Either you can stay here or you can go to that – you know, to that other place." "How can I decide?" said the writer. "You must show me so that my choice will be an informed one." So they took him to hell, and there were rooms full of writers, and demons, you know, lighting fires, torturing them kind of thing, with those sort of big forks. So back the writer went to heaven, but it was just the same there! The demons! The fires! The forks! "What's the difference?" said the writer. "Heaven and hell, they're the same." "Oh," they told him. "There is a difference. Here in heaven, the writers are published."'

❖

To find a Berta storyteller, we had to set off early in the morning and bump along a pot-holed, red-earth road some distance from Asosa then leave the vehicle and walk down a path between high stands of maize. This opened out suddenly into a clearing, where a few conical huts, roofed with shaggy thatch, seemed at first to be deserted.

---

[39] Mesfin wrote a delightful collection of folk tales during the years he spent in Canada. Titled *The Rich Man and the Singer*, it was illustrated by Christine Price and published in the USA by Dutton in 1971.

A moment later, an ancient man came slowly out of the largest one. He wore a long white robe and a green cardigan. With age and strong sunlight his dark skin had been burnt to blackness, and his face was as fine-boned as the bust of a Pharaoh sculpted from obsidian. He was ninety-six years old.

'Ninety-six, Liz! Think of that. He makes me feel like a juvenile,' said Mesfin, bowing with great respect.

I too was awed. Menelik had been on the throne when this man was a child and the British were the masters of Sudan. Slave raiders had come this way many times. Had rumours of wars and nuclear bombs, moon landings and revolutions of all kinds reached this place?

The old man's name was Abdu Rahman Ibrahim. He greeted us in Arabic. From the opposite hut Abdu Rahman's wife emerged, moving with the caution of the very old. During the years of my mother-in-law's frailty, and now my own mother's, I'd become used to the feel of a tiny old woman clinging to my arm. Both mothers had had the benefit of every modern comfort: heated houses, soft beds, medicines, a TV for amusement. This old woman held on to the doorpost as she stepped across the lintel of her hut, feeling for the ground with the toe of her pink plastic shoe. I wanted to run forward and help her. Then I heard the voice of a younger woman inside. The clattering of pots suggested that she was cooking. I saw that Abdu Rahman and his wife had the only thing in their old age that really mattered: the constant presence of their children. Hot radiators, soft beds, TV sets and even medicines were meaningless in comparison, and I felt ashamed when I thought of our old people at home.

This little family compound was hemmed in on all sides by standing crops of sorghum and maize, as well as a plantation of banana palms. It felt remote and enclosed. A man in his late middle age appeared suddenly from a hidden path.

'The old man's son,' Mesfin murmured to me. 'Look! A sickle there on his shoulder. He's a farmer, wouldn't you say?'

Abdu Rahman's son did not look in the least surprised to see a group of city dwellers outside his parents' house. He greeted his father with deference before he turned to welcome us. He was in his working clothes: a pair of shorts and a red Liverpool football shirt sporting the number ten. An exquisitely woven sash was tied round his waist and over one shoulder, the end tucked into the waistband of his shorts.

He had inherited his father's dignity. He called out a greeting to his mother and squatted down beside the old man, smiling up at us in a leisurely way, as if ferenji story collectors came by every day of the week, then went inside the hut and I heard the splash of water.

Here is one of Abdul Rahman's stories:

A snake on the road asked a man to carry him. The man agreed, but when he became tired, the snake refused to uncoil himself from the man's neck, and threatened to bite him with his poisoned fangs. The pair went to the other animals to ask for judgment, but all were afraid of the snake, and found in his favour.

At last the fox said, 'I can't give my opinion unless I hear the man speak, and he cannot speak as you are constricting his throat. Let him speak, and then I will judge.'

At this, the snake slid off the man onto the ground. The man seized his chance and killed it, promising the fox a lamb as a reward.

The fox sat and waited for his reward, but when the man returned, he had a fierce dog with him, who set upon the fox and slashed his throat.

'How wicked is man,' the fox said, and died.

It was appropriate that such an old man was the teller of such an ancient story, surely one of the best-known fables in the world. Similar tales with a varied cast of characters surface in Aesop ('The Viper in the Bosom') and in the medieval stories of Reynard. Richard I, on his return from the Crusades, was said to have told a version featuring a fisherman persuading a malevolent jinn to climb back into the bottle from which he had released it. The earliest examples can be traced back to Sanskrit collections in India. I had gone past the point of being surprised at such universal stories popping up here, in one of the most inaccessible corners of Africa.

❖

Servitude of one kind or another had been on my mind since we had arrived in Asosa – of one ethnic group to another, of slave to master, of woman to man. It was brought home to me as we sat in the house of Fatuma Idris, a shy young woman who had agreed to speak to us. I perched on one of the beds that lined her room while Dires and Mesfin sat opposite me. They leaned back, lounging comfortably, and although I couldn't understand what they were saying, I heard a lordly tone in their voices as they explained what we had come for. Fatuma was worried about providing the right hospitality, and I could see that she was bothered by the men's superior status. I wanted to shoo them away and play with the little girl in a frilled blouse, who was peeping shyly from behind her mother's skirts. I wanted to help Fatuma with her tray and chat to her in a friendly way before demanding stories, but my Amharic wasn't good enough.

Fatuma's best story was the well-known tale about a woman intimidated by an arrogant, violent husband. She seeks advice from all her friends, but at last a wise man tells her that he can only help her if she brings him a hair from the eyebrow of a lion. Alarmed by this advice, she nevertheless sets about the task. She lays out meat beneath a tree, then climbs into the branches to wait. The lion comes and eats the meat. The woman repeats the process day after day until the lion habitually comes to her. At last, when the ferocious creature has eaten well and is deeply asleep, she plucks out one of its eyebrow hairs.

She takes it to the wise man.

'I have done what you asked,' she tells him. 'Now tell me what to do about my husband.'

'You already know,' he told her. 'If you can handle a lion, you can handle a man. Approach him with caution and tact and don't be afraid. You will tame him in the end.'

Studies are made and essays are written on the situation of women in Ethiopia, on the crippling workload they carry, the large number of children they bear, their few chances of education, the cutting of their genitals, the prevalence of kidnap marriages, the common and distressing condition of fistula (caused by early childbearing), which leads to incontinence and social ostracism. Most such reports, valuable as they are, are written by outsiders who have collected data and analysed surveys and statistics. But it was the stories told to me by women in Ethiopia, or by men about women, which told me more than any paper I could read.

There was an ordinariness to many of the stories about marriage. The woman tempted to betray her husband with a rich man comes to her senses when her lover takes the outward form of the donkey he really is. There is forgiveness between husband and wife and the marriage is saved. A quick-witted woman gives her husband clever answers when he is bamboozled by a stupid judge. Sassy girls hide their lovers from their husbands or brush them off with cheeky answers.

There was a dark tone to many stories too. A girl perceives her husband to be lion and flees from him, unsupported by her parents. Another is promised to a river demon, and turns her dogs on her family. Wicked stepmothers try to kill their stepchildren. A daughter-in-law plots to murder her husband's mother. And then there are the sinister characters: the zombie, the hyena woman, the zar, whom I would encounter later, the sorceress, the witch and all the rest of them.

Fatuma's story is similar to many tales around the world celebrating quietness and submissiveness in women. I found it particularly touching. She told it in a soft voice, a pucker in her forehead as she nervously watched the two men opposite her. As we left her house, I saw a pet monkey tied by the waist with a short rope, sitting dejectedly on the ground scratching at a sore. In a world of ranks and hierarchies, this poor little creature was at the very bottom of the pile.

❖

'I don't like to talk about it,' Mesfin kept saying, as we travelled from Asosa to Chagni to search for Gumuz story tellers. He broke open another packet of cigarettes. 'But I am really nervous, really, about a bad road. About the mud.'

I was too, but at the end of the first day's travel, when we neared the place where we had stuck in the bog a year earlier, there was no trace of mud and I couldn't even make out where it had been.

Luckily, the scenery distracted us from our worries.

'There's a mango tree!' Mesfin would cry. 'I've never seen such beautiful mangos. Do you see this river? Really, what a river!

Like Wordsworth. Or Oliver Goldsmith.'

Sometimes, as I looked along the red road unrolling in a straight line into the distance between fields of shocking green tef, above which puffy clouds hovered against an electric blue sky while a white horse trotted across the crest of the hill ahead, I thought I had stepped into a painting by Magritte. At other times, coming to the top of a rise in the road, the land on the far side would drop away, swooping towards the horizon in waves of green, blue and grey, sunbeams shafting down on it in stripes of glory, and it was as if we had been magicked into the idealised landscape glimpsed behind the shoulder of the Mona Lisa.

'I will sing you a song,' Mesfin said, when all danger of mud was behind us.

I settled back into my seat, prepared for an example of fine Ethiopian music.

'It is from Marilyn Monroe.' He cleared his throat and warbled 'Diamonds are a Girl's Best Friend' through pursed lips.

'Now it is your turn, Liz,' he said, when the song was finished.

For some reason, I broke into 'Hark the Herald Angels Sing', which went down well.

Stories came next. My Cinderella held the others spellbound. Dires followed it up with one about bandits, which made me look nervously at each approaching clump of trees. Our driver, who had learned his trade as a tour guide well, told us the names of the birds fluttering above the water in a ditch by the road side.

We stayed that night in Nekemte. Mesfin, who as usual had gone to bed late after 'a couple of beers' in the bar, was in a subdued mood when we set off the next morning. Fears of being trapped in a quagmire on the road still seemed uppermost in his mind, and when we stopped at the petrol station to fill up, I asked him if the prospect of it had kept him awake.

'No, no! It is my haemorrhoids, they are too painful. They are the size of chickpeas, believe me.'

'Haemorrhoids? Oh you poor man. After my first son was born I had them so badly I had to have an operation.'

Dires chimed in.

'Yes, for ladies, it is well known. With childbirth.'

Mesfin wasn't going to have his glory snatched away.

'You don't understand. Mine are worse! Not like chickpeas. Like grapes!'

I was fishing in my sponge bag.

'Here, take this.'

He fingered the suppository.

'How can I swallow it? It is too big.'

'No, you – you apply it – directly. You push it up your . . .'

'Ah! I see!'

He took the suppository off and a few minutes later returned beaming.

'Already they are feeling better.'

A crowd of onlookers had by now gathered round the window of the Land Cruiser, and were staring at me with interest.

'What do they think I am?' I said. 'A film star?'

Mesfin waved a dismissive hand.

'Believe me, Liz, for them, you might as well be anything. A stick. A – a toothbrush!'

To help us through the second day's journey, we began to tell each other our life stories. Dires willingly volunteered his and I listened, fascinated, aware that all Ethiopians in middle age had lived their lives against a backdrop of such violent upheavals that few can have survived unscathed.

Dires's father was a priest. I had guessed already that he came from a priestly family, as his patronymic, Gebre Meskel, means

Servant of the Cross. It had become clear, too, that he was a devout Orthodox Christian, with a strong sense of personal morality.

His father had lived for a while in Addis Ababa, but had disliked the busy, worldly city and retreated to remote Bale in the south-west of Ethiopia. He had settled his family in Goba, a cold little town at such high altitude that frost rimes the ground on many mornings. Dires had started his education in a religious school, studying to become a deacon, an early rung on the ladder of the complex church hierarchy. I could see him as a little boy, his head shaved except for a tuft above the forehead (a prophylactic against the evil eye), running barefoot down a stony path. I imagined him spinning a home-made toy – a circle of wire propelled along the ground at the end of a stick. He must have spent hours nodding sleepily over the great books of saints' lives, standing in the straw by the wall of the church during the endless early morning services, and learning to recite prayers in Ge'ez, the liturgical language.

His father realised that the state school would offer his son more chances, and Dires worked his way right up to twelfth grade in that small, windswept town.

'I thought the most wonderful thing in the world was to be a teacher,' Dires said. 'I did the training.'

He had worked in various parts of Ethiopia, until at last he had been posted to the school in Chagni, the small town in the Beni Shangul region to which we were now heading.

'But I was a political,' he said. 'We had a club of educated men in Chagni. We used to meet.'

They had circulated anti-Derg material among themselves, and when one of them had been caught, and under torture had revealed the names of the whole group, Dires had been arrested.

He had spent a year in prison.

'It was a badge of honour,' he said. 'We were proud. We did it together.'

'Did they beat you?'

'Not much.'

The authorities didn't seem to bear him a grudge, and once he had finished his sentence he was appointed head of the school in Chagni. He was still working there when the Derg fell, and the forces of the government-to-be swept down to occupy the region.

'There were several battles. They fought here and there. We all became frightened, and we decided to go to Addis Ababa.'

The journey to Addis Ababa had taken seven days. They had walked most of the way. They arrived in time to witness the triumphal entry of the battle-weary Tigrayan fighters, as they rode on their tanks into the city.

How strange it must have been, to find the old order, which had kept such a Stalinist grip on the country, suddenly gone.

'Go home,' the new authorities said. 'Everyone should continue with the jobs they were doing before.'

Dires hadn't wanted to leave Chagni, but if you are in government service in Ethiopia, you are given little choice about your place of work. He was posted off to Asosa.

'I hadn't wanted to go,' he said, 'but they froze my salary for three months, so I had to.' He smiled. 'That is my story, Mrs Liz.'

'Not quite,' I objected. 'You haven't told us the most important thing. How did you meet your wife?'

He looked a little embarrassed.

'She is my second wife. My first wife died. After six months only. She had an illness. So, you know, it is not good for a government official to be alone. People are suspicious of him.

They thought bad things about my father when he left Addis and went to Bale. They said, 'It is not good for a man to be on his own. He will do strange things. That is why he sent for his family. It was the same for me. I did things in the traditional way, not like in Europe. I asked my friends to look, and they found my wife for me. They arranged my marriage.'

I didn't see why Dires should be embarrassed. The finding of a life partner in Western society is a haphazard business at the best of times. It suits the confident and the attractive, but in its ruthlessness leaves many wounded and alone. Fortunately, Dires's arranged marriage had brought happiness to both him and his wife.

It was Mesfin's turn next. He seemed uncharacteristically tongue-tied, and proceeded in fits and starts.

'My grandfather was Armenian. I have told you that. He helped the emperor Menelik very much. The emperor gave him a very large piece of land, near Addis Ababa. Very fine. My father was born in a house with twelve rooms. But the Italians came. They destroyed it completely! They left only ashes. My father had no money left. He built a small house, with three rooms only.'

Dires's story was of a climb from being the son of a poor rural priest to holding the solid position of a salaried government post. Mesfin's was a tale of a family's descent, from the life of an imperial courtier to that of a struggling writer. His account was heartfelt, full of thwarted dreams and women loved and lost. He had spent some years in Canada, where he had studied creative writing. I could imagine him cutting a dash in Vancouver, with his charm and wit and good looks. But he had had no choice but to return home to the turmoil of Ethiopia. He had made his mark, however, with his wit, good humour and charm. His broadcasting career had brought him fame, but no fortune.

By now, the road was no longer rolling smoothly along the high plateau, but contorted in death-defying bends as it wound down thousands of feet to the depths of the Nile gorge. With every few hundred feet, the temperature increased until we were all wiping sweat from our faces. At last we arrived at the bridge, under which the thick brown waters of the Nile, clogged with their life-giving silt, were flowing doggedly towards the Sudan. A couple of policemen stepped in front of the car to make us stop. Suddenly, I was missing Tekle and the diplomatic number plates. Some way back down the road, we had given a lift to a mechanic who had thumbed us down from beside a dead truck. His clothes had been so covered with grease that he had insisted on riding on the roof of the Land Cruiser. This being illegal, police further back had stopped us and given our young driver a wigging. I was afraid that our crime had caught up with us, but these hot, thirsty young men were only bored, and wanted to talk to us to break the monotony.

'Now, Liz, it is your turn,' said Mesfin, as we began the long slow ascent up the far side of the canyon. 'Your life story, please.'

I realised, as I mentally ran through the strange combination of people and circumstances which had brought me to this remote place, at this time, in this hot car, crawling up the side of a cliff, that I had no idea what to say. Birth in New Zealand, childhood in a Christian Brethren family in Croydon, a longing for adventure, a snake bite in Malaysia, a few youthful relationships attempted and abandoned, the slog of university, hectic years in Ethiopia, journeys in India, the sheer good luck of meeting David, our lives together in Baghdad, then in war-torn Beirut, babies and cosy domesticity in London, with the slow build-up of a career in writing for children – I couldn't convey it all, and I realised that both Dires and Mesfin had concealed as much as they had told, and that is what we all do, all the time.

We reached our destination, the village of Mandwa, in the middle of the afternoon. Dires seemed to expand. He was a big man here, once headmaster of the school, respected by all. For the last mile or two, we had begun to see Gumuz people. They were darker skinned than the highlanders, and I was shocked to see how thin many of them were; a large number of the children had swollen bellies. Some adults, weaving back to their villages down the road from Chagni, seemed to be drunk. The women wore nothing except for a few beads above the waist and little aprons around their hips. This was, yet again, a different world within the great complexity of Ethiopia.

Everyone knew Dires in Mandwa, and Mesfin and I were swept up into a whirl of welcome and enthusiasm. Belay Makonnen, an official in the Education Bureau, who was Gumuz in spite of his Amhara name, promised to help us if we came back the next day. He wore an orange suit and a sky-blue shirt. His two upper front teeth were missing and his round face was crinkled with scarifications.

'We are not so lucky, Mrs Liz,' Dires told me. 'Tomorrow is national polio day. There are vaccinators going out to every town and village in Ethiopia, and everyone is busy. But they know me. They will do their best for us. You will see.'

We stayed the night in Chagni, further back down the round. Mesfin was in a melancholy mood. There was much translation work to do on the stories we had collected in Asosa, but he was tired, and looking forward to an evening's relaxation in the bar.

He heaved a sigh as I produced my notebook and looked at him expectantly, ready to write down the English translation of the first story.

'This one is about a woman and her husband. He has a problem.

Maybe he drinks a little. She should be more understanding. But instead, she is so jealous!'

'Mesfin, that can't be right.'

'Yes, the woman, in this story, she is not a good wife. A good wife should never . . .'

'That one's not on the tape, Mesfin. Let's move on.'

Early morning found us in a Gumuz village walking through low-growing grass to a round thatched hut. The open space had been swept to perfection and was fringed by a large number of people sitting on stones. A big drum had been brought out, and a bow and arrow leaned against the hut's wall. A man squatted on the ground, sharpening his sickle on a stone.

I felt uncomfortable. The ring of faces was solemn and no one smiled or came forward to greet us. Dires's short account of the Gumuz people, which he had given me on the way to Mandwa, was ringing in my ears.

'They are hunter-gatherers until ten or five years ago,' he had said. 'Nomads. Very fierce murderers.'

He had told me that Gumuz men had long taken a pride in killing, and, like the Afar, had traditionally presented human testicles to their future brides.

'The government is sending civilisers here to show them how to build their houses and plant crops. They don't like it.'

Although I realised that this information had been filtered through Dires's Amhara prejudices and had to be taken with a pinch of salt, nevertheless it made me feel ill at ease. It was not until later that I realised that the villagers had gone to considerable trouble to display their culture to me, bringing out their drums and their traditional weapons and agricultural tools. I should have shown more interest and asked them to demonstrate their use. Instead, I stood awkwardly, letting the men take the lead while dozens of pairs of eyes stared at me unblinkingly.

'The polio team has already come today,' Dires told me, after a consultation with Belay. 'They don't understand what we want.'

I could hardly blame them. The situation must have been baffling. First a bunch of civilisers comes round and forces everyone to eat a sugar lump, then a ferenji appears demanding stories, and it was still only a couple of hours into the morning. Whatever next? I imagined them thinking.

Someone told a story at last, but it wasn't of course until later that Mesfin had the chance to translate it for me.

'It is about a hare and a tortoise,' Mesfin began, holding the tape recorder to his ear as he listened to the start of the Amharic translation which Belay had muttered onto the tape.

'Oh, that old one?'

Mesfin's eyes widened.

'It is obscene, Liz.'

'Really? Let's have it anyway.'

There were two friends, a male hare and a male tortoise, and they were so friendly that they said to each other, 'Let's have sex and see who can do it the fastest.'

The hare, knowing how fast he was, said, 'I'll go first.'

The tortoise thought, 'I'm slow, and I've got a shell on my back, but I know I can beat him at this.'

Out loud, he said, 'My penis is much stronger than yours. You won't be able to win.'

They agreed in the end that the hare should go first.

'But I'll go and bring water from the river, so we can do it better,' said the hare, so off he ran to the river.

While he was fetching the water, the tortoise hid, and when he heard the hare coming, he called out for the water but he didn't let the hare find him.

'We agreed to meet but you're not here!' the hare called out angrily.

'It's the wrong place anyway for having sex,' the tortoise shouted back. 'Go back to the river and get some more water.'

The hare obeyed, but while he was away, the tortoise hid again. The hare came back once more, but when he couldn't find the tortoise, he was very angry.

'This stupid slow animal, if I catch him I'll break his shell for sending me to the river so many times,' he said, and he gave up and ran off.

This story still makes me laugh, years later, but no smile had cracked the thin cheeks of the circle of Gumuz villagers. I've often wondered whether this is the ur-story which was cleaned up by the likes of Aesop. Is there more to the story than the ponderous old moral we grew up with: 'Slow and steady wins the race'?

At last, however, a woman who had been sitting in splendid isolation on a boulder in the middle of the swept area, cleared her throat and began a story. Her name was Egassi Reta.

In the old days, she said, the people used to go to the river and throw fruits from the birbira tree into the water to intoxicate the fish, so that they could catch them. One day, as they were doing this, the water began to rise and rise. Then the water opened and divided in two to the left and the right. The men were pulled into the river and it carried them away. Some of them were changed into elephants, some into crocodiles, while some grew tails and became monkeys. They stayed under the water and built houses and they live there still.

Was this story a folk memory of a natural event, a sudden flood followed by a river blockage caused by an earthquake? Or was it a distant relative of the story of Moses and the crossing of the Red Sea? Perhaps it was a remnant of one of the many flood stories from ancient times. There are, of course, countless stories from around the world of enchanted lands under the sea. Whatever the origin, I had the feeling that for Egassi Reta, mythical time and present time were seamless and that in her mind the river was still the haunt of the shape-shifting fishermen.

When she had finished speaking, silence fell again. The situation was awkward. Mesfin, Dires, Belay and I sat on a log on one side of the open space, with Egassi Reta and the villagers on the other.

'We should have brought a crate of soft drinks,' I muttered to Mesfin. 'It feels rude, to have come without a gift.'

He stood up.

'You are right, Liz. This is not successful. We should go.'

I was worried as we headed back to Chagni in the car. What had we done wrong? Were the stories too precious to be imparted to strangers? Should the elders have been asked first? Should we have taken time to explain our purpose more carefully? Should we have brought gifts?

We in the west have a changing sense of what is forbidden in stories. Religious texts, such as the Bible or the Koran, are on the whole treated with reverence, but in general we accept without a blink levels of violence, sexual explicitness and political criticism which were once considered unacceptable. Old taboos, in fact, attract our artists, who break them in order to shock, albeit with diminishing returns. But for many peoples in the world the telling of stories is hedged about with restrictions.

Stories may 'belong' to a certain group. They may be revealed only to initiates, or on certain ceremonial occasions. Those who know them may not wish to hand them out to strangers and so lose control of them. Some stories may be told only to women, or to men. There may be fears that stories will be misunderstood, misrepresented or ridiculed. Our failure to collect many Gumuz stories could have been for a variety of reasons.

Belay himself told us two more stories. The first, a 'how things began' fable, explained the origins of man. Creation stories intrigue me, perhaps because I was brought up with the poetry of the first chapter of Genesis ringing in my ears. (I can still hear that old clock in the meeting hall ticking away, its hand crawling round the face on which was written 'It is time to meet the Lord'.) I enjoy the way that a good creation myth lays bare the thinking of people with no scientific knowledge, equipped only with their observations of nature and the deductions they have made from the environment that surrounds them.

Belay's story evoked the memory of the cream and red dust jacket with the elephant medallion on my childhood copy of Kipling's *Just So Stories*, of the warm pleasure of the funny tales of the camel and his hump, and the leopard and his spots. Here is Belay's story.

When the first man began to grow his crops, the baboons would come and steal them. He chased them away.

One day, when the baboons were fleeing from him, a baboon child was left behind. The man was enchanted by the little creature. He made friends with her, took her home and fed her. The next day she came out to the field with him, but as he sowed his seeds, she picked them up from the ground and ate them.

'No, that's not the way,' he told her. 'The seeds must grow and make more seeds.'

Thus he taught her. As the plants grew, she helped him to weed them.

When she reached puberty, the man had sex with her, and she gave birth to a boy child who looked like a man and walked on two legs. They had a second child who was a girl. When the children grew up, they married each other, and the grandchildren married each other and so they increased. Forgetting that they had been baboons, they lived as men and went on together very happily.

I liked this acknowledgement of our close relationship with other primates. I spent a few days once in a refuge for orphaned chimpanzees in Zambia and I made friends with one little male called Junior. We spent hours sitting together, grooming each other. I loved to feel his deft fingers searching in my hair, and I did the same for him.

'Why don't we humans groom each other like apes do?' I asked Shirley Strum.[40]

'We do it all the time,' she said. 'It's called language.'

Belay's next story opened other doors for me, into the world of magic. Shape-shifting magicians, with the power to transform themselves into animals, had crept up on me with the donkey man in Bahir Dar, and Nyakwiy's cannibalistic brother-in-law in Gambela. There had been several hyena woman stories along the way too. But here in Mandwa the porcupine man story had an aura of mystery and sadness which has always remained with me.

A man went to hunt for honey in the forest. The honey bird lured him to a hive and the man harvested plenty of honey, but he had nothing to carry it in, so he left it under the tree while he

---

[40] Strum is an internationally known biological anthropologist who has made ground-breaking studies of baboon communities. Her best known book is *Almost Human: A Journey into the World of Baboons*, first published by Norton, 1990.

went to fetch his goatskin sack.

While he was away, a porcupine stole his honey. The man followed its trail to a cave. Inside the cave was an evil spirit (zar) disguised as a woman. She was baking grain to make beer.

'I want my honey,' the man told her. 'The porcupines have stolen it, and I am going to kill them.'

The zar said, 'These porcupines are my food. They are to me as sheep are to you. Don't harm them.'

She gave him bread to eat. Immediately he was turned into a porcupine and spines grew all over his body. He went to find his people but on the way he passed through a fire. The spines were burned off him, and to put out the fire, he jumped into a lake. When he came back to the shore he looked like a man again.

But he was now neither a man nor a porcupine. He lives still among the bushes, gathering his food. He cannot speak like a man. He is lost. He lives like a savage. He still lives.

There is a Greek feel to the metamorphosis of the porcupine man. He suffers the fate of Odysseus's sailors who eat and drink at Circe's table and are transformed into pigs. Unlike the sailors, however, who are rescued by Odysseus and return unscathed to their human form, the porcupine man, having survived ordeals by fire and water, lives in a half world, neither man nor beast. He loses the prestige of the hunter, and must gather his food like women do.

I was touched by this story of a lost soul living on the fringes of human society, unable to speak. From our Western perspective, we can read into this story a depiction of mental illness. But the porcupine man frightens, too, showing the consequences of his foolish brush with the forces of magic. Lured by the honey bird, he broke the taboo that divides mortals from the supernatural world, and is duly punished.

Later, on one of our long journeys around the region, I asked Dires about the zar in the story. I wanted him to outline for me the different kinds of magicians, ogres, wizards and were-people I had encountered. He collected his thoughts for a minute or two, then he offered me this fascinating rogues gallery of magic and mischief, groping for the English words to describe the various characters.

He chose 'wizard' for the first character. This person, a man or a woman, can be consulted as an oracle. He or she sits in a dark place out of sight. People bring gifts, usually of incense, and he makes them wait. While they are waiting, the wizard's servants befriend the client and cleverly extract as much information as they can. When at last the wizard consents to the interview, he has learned all about the client and can make an impressive display of 'magical' knowledge.

'He knows how to show cleverness to others, but he is not clever for himself,' Dires concluded, with the scorn of a son of the Church.

A 'witchman' makes medicine. He performs a kind of voodoo with chicken blood smeared on his face. In Arsi, Dires said, there was a female witch called Yegnana Mebet. Childless women would come from all over Ethiopia to consult her in the hopes of becoming pregnant, bringing lavish gifts. This woman died years ago, but her spirit passed to her son, and then to her grandson. The church had always condemned her, and the names of her clients were published in the newspaper to shame them. That is why people crept off to consult her in the night.

Jinns, so familiar from our own childhood tale of Aladdin and his lamp, haunt dirty places where animals are slaughtered or where ashes are thrown, as their food is blood, the dregs of tala, and the ashes of the cooking fire. They are malign, and if you encounter a jinn you will fall sick. Here at last was an explanation for something that had long puzzled me. I had often seen fireplaces, marked by a pit or a circle of stones in the centre of a hut, from which the ashes had been scrupulously cleaned away. Was this for fear of jinns? And is it in order to hide from jinns that cooking fires are lit in the darkest place within the hut where the jinns cannot find them? Jinns, Dires said, also like to live near churches, and if a priest goes to his church at midnight they will give him a kicking.

The saitan is the river demon I had encountered many times before who comes out of the water at noon to catch girls.

We had arrived at the end of our journey before I had plumbed the depths of Dires's knowledge. Where did shape-shifters fit into this gallery? And what about the zombie masters and purveyors of the evil eye?

In many ways, the belief system of Dires, brought up within the dogmatic confines of the Christian Church, was the same as the one I had imbibed from my Bible-based childhood. We had both been taught to see Man in the centre of the cosmos, with the animals beneath and an ascending hierarchy of saints and angels rising to the Trinity of Father, Son and Holy Spirit at the apex. We were imbued with the idea of intercession, either through prayer to saints, the Virgin Mary, or, in my Protestant tradition, directly through Christ himself.

In Europe, the Christian religion has been virtually universal for so many centuries that the Roman and Viking deities, the shamans, fairies, sprites, elves, witches, trolls and all the rest have either been forgotten or have been relegated to the cosy world of legend and folklore. Even in Europe, however, they took a long time to disappear. The witch trials of the seventeenth century saw ancient terrors bursting out of the dungeons of religion, and interaction with the 'wee people' persisted in remote areas well into the modern era. Belief in ghosts and all kinds of supernatural phenomena, dismissed by the Church as 'superstition', not only persists but gains new strength as the hold of the Church weakens.

The Ethiopian Orthodox Church, unlike its counterparts in the West, existed as an island in a sea of very different cosmologies. Priests like Dires's father had no doubt frowned on 'superstitious' beliefs and practices, but they had less chance of discouraging them than their European colleagues. Even in the Christian heartland of Amhara Bahir Dar I had found that the zombie myth was vigorously alive. On the fringes of the Ethiopian Orthodox world, so recently and imperfectly absorbed into the Ethiopian state, the array of magical and demonic beings listed by Dires must have seemed more real to him than they could ever have done to me.

❖

On our way back to Addis Ababa, Mesfin and I broke our journey for lunch in a cavernous, post-communist dining room in a government hotel. As we picked the bones from our Nile perch, a Russian came to sit at our table. He seemed lonely and showed us a photo of his little daughter. His English was poor but he was eager to tell us jokes.

'Three men. American, Japanese, Russian. American say, "I go to work in Ford car. I go holiday in Chrysler. When I go abroad, I go in Cadillac." Japan say, "I go work in Honda. I go holiday Mitsubishi. I go other country in Toyota." Russian man say, "I go work in bus. I go holidays in train. When I go abroad, I go in tank."'

He attempted several more jokes, in which vodka, shipwrecks

and the balls of a male mosquito had starring roles, but they were too obscure to make much sense.

After he had gone, I wondered about his urge to accost strangers and tell stories through the medium of his few words of our shared language. I guessed that he was in a team of engineers servicing the Russian MiG fighters, Ethiopia's prime weapons in their tragic conflict with Eritrea. Had he hoped that I was a Russian, like him, and could talk to him in his own language? He was clearly lonely. With his stories he had wanted to make us laugh, to invite us to share in his ironic view of himself as a Russian, to make friends. Telling stories was the next step, beyond a simple greeting, towards a friendship.

The road back to Addis Ababa took us over the second bridge across the Nile. This was hedged about with greater security than the first. Only one vehicle was allowed across at a time, and our driver warned me to keep my camera out of sight. Once we had made it to the far side, three soldiers flagged us down and asked for a lift. They piled into the back seat of the Land Cruiser beside me. All were carrying Kalashnikovs. One considerately broke his before climbing in, but the others sat hugging their guns between their knees, resting their chins from time to time on the muzzles. Once or twice, I leaned across a young soldier to push the barrel of his gun away from where it was pointing directly at Mesfin's head in the front seat. We dropped them at the top of the long climb out of the gorge. They thanked us politely, and waved goodbye.

· 12 ·

THE BARD OF BONGA

More than a year was to pass before I could return to Ethiopia, and much had changed in the intervening months. Michael Sargent's replacement as director of the British Council in Addis Ababa had been in post long enough to decide on her priorities.

'Books are boring,' I heard her say to a visiting delegation of sports people. 'We're interested in football now.'

The reader project needed 'strategising', she told me. The finances were wrong. She didn't feel that she *owned* it.

For the sake of completeness, however, it had been decided that I should make one more major journey, this time to the south.

Back in the comfort of England, I had had to steel myself to set off on my travels again. It was February. London was cold and gloomy, and I was afflicted with a winter lethargy, wanting only to wrap myself in jumpers and pile logs on the wood stove. I thought with foreboding of the long days ahead cramped up in a car, the difficulties of finding storytellers, the uncertainties of where to stay and what to eat, the danger of sickness and bandits and impassable roads. But I told myself not to be feeble.

'The minute you step out of the plane and feel the sun on your face and someone says hello in Amharic, you'll wonder what you were fussing about,' David said unsympathetically as I stood in our bedroom in London, holding my old canvas trousers up to the light to check if they would last another journey. He might have added, 'Get a grip,' but kindly spared me.

❖

The south-western corner of Ethiopia is a crazy paving of different cultures, languages, traditions and even climates. The government has not attempted to give each zone its own administration but has grouped them into one region called the Southern Nations, Nationalities and People's Region, or SNNPR for short. If this name is a little clumsy, it has the virtue of including everyone's view of themselves and avoiding demeaning words like 'tribe' and 'ethnicity'.

To my delight, Tekle was to be the driver on this journey, and Mesfin was to be the translator. I would be with friends. There would be stories and laughter to alleviate the long boredom of the road, and the translations when they came would be carefully respectful of the narrators' voices.

Bonga, the old capital of the kings of Kafa, was our first port of call. Coffee originated in Kafa (the name says it all). Life would be a sadder thing without this gift to the world from Ethiopia, so next time you brew up the life-giving elixir, raise your mug in a toast of thanks. The history of this kingdom, which dates from the fourteenth century, is long and complex. It lay on a great trading route, between Shoa to the north and Sudan to the west. It reached the zenith of its power at the end of the eighteenth century but a hundred years later fell victim to Menelik's expansionist ambitions. Its last king, Gaki Sherocho, was defeated in 1897 and taken in silver chains to Addis Ababa. Kafa was incorporated into the Ethiopian empire.

'We were a great nation once,' the regional cultural officer had said to me wistfully. 'There was a big market here, for coffee and musk and slaves.'

'Slaves!' Mesfin had exclaimed, waving an airy hand. 'My Armenian grandfather, Merkurian, was given eighty slaves by the Emperor Menelik.'

He saw the expression on my face.

'In those days, everyone thought differently about such things. Now, of course . . .'

During our first story session in Bonga, a young man had been sitting quietly, listening to the others, but after some time he cleared his throat and indicated that he had a story to tell. I looked at him properly for the first time. He was wearing a lemon-yellow shell suit, and he had a habit of rolling his large eyes, his hands fluttering as he spoke. His name was Worku Alemu.

'He is a special person,' someone explained. 'His ancestors were storytellers to the kings of Bonga.'

'You mean like bards?'

'That is it, exactly! This boy learned the stories from his great uncle. He is determined to preserve them.'

Worku blinked nervously while this explanation was going on. He looked eighteen or nineteen, young to be the carrier of Kafa's oral treasures. I thought of my own two sons, who were only a year or two older than Worku. They were busy soaking up the culture and tastes of their peers. I had somehow failed to impart to them a sense of the beauty and meaning of the stories of Christianity which had underpinned my own life. I imagined Worku as a little boy, rapt beside his ancient uncle, his mouth open, his eyes glazed as he drank in the stories that once had been told to kings.

The first of Worku's stories had a plot as complete as any in *The Decameron.* Shakespeare might have knitted it into a play. It starts in the good old way with a tyrannous act by the King of Kafa, who becomes suspicious of his advisors and murders their entire tribe, the Mattos, except for one little boy who escapes and is brought up in hiding by a humble tribe of outcast tanners.

The king wants to build a palace grander than any seen before, and for this he needs a central pole to hold up the roof. He orders his servants to bring him the longest pole in the world, one that will reach the sky, and not to return without it on pain of death.

His terrified servants spend ten years in the forest, living on berries and the flesh of wild animals, searching for a pole that will reach the sky. They do not even pause to clip their nails or cut their hair, which grows so long that it falls like robes over their backs. At last, exhausted, they give up and seek refuge in the very village of tanners where the Matto boy is now half grown.

The tanners are afraid of these strange people with claws for nails and hair so long, and they run away, but the Matto boy asks the strangers what they want.

They tell him.

'You mean you have been hiding in the forest for ten years for such a little problem?' asks the boy. 'The solution is simple. Go back to the king banging a drum and singing "Yubbo, yubbo," a song of triumph. Say to him, "O King, may you live for a thousand years. We have got the pole you asked for. But we cannot be sure that it is the tallest pole in the world unless you give us a rod to measure it with." Do this, and see what the king will say.'

The advisors do as the boy suggests. The king frowns as he listens to them. He knows he has been tricked.

'Only one of those rascally Mattos could have thought of

this,' he says, and orders the advisors to tell him who gave them the idea. They describe the Matto boy, and the king sends his soldiers to fetch the child.

Fearlessly, the boy confronts the king.

'You are right. I am Mattoni,' he says, 'but I have grown up among the tanners to escape from death.'

The king is so impressed by the boy's wisdom and fearlessness that he repents his actions.

'I need you and your people to be my advisors,' he says. 'From now on you will live with me in my palace and those in exile will come home.'

This story, most probably, is a poetic version of a historical reality. My generation in Britain was brought up on a diet of stories about 'our island race', featuring characters such as Alfred and his cakes, Canute holding back the waves and Robert the Bruce with his spider. Myths about history are more influential – and potentially more dangerous – than truths. One has only to think of the sagas underpinning such concepts as the British 'white man's burden', 'the American dream', the Aryan nightmares of Nazism or the expansionism of Israeli settlers to see how powerful they are. Poetic history is an important source for Ethiopia's academics now working in universities around the country to uncover and record their nation's story, but it is full of pitfalls too. It's a good thing that our school curriculum now attempts to give children tools to study history with objectivity, teaching them how to use sources and draw conclusions from evidence.

The young bard of Bonga's tale of persecution and exile comes back to me whenever I hear of one of my old students from the 1960s, that generation of clever, idealistic, ambitious young Ethiopians who were slaughtered in their thousands during the

terror purges of Mengistu Haile Mariam. Many fled to find a
precarious existence as refugees in Europe or the United States,
living like the Mattoni boy with the 'outcast tanners' of the
Western world. Sometimes I'm lucky enough to meet one of
those who have been too resourceful to succumb to the hardships
of the refugee life, and have become settled and fulfilled in their
work. The current government of Ethiopia casts longing eyes
on this pool of overseas talent, and tries to lure them home.
Some have gone back and are investing their talents and savings
once again in their homeland.

It was in Bonga, too, that I met Imahoy Zewditu, an elderly
nun of the Ethiopian Orthodox Church.

This powerful old lady was waiting to receive us in her house.
Like the homes of so many old people, hers had seen better
days. The walls, made of wattle and daub, had settled and were
now a little askew. The newspapers which had been stuck on as
wallpaper were blackened with smoke from the fire in the centre
of the room and were coming adrift, while the floor of beaten
mud was uneven and holed in places. It reminded me of my
mother's small flat in her sheltered housing complex. She had
hidden the stains in the carpet with a rug, her loose covers were
old and torn, and the bone handles of her knives had split and
were falling apart, but she didn't see anything amiss, and would
have hated to make changes.

Imahoy Zewditu was sitting cross-legged on her bed under
a simply painted portrait of an old man. A snowy shamma was
draped round her shoulders and a tangle of handsome necklaces
fell over the blue cotton top of her dress. White curls crept out from
under the yellow cotton nun's cap, decorated with a red appliqué
cross which she wore at a rakish angle on her head. She greeted us
graciously and called to a young girl to set out stools for us.

She began to tell us her life story. Her father had been a counsellor to the last King of Kafa. He had died, an old man, when she was still a small child. Because of the family's high status, she had not been allowed to play with the maids or go around with the other small children. Instead, she had passed her time at home, listening to the stories the old people told each other and learning them by heart. She had received some education, and had been introduced to Haile Selassie himself when he had visited Kafa. She could remember the Italian occupation.

I guessed she was in her seventies. She was proud of her great age, and had clearly decided that she had earned the right to spend the rest of her days in bed to be waited on hand and foot.

Imahoy Zewditu was a good hostess. She called on the girl to supply us with drinks, and asked me many questions about myself. I couldn't resist this zesty old woman's charm. I wished even more fervently than usual that I could speak to her in her own language and glean her wisdom. Tekle approved of her, I could tell, and I had come to learn that he was a good judge of character.

Imahoy Zewditu's best story contained such striking images that I see them still in my mind's eye – bright pictures in primary colours as if they had been painted by Matisse.

The story starts with the familiar theme of a dying man's bequest to his three sons. He gives each young man a box. In one there is soil, in another money, and in the third pieces of gold.

The man dies, and his puzzled sons can't work out the meaning of the boxes. They go to find a wise man who can explain them. On the way, they pass a river. A crocodile is on the bank licking drops of water from the grass. Next they come to a rich pasture, where a horse, thin to the point of starvation, stands without eating. After this, they cross a desert in which a fat donkey roams, with no means of nourishment. At last, they find the wise man they are seeking.

'We human beings run here and there and think a lot, but the time of our death is a decision for God. However we toil, whatever we do with our lives, in the end it's God's will,' the old nun put in at this point.

Just what my mother would say, I thought.

The wise man examines the boxes. The one whose box contains soil, he says, inherits the land and becomes a farmer. The one with the money must buy cattle and be a herdsman. The brother with the gold is destined to be a merchant.

The brothers return to their village and carry out their father's will. But things do not go well for them. The herdsman has no grassland on which to feed his cattle, and they become thin and hungry. He remembers the starving horse he had seen in the lush field. He goes to his farmer brother and asks for land. The farmer, having no cattle to keep down the weeds, has been bothered by wild animals invading his land to graze. He remembers the crocodile licking the grass beside river. The merchant, meanwhile, travels rootlessly about on his business, with no home to return to. He remembers the fat donkey living alone in the desert. And so the three brothers pool their resources. The farmer offers land to the herdsman, who gives him some cattle in return, and the farmer lets his merchant brother buy a plot from him on which he can build his house. In this way the three support each other and live together in peace.

Another short sermon wrapped the story up.

'The first of the Ten Commandments is "Respect your father,"' Imahoy Zewditu said, her curls bobbing about her face as she nodded at us. 'Children in the past were good and listened to their parents and never quarrelled, and so they lived happily. But these days people disagree with each other and make a world of misery.'

I would have drawn a different moral from this story, one about the division of labour and the roots of the Co-operative Movement. I thought of those thousands of lonely, selfless Africans packed off overseas to work in the heat of the Gulf or the cold of Europe, stinting themselves to send back their remittance money for the good of all their relations. Then I remembered the portrait on the wall above Imahoy Zewditu's head. Was it of her father? And surely she had learned her commandments well enough to know that the injunction to honour one's father (and mother, by the way) is not the first, but the fifth? I was learning again how much a story could reveal about the storyteller.

Imahoy Zewditu had by now crumbled into a state of decrepitude. We had exhausted her, so we thanked her and stepped back out into the sunshine, our eyes dazzled by the light. I ran a checklist through my head. How did my brother and sisters and I match up to Imahoy Zewditu's story? How did we do on mutual support, on sharing and co-operation?

Not bad, I thought, as Western families go, but miles behind the Ethiopian ideal.

Mesfin had sat up till the small hours again on the night before we left Bonga. The pace he was keeping up would have flattened me, but he was on terrific form.

'I did it my way,' he crowed, in a credible imitation of Frank Sinatra as we drove out of town, the slanting sun of early morning picking out vignettes of Ethiopian life as vivid as the panes in a stained-glass window: men driving pairs of oxen behind their ploughs, clouds of golden chaff rising from the threshing floors, trotting donkeys laden with sacks of grain, women appearing at the doors of their huts to throw arcs of water from their pans, and children running to school with dog-eared books in their hands, ambition in every small heart.

The drive to Welkite, our next stop, took four or five hours, and Mesfin never stopped. He sang. He recited poetry. He egged me on to do the same. I gave him my party piece – Tennyson's 'Battle of the Revenge'. I had learned it by heart (all twenty minutes of it) from my brother while we did the washing up together fifty years earlier. When I came to the lines, 'With a joyful spirit I Sir Richard Grenville die!' Mesfin yelped with emotion and sucked in his breath.

'Again! Say that part again!'

He was a literature man through and through, in love with words and stories.

❖

Welkite is the capital of the Gurage Zone. The Gurage people are known throughout Ethiopia as merchants and traders. They are untypical in a country where the vast majority of people are farmers, in that a high proportion of them (perhaps more than a third) live in towns and cities, where they can be found running every kind of business. The Gurage have adapted themselves to the different regions in which they have settled. They have learned the appropriate languages and been influenced by the locally prevailing religion.

The Gurage, who still live in their own heartlands and farm in the traditional way, speak one of several dialects which in the written form use the Ethiopic script. Their staple crop is ensete. Plantations of this banana-like crop abound here. The edible part is not the fruit, however, but the stem and root. The 'false banana', as it is often called, is a winner for Ethiopia, being highly nutritious, resistant to drought and easy to grow and harvest. The current government would like to introduce ensete into other regions, but those used to eating tef-based injera are naturally resistant to such a change. One only has to think of the difficulty in weaning the British off their fat-soaked chips and burgers to realise what an uphill task the government of Ethiopia faces. In fact, people have adapted already to new foodstuffs, introducing foreign vegetables such as potatoes and carrots into their diet, and I was constantly surprised to see how much fruit was being eaten and sold compared with thirty years earlier.

The entrepreneurial streak of the Gurages is evident as soon as you drive into Welkite. It's a thriving place, pushing towards the modern world, with excellent small hotels, well-stocked shops and a magnificent public library. In many parts of Ethiopia the most common vehicles are the white Land Cruisers and Range Rovers of foreign NGOs, which dash importantly about the country (as indeed we were doing in our British Council Land Rover) transporting foreigners from one project to another with bright ideas cooked up abroad and pockets full of aid money. In Welkite, the NGO vehicles were less evident. This town was going somewhere fast, under its own steam.

The traditional dome-roofed houses of Gurage villages, however, are more wonderful than anything you will see in the towns. When you step inside one of these extraordinary constructions you can only look up and gasp. A massive mast of wood, supporting the roof, rises from the centre of the space. It's like the pillar of a cathedral, and the wooden spokes that spring from it create an effect of fan vaulting. These are tied laterally with cross beams and thatch is laid on top. A wall of hewn planks divides the interior space in two. The cattle are housed in the back part, along with the cooking area and store. There is little furniture, seating mainly being provided by the raised bench of mud along the walls, which, like the wide expanse of floor, are finished with an application of smoothed mud. Mud has also been used to mould the fireplace in the middle. Created from the materials at hand – mud, sticks and thatch – these houses leave a light footprint on the land but are beautiful, commodious and perfectly suited to the climate. They join in my personal canon of architectural excellence the reed house in the Iraqi marshes where David and I spent a memorable night long ago, the bamboo kampong house on stilts in Kelantan, Malaysia where I once stayed with the family of a Malay friend, and the 'black house' on the Isle of Lewis built of rough dressed stones with a crux beam roof.

Here is my favourite story from Gurage. It was told by Shirgama Sorama, an old man wearing a Stetson and carrying a fly whisk.

The hero of his tale is a poor man who meets a beautiful woman while travelling down the road.

'What are you seeking?' she asks him.
'I want to work and become rich.'

'I will make you rich,' she says.

She gives him seeds and tells him to plant them on a hill. As he climbs the hill, he sees a man collecting firewood. But this man is gathering more and more sticks, too many for his bundle, which is now impossible to lift.

'Why don't you take some sticks off your bundle so that you can carry it?' the poor man asks him, but the stick gatherer tells him to mind his own business.

Next the poor man passes a farmer cutting his crops with a sickle, but instead of harvesting only the tef, which is ripe, he is cutting the unripe barley too.

'Why don't you leave the barley to ripen, and only harvest the tef?' the poor man asks, but the farmer tells him to go away.

He sees a third man trying to push a rock up the hill, but the rock is so heavy that it cannot be shifted, even by an inch.

'Are you crazy?' says the poor man. 'You'll never be able to move such a heavy rock.'

'What's it to you? Leave me alone,' the rock pusher replies.

The poor man comes at last to the field and sows his seeds. On the way home he meets the beautiful woman again. He tells her about the three men and the strange things they were doing.

'The first was a moneylender,' she explains. 'He is never satisfied with what he has but demands more and more. The second man is death. He kills the young and old alike, taking the weak and the strong, the rich and the poor. The third man is one who is too ambitious. He wants to be rich and is weighed down by the cares of his desires.'

'So what should I do?' the poor man asked.

'Sow your seeds. Care for them. Harvest them, and you will become rich.'

Shirgama tapped his stick on the ground as he ended his story, and smiled as he recited the closing formula.

'*Biya waret bahe kerach*. Good sleep for me, and may the fleas all jump on you.'

There must be reasons why vegetable growing has become such a passion with the British. After years of neglect, allotments are now sought after. Garden centres and seed merchants report rocketing sales of fruit and vegetable seeds. I have long been addicted to my five small raised beds. I plan out my crop rotation and exterminate slugs. I weed, water, net against the pigeons and drone on to anyone who will listen about the sourness of the

London soil and the plagues of cabbage white butterflies which hamper my efforts. Is this urge to grow vegetables a reaction to our consumerist culture of greed and ambition? Are we tired of gathering more sticks than we need and rolling rocks uphill? Are we trying to rediscover the certainties of life in the face of the unpredictability of death? I was amused that this story came from the Gurage, that most business minded of all the sub-cultures of Ethiopia.

❖

To reach Jinka, in the far south-west, Tekle had to drive Mesfin and me for two long days. Anyone passing this way will remember above all the Konso region. The Konso people have sculpted their hills into perfectly engineered terraces. The farmers ploughing these small, productive fields wear dashing blue-and-gold striped shorts, and their hair is tied in plaits. The women striding along the road wear many-layered skirts flicking out around their legs, and pale circlets are tied around their heads.

Not surprisingly, the stone terraces of Konso, which date back half a millennium, are in the impressively long list of UNESCO World Heritage Sites in Ethiopia.

In Jinka, the town where we were to stay, the hotel followed the standard layout for such establishments. Two long, single-storied rows of rooms, set back behind a covered walkway, faced each other across a courtyard. This was a pleasant space with a pergola bright with bougainvillea flowers, and tables and chairs set out in the shade of trees. At night, the guests' cars and trucks could safely be parked here behind the iron gates which closed the courtyard off from the street. The bar was at the front of the hotel, with an entrance onto the street. At the back end a traditional round hut with a conical thatched roof made a pleasant meeting place. In the backyard by the kitchen, chickens scratched in the dirt and cereals were laid out in pans to dry.

The hotel courtyard was the smart hang-out for the middle class of Jinka, and groups of young men lounged at the next table. One evening, as Mesfin and I worked on translations, some of them began to listen. Too conscious of their own dignity to crowd round us, they craned their necks and cupped their ears. One leaned so far back in his chair that it teetered dangerously and nearly crashed to the ground.

Ethiopian hotels outside Addis Ababa are improving all the time. The bed is usually a small double, with a blanket tightly tucked in over the sheets. I often need more warmth in the highland regions, and I take my own patchwork quilt, made for the purpose over many long evenings at home. There's often an overwhelming smell of insecticide, and it's rare to be attacked by fleas. The Ethiopian pillow, though, is a horrible object, round as a barrel and nearly as hard, usually covered with a polyester pillow case, which, even when washed, remains grey and greasy. I travel now with my own pillow case, which I wrap round a fleece or a cardigan to make my own pillow. In my fussy way, I take time to customise my room. In malarial areas I look for a projection from which I can hang my mosquito net. This usually means dragging the bed near a switch or hook, or towards a window shutter. Then there's the problem of making sure that the weak light bulb is directly above one's head so that reading is possible. If the hotel offers a personal shower room, a little bar of soap and a small towel are usually provided along with a few hand turns of toilet paper, no more than twenty squares. There's always a stout bolt on the door and on the shutter across the window, and you know you are perfectly safe.

The only real problem is the noise. The bar blares on until the town generator packs up at midnight, with luck, but sometimes not until two in the morning. Then there are the drunks noisily rolling home, and the night watchman who might tap his stick on the metal grill across your window as he walks past. The game is up at dawn, when the lorries that have been secured overnight in the hotel compound rev up for departure, and the hotel servants wake the residents who are leaving town on the early buses.

You can't expect good roads in such remote regions, and Tekle had to show off his virtuosity in negotiating dry fords and steering the Land Rover in cat-like climbs up steep slopes on our way to a village of the Male people.

'Ai-ee! We are going to fall backwards!' Mesfin the townie would moan, clutching the rim of the open window. And then, when we had made it to the top, he would cry out with admiration and pat Tekle on the shoulder.

We pulled up in the middle of the village. A horde of children surrounded the Land Rover, tapping on the windows.

'Mother! Sister! Father!' they whined, holding out their hands.

I felt an ignoble urge to swipe out at them, followed by another urge, even less realistic, to sit them down in a ring and say, 'Now, children, your methods are counter-productive and you're only being annoying. If you *really* want me to give you some money, here are a few tips.'

Mesfin magnificently ignored the irritation while Tekle smilingly engaged with the children, asking them questions and making them laugh so that they momentarily forgot about me.

An old man in this village told us a tale about the chameleon, that dodgy character who weaves in and out of folk tales from Zululand to Kenya, and across to West Africa too. In most such tales, the chameleon fails in his commission to take a message from the Creator to Man, and is condemned to hide thereafter from fear and shame. But in Oesha's story the chameleon is the guiltless victim.

A 'thunderstorm spirit' has lost one of his sheep. The lizard can't tell him where to find it because he's too busy basking in the sun, so the thunderstorm spirit goes to find the woodpecker.

'I'm doing my job here, pecking. I haven't seen your sheep,' says the woodpecker. 'Why don't you ask the chameleon if he has stolen it? He's always hiding himself. He must have done something bad.'

The thunderstorm spirit goes about in a rage, shouting for the chameleon, who hides behind a tree. At last the thunderstorm spirit finds him and tears the poor chameleon to pieces.

'And to this day,' the storyteller finished, 'there is a saying in the Male language. "Don't go and stand under a tree when there is lightning because it is looking for the chameleon in the trees who stole his sheep."'

In the usual discussion which followed, it was agreed that the moral of the story was that one should not be like people who do bad things and hide themselves. I thought this tacked-on moral missed the point of the story, which, surely, is to warn people not to stand under trees during storms where they risk being struck by lightning.

We were, in fact, sitting under a tree in the compound of the village school. The old men surrounding us, barefoot or shod in sandals made from the rubber of discarded tyres, were occupying themselves absent-mindedly in running their fingers down the seams of their shorts and picking out the fleas and lice. I knew the feeling. I had done the same every time I'd returned from a visit to a church, where the straw which covers the floor abounds with insects. When one of them was ready to tell a story, he would raise his long forked stick, polished with use, and tap it down on the ground.

I looked round at the group as the stories flowed. This would be one of the last times I would be in such a situation, sitting in a circle of people with unknowably different lives from my own, garnering their wisdom and humour and history. I watched the fluffy white curls on the storyteller's chin move up and down as he spoke. I followed his tentative gestures, and smiled at the sight of everyone rocking with laughter. I felt humbled by the honour they were doing me. I had no conception of the houses they lived in, the food they ate or the work they had done all their lives, and they had no idea of mine. I was longing for the moment in the evening when Mesfin would puzzle over each word, pausing the tape recorder for long moments as he found the exact meaning, bringing out the small twists and details which gave character to the individual storytellers' voices.

Here is one from that Male village.

At the beginning of time, baboons and monkeys lived together in one troop. They looked identical, except that the baboons were bigger. Often, the whole troop would gaze up at the sky and wonder how they could get up there to explore it.

One day they agreed that the best way to reach the sky was to make a tower of their bodies. The monkeys said to the baboons, 'You're big and strong, so you'd better make the base of the tower and we'll climb on you.'

So the baboons piled on top of each other, higher and higher.

The one at the very bottom of the tower was bent over, with his bottom sticking up into the air. A naughty monkey saw the round hole of his anus and, unable to resist temptation, stuck his finger into it. The baboon shouted and leaped up and of course all the others fell to the ground. They were furious with the monkeys and began to chase them into the forest.

'We'll kill you for this! Wait till we catch you!' they shouted.

Hidden among the trees, the monkeys prayed to God.

'Help us, God! We have nowhere to hide and the baboons are going to beat us to death!'

God heard their prayer. He changed the monkeys' faces, putting white brows over their eyes and giving them tails. And he changed the baboons too, making their bottoms red and hairless. The baboons didn't recognise in the transformed monkeys the animals they wanted to punish, and so the monkeys were saved. And from that time on, the two species have lived separately from each other and in peace.

This has to be one of my favourite of all the 'how things began' stories I heard in Ethiopia, with its humour and its tantalising echo of the Tower of Babel story in Genesis.

By the time the precious tape had been translated, both Mesfin and I were tired. Tekle appeared. I asked him if he would go out and walk with me, and he stretched out his arms, cracked his knuckles and said that yes, he too needed some exercise.

We strolled along a flat swathe of grass on which cows were grazing. A windsock and a corrugated iron 'air terminal' announced that this was the airstrip. The air was still warm. Clouds obscured the sun, which was now quite low above the horizon, and was trailing stripes of pink and gold across the deepening blue.

'Off you go,' Tekle would say to the begging children. 'Look, your cows are needing you. Does your mother know where you are? It's time for you to go home.'

We turned off the airstrip and found ourselves in a more rural area. It was quiet here. People were going about their evening chores, hobbling their donkeys to prevent them from running off in the night, fetching in the washing hanging on fences, watering the flowering plants growing in old kerosene tins by the hut doors. One family, a father and mother and children, were sitting together on the grass outside their hut under a soaring eucalyptus tree, talking and laughing. They could have been posed by Constable for a portrait of rural family life. They nodded at us politely as we passed by.

As we neared the hotel, walking back down Jinka's dusty main street, a young man caught sight of us. He had been setting off down a side lane, but now he turned and hurried towards us. Tekle increased his pace, and we reached the gates leading into the hotel seconds before he did. Tekle barred the young man's way.

'What are you doing? I want to talk to her. The ferenji. Maybe she can help me.'

'Help you? What do you want?' said Tekle.

'I want to go abroad. A scholarship. Anything. Why are you stopping me? She has money.'

I slipped away towards my room leaving Tekle to it. I had known at the back of my mind how hard it can be for Ethiopians whose job it is to bear-lead ferenjis round their country, but this incident brought their situation starkly to mind. To the young man barred from the Jinka Hotel I represented a rare career opportunity. I might be able to arrange a scholarship for him abroad. I might have the key to acquiring a visa to America, that land of dreams. I might at the very least have some money to give him. Tekle, barring him from me, had to endure his resentment. He had done it dozens of times before without a word of complaint.

I retired to the veranda outside my room after dinner, where the light was better for reading and writing. Mesfin had made for the bar, the source of the rackety music. I lifted my eyes from the diary I was writing after an hour or two and saw him coming towards me.

'Really, I had to do it, to call you to come and see.'

'See what, Mesfin?'

'Just come.'

Reluctantly I followed him to the bar where some children were dancing.

'Look at them! So clever! See how that one is shaking his shoulders, just like a man. You had to see it. I said to myself, she has to see this.' The children jumped around him, entranced by his admiration for them.

As we stood there, a Toyota Land Cruiser roared in through the open gates of the compound. A fat man in a leather jacket, incongruous in the heat, leaned out of the passenger seat. He was holding two bottles of whisky in one plump hand. Whooping with joy, he waved them at the group of men sitting at a table in the courtyard.

I slipped away, back towards my room. It was nearly dark, but sunlight was still lighting up the long veranda that fronted the row of bedrooms. At the far end I saw the man who had cleaned my room that morning. He was sitting on the floor, his back against the wall, in an attitude of complete exhaustion. One leg was stretched out in front of him, the other was crooked up at the knee. An arm rested on this knee, and the hand dangled loosely down from the wrist. His head was leaning back against the wall and half turned away from me so that he was looking out over the green valley beyond where, as night fell country people were returning from their day's labour in the fields, or driving home their cattle, and looking forward to their supper and the glow of the fires in their huts.

I was thirsty. A girl in a tight blouse was passing down the garden. I had seen her the day before carrying beer bottles to the men in the bar so I signalled to her, meaning to ask her to bring me some bottled water. She made a crude gesture and cackled loudly. I realised with embarrassment that she was rather more than a waitress, and was on her way to the bar for her long night's work of servicing the drunken men.

This place is the like the Wild West, I thought, brash and new, full of whores and drunks and encircled by a hinterland of tribal peoples still living according to their ancient customs.

❖

'*Eri ertote*' (Let's narrate the old stories), an elderly Ari speaker said to me the next day. He wore a broad-brimmed hat blazoned with the letters USA. On his feet was a pair of plastic sandals which were too narrow as his toes were splayed out in the manner of one who has always walked barefoot. His little toes were forced to stick out almost at right angles through the plastic webbing. They must have hurt. He had walked forty-two kilometres into Jinka to tell me stories. I hope it was worth it for him, because it certainly was for me. His name was Metekia Libri.

An orphaned brother and sister lived together. A hyena came each day and left food for them. The brother hid up a tree one day to see who their benefactor was. He watched the hyena cook food by magic means. If she wanted a knife, she called for it and

it came to her. The chopper, the ladle, the pot of butter – they
flew through the air at her command. The boy was frightened
and wet himself.

The hyena looked up and saw him.

'Come down,' she said. The boy obeyed.

The girl came home with the cattle, and found the boy with
the hyena.

'We can all live together,' the hyena said to them.

She slept with them that night.

The boy and girl were frightened of the hyena and decided to
run away. The next morning they took their cattle out as usual
to graze, but instead of returning home they went on into the
forest, hid the cattle and went to stay with friends. The hyena
followed them. She had changed herself into a woman, and they
didn't recognise her. She carried a long thin rod in her hand.

'I'll marry whoever can break this wooden rod,' she said.

Many tried, but only the boy could break it. And so he married
the hyena, and his sister lived with them.

One day, when the sister was away and the boy was sleeping,
the hyena woman put a sharpened iron poker into the fire to heat
it. She intended to drive it into the boy to kill him.

A rat came out of its hole and tried to warn the boy, but he
didn't understand, and killed it. A chicken tried to warn him,
but he killed it too. Then the hyena killed the boy and hid his
body outside in the field. When his sister came home, the hyena
pretended that she was sick.

'Your brother has gone to market,' she said. 'I'm going out to
buy some medicine. Grind the tef till I came home.'

The hyenas took a hair out of her vagina to make a lock and
tied it round the bolt of the door so that it could not be opened.
Then away she went.

Another rat came out and said to the girl, 'She has killed your brother and is calling to her relatives so that they will eat his body. She's going to kill you too. I know how to unlock the door. Go out, take a hollow gourd and fill it with your brother's blood.'

The rat opened the door and let the girl out. She found her brother's body and filled the gourd with his blood. Then she ran away.

The hyena returned with her relatives, but the girl had gone. She began to chase after her. The girl met God. He was sitting on a rock. He had split his penis with a knife.

'Where are you going?' God asked the girl.

She told him the whole story.

'Give me the gourd,' said God. 'I will bring your brother back to life. Hide in the bush and leave the hyena to me.'

The hyena woman came and said to God, 'Have you seen a girl passing by?'

'You will find her there,' said God, pointing to the gorge, and when she had reached the edge, he said, 'Jump!'

And so the hyena jumped into the gorge and was killed.

God put the gourd full of blood into a grain store, and it turned back into the boy. He came out of the grain store and joined his sister, and they lived happily ever after.

The moral of the story is that God can do many things for us. It was he who created the harvest.

'*Erina kosemakse.*' (I have come to the end of my story.)

'Are you sure that's right?' I asked Mesfin as he translated this extraordinary tale. 'Is that really God sitting on a stone slitting his penis with a knife?'

He screwed up his face, holding the recorder even closer to his ear.

'Yes.'

It would be hard to spend any time in Ethiopia or East Africa without sooner or later confronting the question of genital surgery. I had recently been on a separate quest in a Samburu village in Northern Kenya, where I was researching the Grevy zebra for a children's novel I was writing.[41] I was travelling with Dr John Waithaka, an expert from the Kenya Wildlife Service. We had been chatting with a group of Samburu warriors. The topic of circumcision came up. All the lads had been circumcised at the age of fifteen in a public ritual without the benefit of any anaesthetic.

'It is not *so* painful,' one said. 'It is painful, but it is compulsory. They use a special knife. You mustn't be afraid. Your daddy tells you, "If you don't do this thing, you will be nothing. You will be ashamed." Those who are not circumcised are not friendly with those who are. Even those who are circumcised in a hospital, their circumcision is not real.'

The conversation turned to female circumcision.

'We Kikuyu,' John Waithaka said, 'we don't circumcise girls. You boys don't know what you're missing. It's so lovely to have sex with an uncircumcised woman! You can't imagine.'

The boys looked startled, and interested.

I felt I had to do my bit for my African sisters.

'An uncircumcised woman,' I said, 'has the same pleasure as a man. And the man's pleasure is so much greater when the couple has it together.'

'Wah!' the boys said, drawing in their breath, but as they looked at me, with my grey hair and wrinkles, they could see that I was hardly a sex object, after all.

'Pity my husband isn't here,' I said, feeling defensive. 'You

[41] *Zebra Storm* was published by Macmillan Children's Books in 1999.

could have asked him.'

John came to my rescue.

'What you cut away when you circumcise the girl, it is the . . . the . . . you know – the head, where you feel everything.'

We had left them talking earnestly among themselves.

'You know what, Liz,' John said with a guffaw, 'I think we have done more in the fight against female circumcision than any lecture from a doctor. They'll be talking about this in the manyatta[42] for months to come.'

Circumcision seems to have originated in north-east Africa, from whence it spread south and east across the Red Sea into the Arabian Peninsula. An Egyptian frieze from 4000 BC illustrates the practice, which is given great importance in the Old Testament and the Jewish religion, and has become obligatory for Muslim men, although it is not mentioned in the Koran. Remarkably, it is also traditional among many Aboriginal people in Australia, prompting some to speculate that the custom is so ancient that it predates human migration out of Africa. No one knows what prompted people to start cutting off parts of their genitalia, and many theories abound, with all kinds of medical, religious and ritualistic theories produced to explain it. In East Africa, circumcision is an important rite of passage for adolescents. A man or a woman who has not been circumcised is considered immature and unclean.

Metekia Libri's story seems to refer to penile subincision, in which the underside of the penis is slit open. I found it particularly intriguing that the self-slitter in this case is God.

Even more fascinating in this story is the role of the were-hyena woman. Though I had met these creatures before,

---

[42] A Masai or Samburu village settlement.

Metekia's story gave the fullest account. It did not surprise me that the animal most associated with this malign form of magic is the hyena. In Europe, after all, wolves must have been the most terrifying of all the wild creatures in the forests of our ancestors, and it is were-wolves who abound in our stories. Lions might be dangerous, and hippos cause more human death than any other animal in Africa, but there is something uniquely frightening about hyenas. In the 1960s I could hear them whoop in the hills above my house in Addis Ababa, and there were reports of attacks on people out at night, even in the city. Limbs would be snatched off and bellies ripped out by the hyenas' fearsome jaws.

Like were-creatures elsewhere in the world, the hyena women in Ethiopia are capable of all kinds of magic beyond their transformation into humans. Metekia's hyena can spirit kitchen utensils out of the air. Others have supernatural powers of speed. Were-creatures are creations of our darkest imagination, clothing our fear of 'the beast within' in concrete form. They are a staple of folklore everywhere. There are were-tigers in China and were-jaguars in South America. Even in Western cultures, which pride themselves on their scientific rationalism, they refuse to go away. From Stevenson's Mr Hyde, through the fantasies of Hollywood, to the horror stories beloved by teenagers today, the werewolf continues to stalk.

I had long ago realised that there was little connection between the endemic wild animals in Ethiopia and the characters in animal fables. The walia ibex, which lives on the insanely sheer cliffs of the Semien Mountains, the wild ass of the Danakil Desert, the mountain nyala, the gelada baboon, the colobus monkey and the 'Semien fox', which is in fact a wolf, are not real counterparts to the lion, the fox, the monkey and the baboon, which are the stock characters of the stories and have ancient origins, their cousins existing in Aesop's fables and the unknowably old Sanskrit tales of Kalilah and Dimnah in the Panchatantra.[43]

The same is true in European folklore, where the cunning fox, the malevolent wolf, the cheeky rabbit and the wise owl are familiar fictional characters. No one with knowledge of wild creatures (which our ancestors certainly had) would impute to them the kind of moral and intellectual characteristics bestowed on them in stories. It is enough that the listener and the storyteller can conjure a picture of the creature into their minds on which fictions can be built. I did notice, however, that when I heard the same story in two different areas, one animal character might be substituted for another which had recognisable relatives in the area.

The were-hyena woman of the stories, however, seemed different in kind from the animals of the fables. She was born of the fear of real hyenas and was closer to the magical world of wizards, jinns and demons which Dires had outlined for me on the road to Chagni.

It was in Jinka that I discovered at last the secret of Tekle's mysterious evening disappearances. Having heard me groan aloud at the thought of another dispiriting meal in the hotel, he shyly invited Mesfin and me to come out and dine with him.

We followed him through the hotel gates and round a few corners until we were standing outside a small wattle-and-daub house. Tekle coughed politely and a woman came to the door.

---

[43] The Panchatantra is an ancient collection of Indian animal fables. The written version in Sanskrit probably dates from the third century BC but it is based on a much older oral tradition.

She hid any surprise she might have felt at seeing three people instead of the one she was clearly expecting, and invited us in.

This was no restaurant in the usual sense of the word, but a family home. The floor, a smooth cork-like surface made of a hardened mixture of mud, dung and blood, was swept to perfection, the walls were freshly plastered with cow dung, and grass was strewn in front of the little tray on legs set out for the coffee ceremony. This celebratory touch was because today was the first of Lent.

'How did you find this place?' I asked Tekle.

He didn't quite know how to answer, but I could see that with his usual care and good judgment he had found a way to escape from the tawdriness of hotels and restaurants and enjoy home cooking where he could be sure that all the stringent dietary requirements of his Orthodox faith would be observed. I realised that he must have set up for himself a network of such homes in every town where his work took him. I also realised that it was an honour to be let in on his secret system, and to be allowed to share in it.

Ethiopian Orthodox Christians fast throughout the whole of Lent, keeping to a vegan diet. This is viewed as a hardship, but I found the fasting dishes among the most delicious I ever ate in Ethiopia, and our dinner that night was one of the best meals I had had on my travels. Our hostess's injera was light, with the tangy sourness that complemented the spiced pulse and vegetable dishes. Even Mesfin, a dedicated meat eater, was impressed. He praised every mouthful and his spirits rose as his stomach filled. He took off on one of his flights of comedy, imitating women he knew in Addis Ababa. I had taught him the phrase 'mutton dressed up as lamb', an expression he adored, and he chanted it as he pursed his lips, wriggled his shoulders and minced across the floor, speaking in a girlish voice which brought squeals of laughter from our hostess, who had no idea, I am sure, that she was offering dinner to a celebrated entertainer.

Having paid an embarrassingly modest sum for our meal, we strolled back to the hotel, I to my bed and Mesfin to entertain the locals in the bar.

It was always difficult to achieve a balance of stories, making sure that we had a representative sample from the different small language groups. We were pursuing Bena and Tsemay stories in a small town called Key Afar. It was pleasant to be there in the bright cool air of early morning. Two small children, no more than three or four years old, dashed up to me as I stood alone beside the Land Rover, my companions having gone off in search of storytellers. I looked down suspiciously at their upturned faces, waiting for their hands to be held out and the begging whine to begin, but instead they simply took my hands in theirs, and stood looking wonderingly up at me. I was so touched by their sweetness that I wanted to scoop them up into my arms and hold them close, and I thought regretfully of our loss of innocence in Europe, where the parents of such children, terrified of paedophiles, would have rushed to snatch them away from me.

Our Bena storyteller was a beaming young man who crushed my hand in a hearty Evangelical grip. I observed with dismay his newly washed jeans, brass-buckled belt and the honed pectorals bulging beneath his whiter than white T-shirt. He looked no more like a Bena storyteller than my late Auntie Mona. I thought of the Bena people I'd seen on the road: of the women with their ochred ringlets and gourd helmets, their leather clothes overstitched with cowrie shells, their tight brass bangles, strings of beads and cow-skin rucksacks. The young men were even more magnificent in their high-collared T-shirts with the sleeves sliced off, their striped loincloths just long enough to cover their buttocks, and leather bandoliers round their waists. Brass bangles like the girls' encircled their magnificent biceps, and their hair was cut in a straight line across their shoulders, then plaited, while their heads were shaved at the front. Some wore feathers shooting up from a topknot. They too wore beads, more elaborate than the girls', and some had long bead earrings dangling from their ears. I had watched them loping along the road after their cattle, appearing and disappearing like phantoms in clouds of dust, whirling their long sticks round their heads.

Evangelical Christian missionaries are irresistibly drawn to small ethnic groups like the Bena.[44] They are busy sweeping aside the ancient religions, whose tales I was so anxious to hear. I sat discontentedly as Mesfin coaxed stories out of the young man, whose name, appropriately enough, was Iyasu (Jesus). Eager and helpful though he was, he only made me feel cantankerous.

'He'll be full of westernised stuff learned from the missionaries,' I told myself.

But I was wrong. Iyasu had time to tell only a few stories, and I had heard none of them before. The first was very short, no more than a fragment. In it, a wizard tells a man to go to the river where he will find his future wife. She will scoop water with her gourd and he must ask her to let him drink from it. If she agrees, she is the right woman, and they will marry.

---

[44] The government of Ethiopia is aware of the impact that Western evangelicals, as well as hard-line Wahabi Muslim missionaries from Saudi Arabia, can have on the more tolerant millennia-old traditions of their Muslim and Orthodox Christian communities, but it is not an easy situation for them to deal with.

This story reminded me of the meeting of Isaac and Rebekah in the Book of Genesis. Isaac's father, Abraham, has sent his servant to find a wife for his son from the family of his brother, Laban. The servant arrives at the place where Laban lives and makes a pact with God. If the first girl who comes to the well agrees to draw water for him, and then offers to water his camels too, then she is the chosen bride. Rebekah duly arrives, and the wedding with Isaac is arranged.[45]

Iyasu's last story was the most fascinating. It was the origin myth of the Bena people.

There was a drought which was so severe that the only survivors were a queen and her two grandsons. To ensure the survival of her people, the queen slaughtered a sheep and put its hide over her eyes to blind herself. Then she said to her grandsons, 'Come and sleep with me one by one, when my menstruation is over.'

A daughter was born, then another. The queen gave one of her daughters as a wife to one of her grandsons. This couple gave birth to a son and a daughter. But living nearby was a dragon, named Golja, who ate people. The queen knew that, while the dragon lived, there would be no future for her family. She prepared a pit trap, and put her unmarried daughter into it as a lure. The dragon came, jumped into the pit and impaled himself on the spears. As he died he fell upon the unmarried daughter, killing her. But the children of her surviving sister grew up and multiplied and the Bena people are descended from them.

It took a while before the association, knocking at the door of my memory, came to me. And then it was there – Abraham's nephew, Lot.

---

[45] Genesis, chapter 24.

And Lot went up out of Zoar, and dwelt in the mountain, and his two daughters with him; for he feared to dwell in Zoar: and he dwelt in a cave, he and his two daughters.

And the firstborn said unto the younger, 'Our father is old, and there is not a man in the earth to come in unto us after the manner of all the earth. Come, let us make our father drink wine, and we will lie with him, that we may preserve seed of our father.'

And they made their father drink wine that night: and the firstborn went in, and lay with her father; and he perceived not when she lay down, nor when she arose. And it came to pass on the morrow, that the firstborn said unto the younger, 'Behold, I lay yesternight with my father: let us make him drink wine this night also; and go thou in, and lie with him, that we may preserve seed of our father.'

And they made their father drink wine that night also: and the younger arose, and lay with him; and he perceived not when she lay down, nor when she arose.

Thus were both the daughters of Lot with child by their father. And the firstborn bare a son, and called his name Moab: the same is the father of the Moabites unto this day. And the younger, she also bare a son, and called his name Ben-ammi: the same is the father of the children of Ammon unto this day.[46]

There are striking similarities here. Both stories start with a disaster. The Bena queen has survived a drought. Lot and his daughters have fled from the holocaust of Sodom and Gomorrah. A decision is made that only incest will ensure the future of the race, but the deed must be performed with the senior party blindfolded, or blind drunk. There is one member of the older

---

[46] Genesis, chapter 19.

generation, and two of the younger. These forbidden unions are the origin of the tribes.

The dragon and the maiden in the pit, in the Bena story, introduce the motif of St George, the patron saint of Ethiopia, a character who appears repeatedly in ancient manuscripts, on church murals, and on flags throughout Ethiopia.

Later, a storyteller from the Tsemay, another small cultural group, gave a similar account of the origins of the Tsemay people.

There are nine kin groups of the Tsemay people. At the beginning of time, they lived without death. Then they committed incest, a mother with her son and a father with his daughter. God said, 'You have sinned with incest and you will be punished.' After that all the diseases were created and people began to die. Then God gave nine girls to the nine original men, and after that people refrained from sin and lived happily.

A golden age of immortality. Sin brings death into the world. Another biblical parallel.

The bright young Evangelical Tsemay casually revealed that until the age of fifteen he had lived the life of a herdboy, subsisting, like the Masai, entirely on a diet of blood and milk. He had been taken up by the missionaries who had sent him to the town of Konso and paid for his schooling there. He had now achieved the holy grail of a government post.

❖

On the first day of our return drive to Addis Ababa, we stopped at the crossroads where the road to Jinka meets the southern route through the Omo valley and on into Kenya. A small town had been planted here. The only building of note was the police station, placed here no doubt in order to keep an eye on smugglers, although the town's most disruptive visitors were probably the tourists on their way to view the exotically dressed peoples of the Omo valley. The only other signs of habitation were a few mud huts surrounded by thorn fences.

We were on the hunt for Birale storytellers. One of the unsung tragedies of globalisation is the death of languages. No one knows how many there are in the world, though experts calculate the figure to be around 6,000. Of these, UNESCO estimates that around 2,500 are endangered and are likely to die out altogether within a century. This mass extinction is happening under our noses and with barely a sigh of regret. It is estimated that around 75 languages are spoken in Ethiopia, but many of these must be on the verge of being lost, along with their stories and their poetry, their history, their grammars and phonetic systems, their proverbs, riddles and the unique world view they embody.

We had been told that only seventy members of the Birale people were left alive in the world, and of these only eight or nine could speak the Birale language. Our hope was that we might find one of them here, in this hot, dusty little town, and that he or she might be persuaded to tell us a story or two.

Our arrival had not gone unnoticed by the pair of policeman sitting in the shade of a concrete wall. They rose to their feet and came over to investigate. The cultural officer in Jinka had thoughtfully provided us with a letter for the police captain, explaining our mission. He read it through a couple of times.

'The Birale village is too far away,' he told us. 'Three or four hours by walking.'

He assured us that if he had known we were coming he would have sent for someone to meet us. It wasn't easy to catch hold of a Birale. They were rare creatures and only seldom came into town.

At that point, two women, who had been sitting under a tree near the police compound, and who, by a process of aural osmosis, had gathered what we wanted (although I would have thought they were way out of earshot), called out that a Birale speaker was walking past the police station at that very moment. They ran off to catch him.

I could feel myself breaking out into a sweat of excitement. Yet again, I was conscious of treading in the footprints of the Brothers Grimm, catching at the tail feathers of stories before they took wing and fluttered out of sight forever, but never before had I been on the trail of something so rare and thrilling.

The women returned to their vigil under the tree and the Birale man came towards us at a trot. He was small with a wizened face, flared nostrils and heavily lidded eyes through which he watched us warily. His tan poplin jacket was very old and his knee-length trousers worn and frayed. His calf muscles looked as hard as if they'd been carved from mahogany, and his bare toes were splayed, the nails as thick as horns.

By this time, we were sitting near the Land Rover under a small thorn tree, which offered only sparse protection from the grilling heat of the sun. Several rubber tyres were piled up at the edge of the road and a couple of young Tsemay men, who had appeared as if from nowhere, perched on them, watching what was going on. Their hair was intricately plaited and one wore a long feather stuck in his topknot, which undulated every time he moved his head. The other was loosely wrapped in a striped polyester cloth, and when he stood up it fell away from his perfect young body to reveal his complete nakedness. His head was wrapped, turban like, in a tartan cloth.

Mesfin, Tekle and I sat and gazed at the Birale man, not knowing how to proceed. It transpired that he could speak only

Birale and Tsemay. We had no way of communicating. The minutes passed. This dilemma was soon resolved. More young Tsemay men had joined the pair on the tyres. One of these, who had had a few years of education, explained that he could speak Amharic and offered to translate for us. By this time we had moved into the shade of an even smaller thorn tree, no larger than a bush.

The Tsemay boy translated our request for stories to the Birale man who peered at us doubtfully and muttered something.

'If he is to do something for you,' the Tsemay boy said, 'he wants to know what you will do for him.'

As usual on these occasions I stared into the distance, pretending to be miles away, and let Mesfin take the lead, but I could follow the discussion. The incredible sum of a hundred birr was being whittled down until at last it was agreed that, if he could tell us some really good stories, the Birale would earn thirty birr.

The poor old man was under pressure now. He squatted with his arms resting on his knees, looking down at the dust as if inspiration might come from the ground. He began to speak haltingly in staccato jerks, but as the Tsemay translated, Mesfin and Tekle shook their heads in disgust.

'He knows nothing!' Mesfin burst out. 'He is only saying how he was born in his father's house, how his father gave him milk and sent him to tend the cattle. He doesn't understand!'

We were asking too much of the old man and I was embarrassed. Mesfin could barely conceal his impatience.

'You know, stories about the clever fox and the hungry hyena,' I understood him to say. 'What happened when the Creator made the world.'

The Birale man was sweating, desperate to earn the thirty

birr. He made a couple of stabs at putting together something that might please us, but it was clear that he knew no stories at all.

'This is a dead duck, Liz,' Mesfin said at last. 'He is just saying that hyenas chased his cows, he tried to kill them and they ran away.'

I was so hot that my shirt was clinging to my back. I couldn't understand how Mesfin managed to look so cool in his white shirt and black trousers, balancing on a crude stool which someone had fetched for him from the police station. My head was beginning to ache, I was hungry, and our encounter with the Birale man was making me feel ashamed.

We gave him five birr in the end, which he pocketed with silent dissatisfaction, and away he went, half-trotting out of the police compound with the easy lope of a man used to walking over great distances. I watched him go up the path that led round the edge of the hillside with deep regret, not only for the stories he had been unable to tell, but for his people whose language and very identity was in the process of being swept away.

Just beyond the police compound a thatched, unwalled shelter turned out to be a kind of truck stop serving food and drink. While we had been busy with the Birale man, a minibus had stopped there, and when we went in, craving lunch and coffee, we found a group of middle-aged Italian tourists settling down to a picnic with cans of iced drinks which their tour guide had carried in for them in cold boxes. They were on their way south to the Omo valley, cameras ready to capture photographs of lip-plates, elongated earlobes and exotic headgear. They were happy and friendly, joking among themselves, delighted to see another European and curious about our project, but I watched with mixed feelings as they climbed back into their air-conditioned minibus. There was something cruel about this juxtaposition: the lean, lonely Birale man disappearing along that narrow track, back to his ancestral land whose nature and use he understood so well, and the arrival of these plump foreigners in the luxurious vehicle. The Birale man and his people had no defences against the forces of the modern world arrayed against them, which, with no malice intended, were bringing about their destruction.

It was a two-day drive back to Addis Ababa. By the morning of the second day, Tekle had dark shadows under his eyes, and for once Mesfin's powers of recovery after another late night had deserted him.

'You look half dead, Mesfin. Are you all right?'

'No, no, I am fine, really. I think, therefore I am. Descartes said it.'

'Have you had breakfast?'

He suppressed a shudder.

'No.'

'Have a banana.'

'Oh, how good. Somehow I need something in my mouth after all.'

He took the banana, unpeeled the first quarter and nibbled at it.

'I'm dreaming of milky coffee,' I said.

'Oh, how lovely, the way you say it!' said Mesfin in a hollow voice. 'Anyway, we are busy taking our Vitamin D from the sun. What else do we need?'

We were silent as we drove out of Awassa. The new international road to Kenya was in the process of being constructed and we had to bump along through rubble and dust.

'This is my last cigarette before Addis,' announced Mesfin, crumpling up the empty packet. 'You will see how strong-willed I am.' He drew in a deep lungful of smoke. 'The goddess of reading and writing, let me say, has taught me to understand my own make-up.'

We reached the finished tarmac and Tekle put on speed. I could see that he was longing to be home with his beloved wife and his three clever children. Mesfin closed his eyes and began to breathe heavily and I could see that he was asleep, though he was sitting bolt upright on the Land Rover's hard back seat.

We stopped for breakfast at Zwai in a smart modern bar. Mesfin was recognised. A fan who had seen him on TV came up to shake his hand. A smile lit Mesfin's face and he seemed to visibly expand. He had been wearing his jacket in the usual way, but now he took it off and draped it over his shoulders.

'They see me, Liz, a famous man . . .'

Artistically, he didn't finish his sentence.

'Why didn't you ever go into films, Mesfin?' I asked, as we waited for the plates of fried eggs we had ordered.

'I should have done. People say I look like the old stars – Clint Eastwood, or that other one, Cary Grant. Canadians used to tell me how I was exactly the same, an actual double, of Omar Sharif.'

I couldn't help laughing. He joined in, happy to laugh at himself.

'Those old films, I like them so much.' He pursed his lips and assumed a pinched English accent. '"Good morning, Mr Bond. How do you like my electronic ammunitions?" And Sophia Loren! Oh how I love her. Now I will have to have a cigarette. If I hadn't thought of Sophia Loren, it wouldn't have been necessary.'

As we drove back into Addis Ababa through the outskirts which seemed to have crept further across the countryside even in the few days we had been away, Mesfin fell silent. The end of our travels had come. The worries of his life, of which lack of money was the chief, were pressing in on him. I was preoccupied too with the meetings I would have to set up at the British Council, and the effort it would take to fight for the publication of my readers in the face of the director's indifference.

'I don't know what to say, Mesfin,' I said, as we tapped shoulders in a final farewell in the little car park below the British Council office.

'No, really, Liz, we writers, when it come to words we are helpless.'

A CHANCEFUL PERSON

It's some while now since I sat with Aykabadane Basha, my last Ethiopian storyteller in Key Afar, holding my little tape recorder to her lips. The readers had only used a fraction of the stories I'd collected, and the row of notebooks full of stories, the diaries of my journeys and the boxes of tapes filled a shelf above the desk in my study, gathering dust. I would take them down from time to time and flip through them, refreshing my memory of a moment by a lake, the voice of a storyteller running up and down the range of pitch to imitate the squeak of a mouse or the growl of a lion. I would remember the shock of delight as the translator unfolded a new story.

And all the time the stories were working like yeast in the dark places of my mind. They would recur to me at unexpected moments. I would see the child of a friend emerge from his bedroom, bug-eyed and cross after hours of solitary engagement with a violent computer game, and I would remember Worku Alemu in Bahir Dar, recalling how his mother would put her shamma round his shoulders as they sat in the firelight with the door closed against the night, while she told him stories.

Like so many other people of my generation, I had become interested in my family history.

'A man came from the north,' Auntie Marie had said, passing on the legend of how our family had settled in the village in Renfrewshire where they were to live for hundreds of years.

'A man came from the river,' Lieutenant Akwai Gora had said in Gambela, beginning his story of the mysterious stranger who had arbitrated between two women fighting over a fish, and had gone on to become the father of the first king of the Anuak.

'There was a queen who had three breasts,' Iyasu Origo had told me in Key Afar, introducing his account of the origin of the Bena people, and the grandmother who had had daughters by her own grandsons.

What kernel of truth was there in any of these stories, my own included? Their importance is beyond question. Myths of origin have as much power today as they have ever had.

'God gave us the land from Jordan to the sea,' say the Israeli settlers, justifying the ethnic cleansing of Palestinians from the land.

'We are the sons of Genghis Khan,' say the Khazaks, flexing their muscles against the Russians, their erstwhile rulers.

My childhood recurs more often to me now, and with it the rhymes and jingles of my Auntie Mary.

> *Oh come to church and don't be late*
> *And put a penny in the plate*

she would sing, as we walked to church from her house in Kilmacolm, a clean hanky in one pocket and a sixpence for the collection in the other. Many, many times in Ethiopia storytellers had tried to pass on to me riddles and proverbs and popular rhymes, and I had always spurned them, asking only for stories. How much more would I have learned about the old ways and ideas of Ethiopia if I had taken the time to collect them?

'Once upon a time there were three adventurers,' Auntie Mona would begin, hunched over the steering wheel of her grey

Standard car as she hugged the crown of the road all the way up the A1 from London to Scotland. 'There was the captain, the mate, and the cabin boy.' And she would make the dreary miles fly faster, as Chaucer's pilgrims had done on the road to Canterbury.

'Three men travelled together and when they rested for the night, two of them decided to trick the third. They would tell each other their dreams,' a story from Assayita had begun. It had been one of many celebrating journeys, travellers meeting by chance as they walked along, the adventures that befell them, the tricks they played and the stories they told each other.

And what of the river demons, the witches, ogres, hyena women, jinns and zombies?

'Superstition,' my mother would have said, pursing her lips. But she would have been wary of such creatures too. For her, as for Auntie May and all the other aunties, the Devil was a real being.

'Be sober, be vigilant,' she would have quoted, 'because your adversary the Devil, as a roaring lion, walketh about, seeking whom he may devour.'[47]

I had given up hope that the stories would ever tumble out of my notebooks into the wider world. I feared they would be locked away there forever. I should have had more faith in the Ethiopian way. Time after time, in the course of my journeys, seemingly hopeless situations had resolved themselves.

By chance, I heard of an old student of mine now living in the UK. His name was Wolde Gossa Tadesse. He worked for the Christensen Foundation, which had provided funding for the reprints of my stories.

Taddesse and his family came to lunch with us at home. I took him up to my study and showed him my notebooks and cassettes.

[47] 1 Peter, chapter 5, verse 8.

'You must do something! This is a treasure!' he exclaimed, leafing through the crumpled pages of a notebook.

He urged me to apply to the Christensen Foundation. I received a grant. And everything came full circle, because it was to Michael Sargent, that inspirational British Council director, that I turned for help. Now living in retirement, he took on the job of deciphering all the stories, typing them up and cataloguing the tapes. We created a website, so that anyone anywhere in the world can read and enjoy the stories and listen to the voices of the storytellers in their own languages. [8]

The news that filters through from Ethiopia into our newspapers and onto our TV screens is never good. Climate change is causing droughts and floods, we hear. Famine threatens once more. The government is acquiring an unsavoury reputation for repression and human rights abuses. There is a starkness to these reports which conveys only partial truths. 'Ethiopians are victims,' they seem to suggest. 'The poorest of the poor. We must send them aid. It is our human duty.'

I don't recognise that picture. I think of the jolly old men in Bahir Dar, and their nostalgia for the high old days of Amhara princes with their jesters and their intricate wax-and-gold wordplay. From Tigray I remember stories celebrating women, and in particular the irrepressible Almaz, setting her forty dogs on her cruel parents. However hard life might be in the Danakil desert, the Afar stories were full of zestful raunchiness and humour, a cheerful slicing off of penises, a refusal of wives to be put down. In Gambela, Jinka, and among the Beni Shangul I felt a shiver of awe at the antiquity of the stories I was told, with their echoes of the Book of Genesis,

[48] www.ethiopianfolktales.com.

their stories of tribal origins, their thrilling porcupine men and cannibalistic ogres. From Harar and Jijiga came the smell of the great trading routes which connected them with Yemen, old Baghdad and the Indian Ocean beyond. Here there were jinns and tricksters and blind old kings. The Oromos had taught me about their ancient form of government, so different from the feudal history of the highlands, and their skills in sorting out disputes and achieving reconciliation with the use of rituals and sacred objects. In Bonga I had been thrilled by the youth of the boy who had inherited the mantle of bard to the kings. He had given me hope that the great tradition to which he was heir would not yet die out. In Awassa I had been beguiled by the skills of Yisahak and Abebe. 'Everything changes. Everything passes,' they had told me, and their words have rung in my ears ever since.

Why do I think of my Aunt Martha at this point, with her dark memories of horror on the Indo-Burmese border in 1944? Perhaps it's because I know there were so many stories that I wasn't told. Tens of thousands of Ethiopians were murdered in the Red Terror unleashed by Mengistu Haile Mariam. Many more thousands died in the wars and famines that followed. Only a few glimpses were given me of the sufferings that many of the people I met must have endured.

Aunt Martha left her wartime experiences behind her. She married, had two children, and became a pillar of her church and her community. No one could have guessed, watching her in her sitting room pouring tea for her guests, that she had been the heroine of a jungle hospital, a cyanide pill always in her pocket in case she was taken prisoner. Like her, the men who helped me in my quest for stories throughout Ethiopia had moved on with their lives. They were making the best of things.

The opinion that outsiders have of Ethiopians is a poor match with the way Ethiopians see themselves. If ever I needed a final proof of this, I was shown it on my very last day in Addis Ababa, when, the round of meetings over, I was in my hotel room packing my suitcase. It was October 2000, and the Olympic Games in Sydney had recently ended. Ethiopia's triumphant athletes were due to arrive back that very day, and the air in Addis Ababa was vibrating with anticipation.

Crowds had been gathering at the airport since early in the morning. I had been watching them on the TV set in my hotel room. The families of the famous runners – Derartu Tulu, Million Wolde, Gezahegne Abera and Haile Gebre Selassie, the darlings of the nation, were being endlessly interviewed and filmed. The camera recorded the plane as a speck in the sky. It followed its descent and its landing. The nation waited, breathless, while for long minutes the doors remained shut. They opened at last, and the athletes appeared. They danced down the steps, waving flags, their medals bouncing against their chests on long blue ribbons, their faces shining with the emotion of this glorious moment. The president of Ethiopia and his wife surged forward. Other dignitaries pushed the TV cameras aside, so that the millions of viewers for some moments could see nothing but a forest of arms and flags.

The athletes, transformed into gods, were picked up and were now being carried shoulder high. They bobbed about above the mass of heads. The cameras swivelled upwards for a moment to film helicopters which had appeared in the sky, from whose bellies thousands of sheets of paper were fluttering, feather-like, to the ground. The athletes were set down again and the cameraman managed to part the crowd for long enough to film a view of the long line of welcoming officials who were bending low to the athletes as I had once seen courtiers bow to Haile Selassie.

My attention had been dragged away from the TV screen by the blaring of horns from every passing bus and taxi in the street outside the hotel. Now there were groups of men running together, chanting as they went.

It was time for me to go to the British Council offices to pick up some documents before I could leave. Somehow, I managed to find a taxi. The driver's progress was slow through the seething mass of people. In the end, I got out to walk.

People were waiting in ranks along the sides of the roads to cheer the athletes as they came past. They were quiet, but joyful with expectation. Some had tied ribbons of the national colours (red, yellow and green) round their heads. Others had draped flags round their shoulders. No one called out 'You!' or 'Ferenji!'

An elderly man in a baseball cap smiled at me.

'When will they get here?' I asked him.

'Soon,' he said, listening to the transistor clamped to one ear. 'They are already at Arat Kilo.'

I couldn't bear to go inside the office. I wanted to linger and savour the moment. I walked on into the thickest part of the crowd. I realised suddenly that I was the only ferenji in this mass of people, and I felt a small tingle of apprehension. This part of town could be a tricky place, notorious for pickpockets. Street children had sometimes been aggressive to me here. But I quickly saw that I didn't have to worry today.

'Isn't this wonderful?' someone called out to me. 'What do you think of this? How is it?'

'Wonderful!' I called back.

A woman in a group of others caught my eye. We smiled and nodded at each other.

I worked my way along the street till I came to a corner. Elderly men were perched on the steps of shop fronts and mothers were calling out to their straggling children. Policemen, more used to harassing people for fines, were trying to impose some order on the crowd, but they were too happy and excited themselves to take their work seriously.

Suddenly there were shouts from behind me, then came the chanting of the vanguard of running men. They went past by so fast that I hardly had time to register their faces, catching only the glint of sweat on their cheeks and the flutterings of the flags they carried, whose poles were resting against their shoulders.

'Ah oh!' they were shouting. 'Ah oh! Ah oh! Ah oh!'

Their voices were so loud they almost drowned out the wail of the siren from the car behind them, which was filled with policemen and flanked by outriders.

And now at last three black limousines were abreast of us, and through their sunroofs, one in each car, stood the medalled athletes, garlanded with golden Meskel daisies. Derartu and Million looked overwhelmed, but Haile Gebre Selassie raised his arms and threw back his head. He could have been a Roman emperor at his triumph. At that moment, he was a god.

The crowd roared for him. My skin prickled and my hair stood on end as women began to ululate.

A moment later the cavalcade had gone, rounding the corner, entering Churchill Avenue. We could hear the shouts of the crowd down there, a Mexican wave of sound.

My throat was tight with emotion. An old man was standing next to me. I turned and caught his eye.

'I was here, you know, when Abebe Bekele, the first Ethiopian gold medallist, returned with his medal in 1968,' I told him.

He sucked the air in through his teeth.

'You saw him? You were here then, in His Majesty's time?'

There were tears in his eyes too. We clasped hands. He shook his head wonderingly.

'You are a very chanceful person,' he said.

INDEX